# PREFACE.

THE rapid increase of persons seeking information concerning a department of the history of Plymouth and Rhode Island Colonies not usually found in standard works, has seemed to demand a book of ready reference wherein the names of colonial, county and town officers and professional men should be presented concisely, and in a form the most convenient to the reader. The need long felt for such a work is thought sufficient to justify the present effort to furnish it to the public.

The compiler does not claim for himself the credit of being the first to discover the want referred to; doubtless others have seen and felt it, but have been deterred from undertaking a work requiring so much toil and time, by the fear of their labor being insufficiently requited. The compiler of this work, however, will consider himself rewarded, if he sees his efforts appreciated by the public, for whose convenience mainly he has labored.

The plan adopted in the following pages is to give in brief and in tabular form:

1. The names, residences and dates of election or of appointment of the civil officers of the colonial government, of the several counties and of each town, under the head of CIVIL LISTS, respectively of Plymouth and Rhode Island Colonies.

2.  The names, residences, and dates of commission, of the officers in the local militia, and those appointed to serve in the capacity of commissioned officers in the successive warlike expeditions fitted out by the colonies, under the head of MILITARY LISTS of Plymouth and Rhode Island Colonies.

3.  The names of clergymen, physicians and lawyers ; where and when settled in the practice of their several professions ; under the head of PROFESSIONAL LISTS, respectively of the two colonies.

Should the demand for this work seem to warrant the effort for a further and enlarged publication in the same line, the compiler will probably, ere long, publish in like form the Civil, Military and Professional Lists of the Massachusetts, Connecticut, New Haven and New Hampshire Colonies, which, with this present work, will constitute complete books of reference to all Colonial New England.

EBENEZER W. PEIRCE.

*Freetown, Mass.*, Nov. 12, 1880.

# TABLE OF CONTENTS.

## PLYMOUTH COLONY.

### Civil Lists.

CONTENTS.

## PLYMOUTH COUNTY.

## Military Lists.

# RHODE ISLAND COLONY.

## Civil Lists.

## Military Lists.

## Professional Lists.

# PLYMOUTH COLONY.

## CIVIL LISTS.

# COLONIAL OFFICERS.

## GOVERNORS.

| Name. | Residence. | Term of Service. |
|---|---|---|
| John Carver | Plymouth | Nov. 11, 1620, to April, 1621. |
| William Bradford | Plymouth | May, 1621, to January 1, 1633. |
| Edward Winslow | Plymouth | Jan. 1, 1633, to 1634. |
| Thomas Prence | Plymouth | *Jan. 1, 1634, to March, 1635. |
| William Bradford | Plymouth | March 3, 1635, to Jan. 1636. |
| Edward Winslow | Plymouth | Jan. 5, 1636, to January, 1637. |
| William Bradford | Plymouth | Jan. 3, 1637, to January, 1638. |
| Thomas Prence | Plymouth | June 5, 1638, to March, 1639. |
| William Bradford | Plymouth | March 5, 1639, to June, 1644. |
| Edward Winslow | Plymouth | June 5, 1644, to June, 1645. |
| William Bradford | Plymouth | June 4, 1645, to June, 1657. |
| Thomas Prence | Eastham | June 3, 1657, to April 8, 1673. |
| Josias Winslow | Marshfield | June 3, 1673, to Dec. 28, 1680. |
| Thomas Hinkley | Barnstable | June 7, 1681, to June, 1692.† |

## DEPUTY GOVERNORS.

| Name. | Residence. | Term of Service. |
|---|---|---|
| Thomas Hinkley | Barnstable | June 1, 1680, to 1681. |
| James Cudworth | Scituate | June 7, 1681, to 1682. |
| William Bradford | Plymouth | June 6, 1682, to 1686. |
| William Bradford | Plymouth | 1689, to 1692. |

## SECRETARIES.

| Name. | Residence. | Term of Service. |
|---|---|---|
| Nathaniel Souther | Plymouth | Jan. 3, 1637, to 1647. |
| Nathaniel Morton | Plymouth | December, 1647, to 1685. |
| Nathaniel Clarke | Plymouth | June, 1685, to 1686. |
| Samuel Sprague | Marshfield | June, 1686, to 1692. |

* Thomas Prence was elected Governor, Jan. 1, 1634, but was not to enter upon the duties of that office until March, 1634.
† Save during the interruption in the government made by Sir Edmund Andros.

## TREASURERS.

| Name. | Residence. | Term of Service. |
|---|---|---|
| Thomas Prence | Plymouth | Jan. 3, 1637, to 1640. |
| Timothy Hatherly | Scituate | March 3, 1640, to 1642. |
| John Atwood | Plymouth | March 1, 1642, to 1644. |
| Miles Standish | Duxbury | Aug. 20, 1644, to 1656. |
| John Alden | Duxbury | June 8, 1656, to 1659. |
| Constant Southworth | Duxbury | June 7, 1659, to 1679. |
| William Bradford | Plymouth | June 3, 1679, to 1686. |
| William Bradford | Plymouth | 1689, to 1692. |

## GOVERNORS' ASSISTANTS.

| Name. | Residence. | Term of Service. |
|---|---|---|
| Isaac Allerton | Plymouth | 1621, 1634. |
| Edward Winslow | Plymouth | 1634, 1635, 1637, 1638, 1641–1643, 1645–1650. |
| William Bradford | Plymouth | 1634, 1635, 1637, 1638, 1644, 1658–1681. |
| John Alden | Duxbury | 1632, 1634–1639, 1650–1686. |
| Samuel Fuller | Plymouth | 1632. |
| John Howland | Plymouth | 1634, 1635. |
| Miles Standish | Plymouth & Duxbury | 1632, 1635, 1637–1641, 1645–1656. |
| Thomas Prence | Plymouth *& Eastham | 1632, 1635–1637, 1639–1656. |
| Stephen Hopkins | Plymouth | 1634, 1635. |
| William Collier | Duxbury | 1635–1637, 1639–1651, 1654–1656, 1658–1665. |
| Timothy Hatherly | Scituate | 1636, 1637, 1639–1658. |
| John Browne | Rehoboth | 1636, 1638–1655. |
| John Jenney | Plymouth | 1637, 1638–1640. |
| John Atwood | Plymouth | 1638. |
| Edmund Freeman | Sandwich | 1640–1645. |
| William Thomas | Marshfield | 1642–1644, 1646–1650. |
| Thomas Willett | Plymouth | 1651–1654, 1656–1664. |
| James Cudworth | Scituate | 1656, 1657, 1674–1680. |
| Josias Winslow | Marshfield | 1657–1672. |
| Thomas Southworth | Plymouth | 1655, 1657–1671. |
| Thomas Hinckley | Barnstable | 1658–1679. |
| John Freeman | Eastham | 1667–1678, 1682–1686. |
| Nathaniel Bacon | Barnstable | 1667–1673. |
| Constant Southworth | Duxbury | 1672–1678. |
| James Browne | Rehoboth | 1673–1683. |
| Daniel Smith | Rehoboth | 1679–1683. |
| Barnabas Lothrop | Barnstable | 1681–1686. |
| John Thacher | Yarmouth | 1682–1686. |
| John Walley | Bristol | 1684–1686. |

* Thomas Prence removed to Eastham, in or about 1644.

## MARSHALS.

| Name. | Residence. | Term of Service. |
|-------|-----------|------------------|
| Samuel Nash | Duxbury | 1652, to 1684. |
| William Bassett | Sandwich | June, 1689, to 1692. |

## CORONER.

| Name. | Residence. | Term of Service. |
|-------|-----------|------------------|
| William Collier | Duxbury | Jan. 3, 1637; re-chosen June 2, 1646. |

Duties of Governor's Assistant, as defined by the laws of Plymouth Colony:—

"The office of an Assistant for the time being consisteth in appearing at the Governor's sumons, and in giving his best advice both in publick Court & private Councell with the Gov' for the good of the Colonies within the limits of this government. Not to disclose but keep secret such things as concerne the publick good and shall be thought meet to be concealed by the Gov' & Councell of Assistants. In having a speciall hand in the examination of publick offenders and in contriving the affairs of the Colony. To have a voice in the censuring of such offenders as shall not be brought to publick Court. That if the Governor shall have occasion to be absent from the Colony for a short time, by the Gov' with the consent of the rest of the Assistants, he may be deputed to governe in the absence of the governour. Also it shall be lawfull for him to examine and comit to ward where any occasion ariseth where the Gov' is absent provided the person be brought to further hearing with all convenient speed before the Governor and the rest of the Assistants."

## GOVERNORS OF PLYMOUTH COLONY.

JOHN CARVER, the first chief magistrate of Plymouth Colony, was born in England, but left that country for the sake of his religion and settled at Leyden, where he held the office of Deacon in the Pilgrim Church; and being a very influential member of that body was sent by it to England to negotiate with the Virginia Company for the privilege of settling upon some part of the territory that company had acquired in North America. He took a prominent part in all the arrangements of the Pilgrim voyage to and settlement in America; and, in the cabin of the Mayflower then lying at anchor in Provincetown harbor, John Carver was chosen Governor of Plymouth Colony. He was re-elected at Plymouth, April 2, 1621, and died, to the inexpressible grief of the colonists, a little past the middle of the same month, his wife dying six weeks after.

WILLIAM BRADFORD was born in Yorkshire, England, March, 1588. At an early age he emigrated to Holland, and joined the English congregation at Leyden, sailing with the Pilgrims to America in 1620. The first legal patent or charter of Plymouth Colony was obtained in the name of John Peirce, but in 1630 a more comprehensive charter was obtained in the name of William Bradford, his heirs, associates and assignees. The General Court of Plymouth Colony in 1640 requested that this charter should be surrendered into their hands, which being done it was returned to Gov. Bradford for safe keeping. He was annually elected governor as long as he lived, excepting for five years at different times when he declined, thus holding the office 31 years. He wrote a history of Plymouth Colony, from 1620 to 1647, which remained in manuscript, was carried away by the British army in 1775, and was supposed to have been destroyed or lost; but fortunately it was discovered a few years since, and printed entire by the Mass. Hist. Soc. in 1856. He died May 9, 1657.

EDWARD WINSLOW was born at Droitwich, Worcestershire, England, Oct. 19, 1595, joined the Puritans at Leyden in 1617, and took an active part in all the affairs of their emigration. With piety he combined great energy, and extensive knowledge of the world and of society, whereby he was enabled to render the colonists very great and essential service. He was four times sent to England as an agent for Plymouth and Massachusetts Bay Colonies, and was three times selected Governor of Plymouth Colony. In 1623 he made the first importation of neat cattle into New England. Cromwell appointed Gov. Winslow one of three commissioners to overlook an expedition against the Spaniards in the West Indies, and while on that duty died at sea, May 8, 1655. He was the author of the interesting and valuable works: "Good Newes from New England," printed at London in 1624; "Hypocrasie Unmasked," 1646; "The Glorious Progress of the Gospel among the Indians," 1649.

THOMAS PRENCE was born in England in 1600; came to America in 1621, and settled in Plymouth, from whence he removed to Eastham in 1644. He married 1st, in 1624, Patience Brewster, who died in 1634; 2d, Mary Collier; 3d, in 1662, Mary, widow of Samuel Freeman. He was eighteen times chosen governor of Plymouth Colony, and died March 29, 1673.

JOSIAS WINSLOW, son of Gov. Edward and Susannah (White) Winslow, was born at Plymouth, in 1629, and married in 1657, Penelope, daughter of Herbert Pelham, Esq. He was eight times chosen Governor of Plymouth Colony, and was distinguised for his great talents, energy and usefulness. Perhaps it would not be too much to say of him, that in his day and generation he was indeed "first in peace, first in war," and among the very "first in the hearts of his countrymen." He died in Marshfield, Dec. 28, 1680.

THOMAS HINKLEY was born in England in 1618: came with his father, Samuel Hinkley, to America, and was at Scituate as early as 1635; at Barnstable in 1639; admitted as freeman in Plymouth Colony in 1645. In 1646 he was elected a Deputy or Representative from the town of Barnstable to the Colonial Court, and was repeatedly chosen until 1658, when he was made Governor's Assistant. Promoted to Deputy Governor in 1680, he was next year chosen Governor, and except during the interruption to the government caused by Sir Edmund Andros, Gov. Hinkley held that office until 1692,

# BARNSTABLE COUNTY.

INCORPORATED JUNE 2, 1685.    SHIRE OR COUNTY TOWN, BARNSTABLE.

## COUNTY MAGISTRATES.

| Name. | Residence. | Term of Service. |
|---|---|---|
| Jonathan Sparrow | Eastham * | May 20, 1690, to 1692. |
| Stephen Skiff | Sandwich | May 20, 1690, to 1692. |

### CLERK OF COUNTY COURT AND REGISTER OF DEEDS.

| Name. | Residence. | Term of Service. |
|---|---|---|
| Joseph Lothrop | Barnstable | |

Act of Incorporation :—

"It is also Ordered, That Barnstable, Sandwich, Yarmouth and Eastham, the Villages of Sippican, Suckoonesset and Monamoy shall be a County; Barnstable the County Town and said County shall be called the County of Barnstable, in which County shall be kept two County Courts annually at the County Town, one on the third Tuesday in April, and the other on the third Wednesday in October."

# TOWN OFFICERS.

## BARNSTABLE. Incorporated Sept. 3, 1639. Indian name—Chequocket.

| Date. | SELECTMEN. | CONSTABLES. | REPRESENTATIVES. |
|---|---|---|---|
| 1639 | None Chosen. | William Casey | Joseph Hull, Thomas Dimmock, |
| 1640 | " | John Cooper | James Cudworth, Thomas Dimmock, Anthony Annable. |
| 1641 | " | Henry Rowley | Thomas Dimmock, Anthony Annable. |
| 1642 | " | Thomas Lathrope | James Cudworth, Thomas Dimmock, Anthony Annable. |
| 1643 | " | John Hamlen | John Coop, Anthony Annable, Henry Rowley, Henry Bourne. |
| 1644 | " | William Crocker | Anthony Annable, Henry Bourne, Henry Cobb. |
| 1645 | " | John Barsley | Anthony Annable, Isaac Robinson. |
| 1646 | " | Thomas Huckens | Henry Cobb, Thomas Hinckley. |
| 1647 | " | John Hall | Anthony Annable, Henry Cobb, |
| 1648 | " | Thomas Allen | Thomas Dimmock, Thomas Hinckley. |
| 1649 | " | | Thomas Dimmock, Thomas Hinckley. |
| 1650 | " | Nathaniel Bacon | Thomas Dimmock, Anthony Annable. |
| 1651 | " | George Lewis | Anthony Annable, Isaac Robinson. |
| 1652 | " | James Naighbore | Henry Cobb, Nathaniel Bacon. |
| 1653 | " | John Finney | Anthony Annable, Nathaniel Bacon. |
| 1654 | " | Dolar Davis | Nathaniel Bacon, Thomas Hinckley. |
| 1655 | " | Robert Shelley | Nathaniel Bacon, Thomas Hinckley. |
| 1656 | " | Abraham Blush | |
| 1657 | " | Thomas Huckens | Anthony Annable. |
| 1658 | " | Thomas Allen | Nathaniel Bacon. |
| 1659 | " | Thomas Huckens | Nathaniel Bacon, Henry Cobb. |
| 1660 | " | Abraham Blush | Nathaniel Bacon, Henry Cobb. |
| 1661 | " | Trustrum Hull | Nathaniel Bacon, Henry Cobb. |
| 1662 | " | Thomas Huckens | Nathaniel Bacon, Henry Cobb. |

| Year | | | |
|---|---|---|---|
| 1663 | None Chosen. | Trustrum Hull | Nathaniel Bacon, John Chipman. |
| 1664 | " " | Joseph Lothrop | Nathaniel Bacon, John Chipman. |
| 1665 | " " | Thomas Lothrop | Nathaniel Bacon, John Chipman. |
| 1666 | Nathaniel Bacon, John Chipman, John Thompson, Trustrum Hull | Thomas Huckens | Nathaniel Bacon, John Chipman, Joseph Lothrop. |
| 1667 | William Crocker, John Chipman, John Thompson, Joseph Lothrop | Abraham Blush | Joseph Lothrop. |
| 1668 | Thomas Huckins, William Crocker, John Thompson, John Chipman, Lieut. Joseph Lothrop | Henry Bourne | Lieut. Joseph Lothrop, John Chipman. |
| 1669 | John Huckens, John Thompson, Joseph Lothrop, Ensign Mark Eames | Robert Parker | John Chipman, Thomas Huckens. |
| 1670 | Thomas Huckens, John Thompson, Joseph Lothrop, Ensign Mark Eames | Thomas Allen | Thomas Huckens. |
| 1671 | Thomas Huckens, Lieut. Joseph Lothrop, John Thompson | Samuel Allen | Thomas Huckens, John Thompson. |
| 1672 | Thomas Huckens, Lieut. Joseph Lothrop, John Thompson | John Huckens | Thomas Huckens, John Thompson. |
| 1673 | Lieut. Joseph Lothrop, John Thompson, John Thompson | Jabez Lumbert | John Thompson, Lieut. Joseph Lothrop. |
| 1674 | Thomas Huckins, Lieut. Joseph Lothrop, John Gorham | Barnabas Lothrop | Thomas Huckins. |
| 1675 | Thomas Huckins, Lieut. Joseph Lothrop, Barnabas Lothrop | John Finney, Sr. | Thomas Huckens, Barnabas Lothrop. |
| 1676 | Thomas Huckens, Lieut. Joseph Lothrop, Barnabas Lothrop | Job Crocker | Lieut. Joseph Lothrop, Barnabas Lothrop. |
| 1677 | Thomas Huckens, Lieut. Joseph Lothrop, Barnabas Lothrop | Samuel Hinckley, Sr. | Thomas Huckens, Barnabas Lothrop. |
| 1678 | Lieut. Joseph Lothrop, Lieut. James Lewis, Barnabas Lothrop | Nathaniel Bacon | Thomas Huckens, Barnabas Lothrop. |
| 1679 | Lieut. Joseph Lothrop, Barnabas Lothrop, Lieut. Samuel Allen | Thomas Huckens | Lieut. Joseph Lothrop, Barnabas Lothrop. |
| 1680 | Lieut. Joseph Lothrop, Lieut. James Lewis | | Lieut. Joseph Lothrop, Barnabas Lothrop. |
| 1681 | Lieut. Joseph Lothrop, Lieut. Samuel Allen, Sergt. John Howland | Lieut. Samuel Allen | Lieut. Joseph Lothrop. |
| 1682 | Capt. Joseph Lothrop, Lieut. Samuel Allen, Ens. John Howland | John Barker | Capt. Joseph Lothrop, Lt. Samuel Allen. |
| 1683 | Capt. Joseph Lothrop, Samuel Allen, Lieut. John Howland | Melatiah Lothrop | Capt. Joseph Lothrop, Lt. Samuel Allen. |
| 1684 | Capt. Joseph Lothrop, Lt. John Howland, Ens. Shubael Dimmock | | Capt. Joseph Lothrop, Samuel Allen. |
| 1685 | | Thomas Huckins | Capt. Jos. Lothrop, Ens. Shubael Dimmock. |
| 1686 | | | |
| 1687 | | | |
| 1688 | Capt. Joseph Lothrop, Lieut. James Lewis, John Howland | | Shubael Dimmock, John Gorham. |
| 1689 | Capt. Joseph Lothrop, Lieut. James Lewis, Lieut. John Howland | | Capt. Joseph Lothrop, John Gorham. |
| 1690 | | | Capt. John Gorham. |
| 1691 | | | |
| 1692 | | | |

Thomas Hinkley was Town Clerk of Barnstable in 1644, and probably for quite a number of the succeeding years. Joseph Lothrop was Town Clerk in 1660, and he probably filled that office for several years.

## EASTHAM. Incorporated June 2, 1646. Indian name—Nauset.

| Date. | Selectmen. | Constables. | Representatives. |
|---|---|---|---|
| 1646 | None Chosen. | Samuel Hicks | Josias Cooke, Richard Higginson. |
| 1647 | " | John Smalley | Nicholas Snow, Samuel Hicks. |
| 1648 | " | Job Cole | John Doane, Samuel Hicks. |
| 1649 | " | | John Doane, Nicholas Snow. |
| 1650 | " | George Crispe- | John Doane, Josiah Cook. |
| 1651 | " | William Twiney, Jr. | Daniel Cole, Edward Bangs, Nicholas Snow |
| 1652 | " | Stephen Wood | John Doane, Richard Higgins. |
| 1653 | " | Thomas Payne | Daniel Cole. |
| 1654 | " | John Young | Richard Higgins, Richard Sparrow. |
| 1655 | " | Mark Snow | Richard Sparrow, John Freeman. |
| 1656 | " | Jonathan Sparrow | Richard Higgins. |
| 1657 | " | Henry Atkins | Richard Higgins. |
| 1658 | " | John Mayo | Richard Higgins. |
| 1659 | " | Henry Atkins | |
| 1660 | " | Ralph Smith | Richard Higgins. |
| 1661 | " | John Doane, Jr. | Lieut. John Freeman, Josias Cooke. |
| 1662 | " | Nicholas Snow | Lieut. John Freeman, Josias Cooke. |
| 1663 | " | Edward Bangs | Lieut. John Freeman, Josias Cooke. |
| 1664 | " | Daniel Cole | Lieut. John Freeman, Josias Cooke. |
| 1665 | " | Joseph Harding | Richard Higgins, Lieut. John Freeman. |
| 1666 | John Freeman, Josias Cooke, Richard Higgins | Robert Vixon | Lieut. John Freeman, Josias Cooke. |
| 1667 | | John Bangs | Daniel Cole. |
| 1668 | Richard Higgins, Daniel Cole, Nicholas Snow | Samuel Freeman | Daniel Cole, Jonathan Sparrow. |
| 1669 | | Benajah Dunham | Daniel Cole, Jonathan Sparrow. |
| 1670 | Nicholas Snow, Daniel Cole, Lieut. Joseph Rogers, Josias Cooke | Samuel Smith | Daniel Cole, Jonathan Sparrow. |
| 1671 | Nicholas Snow, Daniel Cole, Thomas Paine, Jonathan Sparrow | John Mayo | Josias, Cooke, Thomas Paine. |
| 1672 | Nicholas Snow, Daniel Cole, Thomas Paine, Jonathan Sparrow, Mark Snow | Jonathan Bangs | Daniel Cole, Thomas Paine. |
| 1673 | Nicholas Snow, Jonathan Sparrow, Mark Snow | | Jonathan Sparrow, Thomas Paine. |
| 1674 | Nicholas Snow, Daniel Cole, Jonathan Sparrow, Mark Snow, Jonathan Bangs | Thomas Paine | Jonathan Sparrow, Jonathan Bangs. |

| Date | Selectmen | Constables | Representatives |
|---|---|---|---|
| 1675 | Nicholas Snow, Jonathan Sparrow, Mark Snow | Joshua Bangs | Jonathan Sparrow, Mark Snow. |
| 1676 | Lieut. Jonathan Sparrow, Mark Snow, Jonathan Bangs | John Doane | Lieut. Jonathan Sparrow, Jonathan Bangs. |
| 1677 | Jonathan Sparrow, Mark Snow, John Doane | Thomas Mulford | Capt. Jonathan Sparrow, Mark Snow. |
| 1678 | Capt. Jonathan Sparrow, Mark Snow, John Doane | Josias Cooke | Capt. Jonathan Sparrow, Thomas Paine. |
| 1679 | Capt. Jonathan Sparrow, Mark Snow, John Doane | William Browne | Capt. Jonathan Sparrow, Jonathan Bangs. |
| 1680 | Capt. Jonathan Sparrow, Mark Snow, John Doane | | Thomas Paine. |
| 1681 | Capt. Jonathan Sparrow, Mark Snow, John Doane, Thomas Paine, Daniel Cole | John Freeman | Capt. Jonathan Sparrow, Thomas Paine. |
| 1682 | Capt. Jonathan Sparrow, Mark Snow, John Doane | | Capt. Jonathan Sparrow, John Doane. |
| 1683 | Capt. Jonathan Sparrow, Mark Snow, John Doane | William Walker | Capt. Jonathan Sparrow. |
| 1684 | Capt. Jonathan Sparrow, Mark Snow, John Doane | | Capt. Jonathan Sparrow, John Doane. |
| 1685 | Capt. Jonathan Sparrow, Mark Snow, John Doane | | Capt. Jonathan Sparrow, John Doane. |
| 1686 | Capt. Jonathan Sparrow, Mark Snow, John Doane | Benjamin Higgins | Capt. Jonathan Sparrow, Mark Snow. |
| 1687 | [Government interrupted by Sir Edmund Andros.] | | |
| 1688 | | | |
| 1689 | Mark Snow, John Doane, Jonathan Bangs | | Capt. Jonathan Sparrow, Mark Snow, John Doane. |
| 1690 | Mark Snow, John Doane, Sr., Jabez Snow, Benjamin Higgins | | Capt. Jonathan Sparrow, Thomas Paine. |
| 1691 | | | Capt. Jonathan Sparrow, Thomas Paine. |
| 1692 | | | |

Nicholas Snow was Town Clerk of Eastham from 1646 to 1663; Mark Snow, from 1663 to 1676; Daniel Doane, from 1676 to 1703.

FALMOUTH. INCORPORATED JUNE 4, 1686. Indian name—SUCCANESSETT.

| Date | SELECTMEN. | CONSTABLES. | REPRESENTATIVES. |
|---|---|---|---|
| 1686 | None Chosen. | None Chosen. | None Chosen. |
| 1687 | [Government interrupted by Sir Edmund Andros.] | | " " |
| 1688 | | | " " |
| 1689 | | | John Robinson. |
| 1690 | | | John Robinson. |
| 1691 | | | John Robinson. |
| 1692 | | | |

## ROCHESTER. INCORPORATED JUNE 4, 1686. Indian name—SIPPICAN.

| Date. | SELECTMEN. | CONSTABLES. | REPRESENTATIVES. |
|---|---|---|---|
| 1686 | Aaron Barlow, Samuel Hammond, Samuel White | None Chosen. | |
| 1687 | | | |
| 1688 | | | |
| 1689 | | | |
| 1690 | | | Joseph Burgess. |
| 1691 | | | Aaron Barlow. |
| 1692 | | | Aaron Barlow. |

## SANDWICH. INCORPORATED SEPT. 3, 1639. Indian name—SHAWME.

| Date. | SELECTMEN. | CONSTABLES. | REPRESENTATIVES. |
|---|---|---|---|
| 1639 | None Chosen. | { George Allen<br>Thomas Amitage | Richard Bourne, Thomas Armitage, John Vincent. |
| 1640 | | William Wood | Richard Bourne, George Allen. |
| 1641 | | Nathaniel Willis | Richard Bourne, George Allen. |
| 1642 | | Michael Turner | Richard Bourne, George Allen, William Newland, Thomas Burges. |
| 1643 | | George Knott | William Newland, Henry Peak. |
| 1644 | | Joseph Holly | Thomas Tupper, James Skiffe. |
| 1645 | | George Bewyt | Richard Bourne, Thomas Burges. |
| 1646 | | Peter Gaunt | William Newland, James Skiff, Edmund Freeman. |
| 1647 | | Thomas Dexter, Jr. | Thomas Tupper, William Newland. |
| 1648 | | James Skiffe | Thomas Tupper, Thomas Burgis. |
| 1649 | | | John Vincent, William Newland |
| 1650 | | Edmund Freeman | John Vincent, Thomas Tupper. |

| Year | | | |
|---|---|---|---|
| 1651 | John Vincent, Thomas Tupper. | Nathaniel Fish | |
| 1652 | Thomas Tupper, Richard Bourne. | Jonathan Fish | |
| 1653 | James Skiffe, Thomas Burgess. | Richard Chadwell | |
| 1654 | John Vincent, James Skiffe. | Thomas Burgess, Jr. | |
| 1655 | Thomas Tupper, James Skiffe. | Stephen Wing | |
| 1656 | Thomas Tupper, James Skiffe. | Myles Blacke | |
| 1657 | Thomas Tupper, James Skiffe. | William Bassett | |
| 1658 | John Vincent. | Thomas Tobey | |
| 1659 | Thomas Tupper, Thomas Burgess. | | |
| 1660 | Thomas Tupper, John Vincent. | William Swift | |
| 1661 | Thomas Burgess, William Bassett. | Benjamin Nye | |
| 1662 | Thomas Tupper, James Skiffe. | Thomas Dexter | |
| 1663 | Richard Bourne, James Skiffe. | George Barlow | |
| 1664 | Richard Bourne, James Skiffe. | Thomas Burgess | |
| 1665 | Richard Bourne, James Skiffe. | Richard Chadwell | |
| 1666 | Richard Bourne, Thomas Tupper. | Henry Dillingham | |
| 1667 | Thomas Burgis. | Edmund Freeman, Jr. | Thomas Tupper, James Skiffe, Thomas Burgis |
| 1668 | Edmund Freeman, Jr. | William Swift | Thomas Tupper, James Skiffe, Edmund Freeman |
| 1669 | Richard Bourne. | Thomas Tupper, Jr. | Thomas Tupper, Sr., Edmund Freeman, Jr., William Swift |
| 1670 | Edmund Freeman, Jr. | | James Skiffe, Edmund Freeman, Jr., William Swift |
| 1671 | Thomas Tupper. | | James Skiffe, Sr., Edmund Freeman, Jr., William Swift |
| 1672 | Thomas Tupper, Jr. | Stephen Skiffe | James Skiffe, Thomas Burgess, Stephen Skiffe |
| 1673 | Edmund Freeman, Jr. | | James Skiffe, Sr., William Swift, Thomas Tupper, Jr. |
| 1674 | Thomas Tupper. | | James Skiffe, Sr., William Swift, Edmund Freeman |
| 1675 | William Swift, Stephen Skiffe. | Benjamin Nye, Sr. | William Swift, Stephen Skiffe, Thomas Tupper, Jr. |
| 1676 | William Swift. | Richard Gibbs, Sr. | |
| 1677 | Thomas Tupper. | Benjamin Hammond | William Swift, Edmund Freeman, Jr., Thomas Tupper |
| 1678 | Thomas Tupper. | Joseph Burgess | William Swift, Edmund Freeman, Thomas Tupper |
| 1679 | Edmund Freeman, Jr. | James Pursnall | Edmund Freeman, Thomas Tupper, John Blackwell |
| 1680 | Thomas Tupper, Stephen Skiff. | James Blackwell | Edmund Freeman, William Swift, Thomas Tupper |
| 1681 | Thomas Tupper, Stephen Skiff. | Ezra Perry | Edmund Freeman, Jr., William Swift, Thomas Tupper |
| 1682 | Stephen Skiff, Shearjashub Bourne. | William Bassett | Edmund Freeman, Jr., John Blackwell |
| 1683 | Thomas Tupper, Stephen Skiff. | | Edmund Freeman, Sr., Stephen Skiff, John Blackwell |
| 1684 | Thomas Tupper, Stephen Skiff. | Jacob Burgess | Thomas Tupper, Stephen Skiff, Shearjashub Bourne |
| 1685 | | Elisha Bourne | William Swift, Sr., Thomas Tupper, Stephen Skiff |
| 1686 | | Jonathan Hallett | William Swift, Thomas Tupper, Stephen Skiff |
| 1687 | | Ambrose Fish | William Swift, Thomas Tupper, Stephen Skiff |

## SANDWICH (CONTINUED).

| Date. | SELECTMEN. | CONSTABLES. | REPRESENTATIVES. |
|---|---|---|---|
| 1688 | | | |
| 1689 | Thomas Tupper, Shearjashub Bourne, William Bassett | | Thomas Tupper, Stephen Skiff. |
| 1690 | Stephen Skiff, Shearjashub Bourne, William Bassett | | Stephen Skiff, Shearjashub Bourne. |
| 1691 | | | Capt. Thomas Tupper, Elisha Bourne. |
| 1692 | | | |

William Wood was Town Clerk of Sandwich in 1649, and probably for several years after; Thomas Tupper was Town Clerk for a time; the office was held by Stephen Wing in 1669; Edmund Freeman, Jr., in 1670; Thomas Tupper, Jr., in 1675; William Bassett, in 1685, who continued in that office until 1720.

## YARMOUTH. INCORPORATED SEPTEMBER 3, 1639. Indian name—MATTACHEESE or NOBSCUSET.

| Date. | SELECTMEN. | CONSTABLES. | REPRESENTATIVES. |
|---|---|---|---|
| 1639 | | William Chase | Thomas Payne, Philip Tabor. |
| 1640 | | William Lumpkin | Philip Tabor. |
| 1641 | | Edward Sturges | John Crow, Richard More. |
| 1642 | None Chosen. | Emanuel White | John Crow, Richard More. William Palmer. |
| 1643 | | | Anthoney Thacher, Mr. Crowe, Sr., William Palmer, Thomas Falland. |
| 1644 | | Thomas Howes | Anthoney Thacher, William Palmer, Job Cole, James Mathews. |
| 1645 | | Richard Templer | Anthoney Thacher, Edmund Hawes. |
| 1646 | | John Joyce | Anthoney Thacher, Edmund Hawes. |
| 1647 | | Trista Hull | Anthoney Thacher, Edmund Hawes. |
| 1648 | | John Marchant | Lieutenant Palmer, Edmund Hawes. |
| 1649 | | | Lieutenant Palmer, Edmund Hawes. |
| 1650 | | William Hedge | Lieutenant Palmer, Richard Hoar. |

| Year | | | |
|---|---|---|---|
| 1651 | | Andrew Hallett | Anthoney Thacher, Edmund Hawes. |
| 1652 | | Benjamin Hammon | Anthoney Thacher, Thomas Howes. |
| 1653 | | Francis Baker | Thomas Howes, Edmund Hawes. |
| 1654 | | James Mathews | Edmund Hawes, Anthoney Thacher. |
| 1655 | | Thomas Boardman | Edmund Hawes, William Nickerson. |
| 1656 | | Richard Taylor | Edmund Hawes. |
| 1657 | | Robert Eldred | Edmund Hawes. |
| 1658 | | Anthony Thacher | Edmund Hawes, Thomas Howes. |
| 1659 | | Edmund Hawes | Anthony Thacher, Thomas Howes. |
| 1660 | | Richard Sears | Edmund Hawes, Thomas Howes. |
| 1661 | | Thomas Boardman | Edmund Hawes, Thomas Howes. |
| 1662 | | Edward Sturgis | Thomas Howes, Richard Sears. |
| 1663 | | Samuel Ryder | Anthony Thacher, Yelverton Crow. |
| 1664 | | Samuel Hall | Edward Sturgis, James Mathews. |
| 1665 | | Joseph Howes | Anthony Thacher, Edmund Hawes. |
| 1666 | | John Miller | Edward Sturgis, Yelverton Crow. |
| 1667 | Anthony Thacher, Edmund Hawes, James Mathews | Thomas Howes | Edward Sturgis, Yelverton Crow. |
| 1668 | Edmund Hawes, Edward Sturgis, James Mathews, Yelverton Crow | Richard Taylor | Thomas Howes, John Thacher. |
| 1669 | Edmund Hawes, James Mathews, Thomas Howes, John Miller, John Thacher | Henry Vincent | Thomas Howes, John Thacher. |
| 1670 | Edmund Hawes, Thomas Howes, John Miller, John Thacher, Edward Sturgis, Sr. | Samuel Sturgis | Thomas Howes, John Thacher. |
| 1671 | Edmund Hawes, Thomas Howes, John Miller, John Thacher, Edward Sturgis, Sr. | Joseph Hall | John Thacher, John Miller. |
| 1672 | Edmund Hawes, Ensign Thomas Howes, John Miller, John Thacher, Edward Sturgis | Hosea Joyce | Ensign Thomas Howes, Edward Sturgis, Sr. |
| 1673 | Edmund Hawes, Ensign Thomas Howes, John Miller, John Thacher, Edward Sturgis | Elisha Hedge | Ensign Thomas Howes, John Thacher. |
| 1674 | Edmund Hawes, Ensign Thomas Howes, John Miller, John Thacher, Edward Sturgis | Edward Sturgis | Edmund Hawes, John Thacher. |
| 1675 | Edmund Hawes, Captain Thomas Howes, John Miller, John Thacher, Edward Sturgis, Sr. | Nathaniel Bassett | Edmund Hawes, Captain Thomas Howes. |
| 1676 | Edmund Hawes, Captain Thomas Howes, Ensign John Thacher | Jeremiah Howes | Captain Thomas Howes, John Thacher. |
| 1677 | Edmund Hawes, John Thacher, Edward Sturgis, Sr. | John Hawes | John Miller, Jeremiah Howes. |
| 1678 | Edmund Hawes, John Miller, John Thacher, Edward Sturgis, Sr. | Edward Sturgis. Sr. | John Miller, John Thacher. |
| 1679 | Edmund Hawes, Ensign John Thacher, Edward Sturgis, John Miller, Jeremiah Howes | Andrew Hallett | John Miller, John Thacher. |

## YARMOUTH (CONTINUED).

| Date. | SELECTMEN. | CONSTABLES. | REPRESENTATIVES. |
|---|---|---|---|
| 1680 | Edmund Hawes, Edward Sturgis, John Thacher, John Miller, Jeremiah Howes | Jabez Gorham | John Thacher, John Miller. |
| 1681 | Edmund Hawes, John Miller, Ensign John Thacher, Edward Sturgis, Jeremiah Howes | Thomas Sturgis | |
| 1682 | Edmund Hawes, Edward Sturgis, John Miller, Jeremiah Howes | John Hallett | John Miller. |
| 1683 | Edward Sturgis, Edmund Hawes, John Miller | | John Miller, Jeremiah Howes. |
| 1684 | Edmund Hawes, John Miller, Jeremiah Howes | | John Miller, Jeremiah Howes. |
| 1685 | Edmund Hawes, John Miller, Jeremiah Howes, Joseph Howes | Elisha Hedge | Jeremiah Howes, Lieutenant Silas Sears. |
| 1686 | Edmund Hawes, John Miller, Jeremiah Howes, Joseph Howes | | Jeremiah Howes, Lieutenant Silas Sears. |
| 1687 | | | |
| 1688 | | | |
| 1689 | Jeremiah Howes, John Miller, Lieutenant Silas Sears | | John Miller, Jeremiah Howes. |
| 1690 | Jeremiah Howes, John Miller, Silas Sears | | John Miller, Lieutenant Silas Sears. |
| 1691 | | | John Miller, Silas Sears. |
| 1692 | | | |

Anthony Thacher was Town Clerk of Yarmouth from 1639 to 1667; Edmund Hawes, from 1667 to 1693.

## MONAMOIT, AFTERWARD CHATHAM.

| Date. | SELECTMEN. | CONSTABLES. | REPRESENTATIVES. |
|---|---|---|---|
| 1681 1682 &c. to 1690 1691 | None Chosen. | John Savage | Gershom Hall. |

## BARNSTABLE.

| Date. | GRAND JURYMEN. | SURVEYORS OF HIGHWAYS. |
|---|---|---|
| 1639 | Samuel Hinkley | |
| 1640 | John Doane | |
| 1641 | Samuel Hinkley | |
| 1642 | Henry Bourne, Henry Ewell | |
| 1643 | Abraham Blush, Isaac Wells | |
| 1644 | Thomas Hinkley | Thomas Allen, Samuel Hinkley. |
| 1645 | Dolar Davis. Nathaniel Bacon | Abraham Blush, Nathaniel Bacon. |
| 1646 | Henry Bourne, Burnard Lumbert | Henry Rowley, Thomas Shaw. |
| 1647 | John Jenkins | Samuel Hinkley, Henry Rowley. |
| 1648 | Isaac Robinson, Isaac Wells | Thomas Burmen, George Lewis. |
| 1649 | | Thomas Lumbert. |
| 1650 | Thomas Burmen | Andrew Hallett, Richard Templer. |
| 1651 | John Gorham | Thomas Allen, Samuel Hinkley. |
| 1652 | John Chipman | Abraham Blush, Dolar Davis. |
| 1653 | John Scudder | Henry Rowley, John Thompson. |
| 1654 | William Crocker | John Finney, John Smith. |
| 1655 | Joseph Lothrop, Thos. Huckens | Henry Bourne, Thomas Burmen. |
| 1656 | Henry Bourne | Samuel Hinkley, John Davis. |
| 1657 | William Crocker | Thomas Allen, Samuel Hinkley. |
| 1658 | Abraham Blush, Henry Bourne | |
| 1659 | Burnard Lumbert | |
| 1660 | John Finney | |
| 1661 | Henry Bourne | |
| 1662 | George Lewis, Austine Bearce | Thomas Lewis, Moses Rowley. |
| 1663 | Abraham Blush | |
| 1664 | John Thompson, Henry Bourne | |
| 1665 | John Smith, John Howland | |
| 1666 | James Lewis | |
| 1667 | William Crocker | |
| 1668 | Jabez Lumbert | John Crocker, Sr., John Finney, Sr. |
| 1669 | Shubael Dimmock | John Chipman, Thomas Huckens. |
| 1670 | James Hamblin | Samuel Fuller. |
| 1671 | Job Crocker | John Davis, Samuel Hinkley. |
| 1672 | John Finney | John Davis, Thomas Hinkley. |
| 1673 | Samuel Hinkley | William Crocker, Thomas Huckens. |
| 1674 | Nathaniel Bacon | Austine Bearce, George Lewis. |
| 1675 | William Crocker | John Davis, Samuel Hinkley. |
| 1676 | John Crocker | |
| 1677 | | John Davis, Sr., William Throop. |
| 1678 | Shubael Dimmock | William Throop, Ens. John Howland. |
| 1679 | Josiah Crocker | Ens. John Howland, James Lewis. |
| 1680 | Wm. Throop, Melatiah Lothrop | |
| 1681 | John Finney | |
| 1682 | John Davis | Melatiah Lothrop, Josiah Crocker. |
| 1683 | Shubael Dimmock | William Throop, Jabez Lumbert. |
| 1684 | Nathan'l Bacon, Thos. Huckens | |
| 1685 | Thomas Hinkley, Richard Child | |
| 1686 | | |
| 1687 | | |
| 1688 | | |
| 1689 | | |
| 1690 | | |
| 1691 | | |
| 1692 | | |

3

## EASTHAM.

| Date. | GRAND JURYMEN. | SURVEYORS OF HIGHWAYS. |
|---|---|---|
| 1646 | | |
| 1647 | John Jenkins | Nicholas Snow, Edward Bangs. |
| 1648 | Daniel Cole | Josias Cooke, Robert Vixon. |
| 1649 | | John Smalley, Thomas Williams. |
| 1650 | Robert Wixon | Edward Bangs, Giles Hopkins. |
| 1651 | Samuel Hix, John Freeman | Edward Bangs, Richard Higgins. |
| 1652 | Edward Bangs | |
| 1653 | Henry Atkins | Nicholas Snow, John Freeman. |
| 1654 | John Smalley | Job Cole, Stephen Wood. |
| 1655 | Nathaniel Mayho | Robert Sparrow, Robert Vixon. |
| 1656 | Samuel Hix | George Crispe, John Mayho. |
| 1657 | Daniel Cole | Thomas Roberts, Mark Snow. |
| 1658 | William Merrick | Richard Sparrow, Nathaniel Mayho. |
| 1659 | Richard Sparrow | |
| 1660 | John Smalley | |
| 1661 | Daniel Cole | |
| 1662 | William Twining | Giles Hopkins, Thomas Paine. |
| 1663 | Edmund Freeman | |
| 1664 | Thomas Paine | |
| 1665 | Samuel Hix | |
| 1666 | Jonathan Sparrow | |
| 1667 | Mark Snow | |
| 1668 | John Doane, Jr. | Jonathan Bangs, William Walker. |
| 1669 | Jonathan Bangs | Richard Knowles, William Walker. |
| 1670 | Thomas Paine | Richard Knowles, Samuel Freeman. |
| 1671 | William Twining | Nicholas Snow, Giles Hopkins. |
| 1672 | George Crispe | John Doane, Daniel Doane. |
| 1673 | John Bangs | John Doane, Daniel Doane. |
| 1674 | Josias Snow | |
| 1675 | John Mayho | Robert Vixon, Henry Atkins. |
| 1676 | Benjamin Higgins | Robert Vixon, Henry Atkins. |
| 1677 | Daniel Doane | Jonathan Bangs, John Doane. |
| 1678 | George Crispe | William Walker, William Merrick, Jr. |
| 1679 | Jonathan Sparrow, Jona. Bangs | William Walker, William Merrick. |
| 1680 | Jabez Snow | |
| 1681 | Joshua Bangs | Thomas Freeman, Jabez Snow. |
| 1682 | Thomas Freeman | Thomas Freeman, Jabez Snow. |
| 1683 | John Freeman | Samuel Freeman, Samuel Knowles. |
| 1684 | William Merrick | |
| 1685 | Samuel Paine | John Freeman, Jr., Thomas Paine, Jr. |
| 1686 | | |
| 1687 | | |
| 1688 | | |
| 1689 | | |
| 1690 | | |
| 1691 | | |
| 1692 | | |

## MANAMOIT, AFTERWARD CHATHAM.

In 1685, Hugh Steward was a member of the Grand Jury for Manamoit.

## SANDWICH.

| Date. | GRAND JURYMEN. | SURVEYORS OF HIGHWAYS. |
|---|---|---|
| 1639 | | |
| 1640 | Thomas Burgess, Thomas Tupper | Richard Bourne, George Allen. |
| 1641 | William Newland | Edward Dillingham, Robert Bodfish. |
| 1642 | John Wing | |
| 1643 | Richard Chadwell, James Skiff | |
| 1644 | Robert Bodfish | Richard Chadwell, Thomas Boardman. |
| 1645 | Thomas Tupper, Jonathan Fish | Thomas Burgess, Anthony Wright. |
| 1646 | Michael Turner | Edmund Freeman, Jr., James Skiff. |
| 1647 | Edmund Freeman, Thos. Tupper | Joseph Holloway, George Buett. |
| 1648 | Thomas Boardman | Thomas Dexter, John Fish. |
| 1649 | | William Newland, Peter Wright. |
| 1650 | George Buett | Thomas Dexter, Michael Turner. |
| 1651 | Peter Wright, John Ellis | Nicholas Wright, Jonathan Fish. |
| 1652 | Thomas Dexter | |
| 1653 | Edward Perry | Edward Dillingham, Richard Bourne. |
| 1654 | Ralph Allen, Jr. | Peter Grant, Anthony Bessey. |
| 1655 | Edward Dillingham | Benjamin Nye, William Swift. |
| 1656 | William Allen | |
| 1657 | James Skiff | John Jenkins, Edward Perry. |
| 1658 | Benjamin Nye | |
| 1659 | Thomas Dexter | |
| 1660 | George Bewett | |
| 1661 | Ezra Perry | |
| 1662 | Thomas Tupper | Thomas Burgess, Richard Chadwell. |
| 1663 | Edmund Freeman | Thomas Burgess, Sr., Thomas Launder. |
| 1664 | Joseph Holly | |
| 1665 | Stephen Skiff | |
| 1666 | Joseph Burgess | Stephen Wing, Thomas Butler. |
| 1667 | John Dingley | |
| 1668 | Benjamin Nye | Miles Blackwell, Edward Perry. |
| 1669 | Nathaniel Willis | Thomas Gibbs, Sr., Daniel Wing. |
| 1670 | Thomas Tobey | |
| 1671 | Stephen Wing | Ralph Allen, Sr., John Blackwell. |
| 1672 | John Blackwell | |
| 1673 | Shearjashub Bourne | Jacob Burgess, William Allen. |
| 1674 | Samuel Briggs, Samuel Freeman | Edward Perry, Stephen Skiff. |
| 1675 | Thomas Gibbs, Jr. | Thomas Gibbs, William Newland. |
| 1676 | William Swift, Stephen Skiff | |
| 1677 | Ezra Perry | Peter Grant, William Gifford. |
| 1678 | Edmund Freeman, Jr. | Thomas Burgess, Samuel Briggs. |
| 1679 | Benjamin Nye | William Swift, Sr., Stephen Skiff. |
| 1680 | William Swift | Ralph Allen, John Jenkins. |
| 1681 | William Wood | |
| 1682 | William Swift | |
| 1683 | Edmund Freeman | William Swift, Sr., Caleb Allen. |
| 1684 | John Briggs | |
| 1685 | Matthias Ellis, Joshua Blackwell | |
| 1686 | | |
| 1687 | | |
| 1688 | | |
| 1689 | | |
| 1690 | | |
| 1691 | | |
| 1692 | | |

## YARMOUTH.

| Date. | GRAND JURYMEN. | SURVEYORS OF HIGHWAYS. |
|---|---|---|
| 1639 | | |
| 1640 | William Palmer | |
| 1641 | William Nickarson | William Clarke, Emanuel White. |
| 1642 | Anthony Thatcher, Jas. Mathews | William Palmer, Gabriell Whelding. |
| 1643 | William Lumpkin | Giles Hopkins, Andrew Hallett, Jr. |
| 1644 | Edmund Hawes | Anthony Thatcher, Hugh Hiller. |
| 1645 | Robert Dennis | Emanuel White, James Bursell. |
| 1646 | Emanuel White | Yelverton Crowe, Edward Sturgis. |
| 1647 | William Nickarson | Gabriell Whelding, John Darbie. |
| 1648 | James Bursell | Richard Taylor, Francis Baker. |
| 1649 | | Samuel Ryder, Richard Templar. |
| 1650 | Edward Sturgis | Andrew Hallett, Richard Templar. |
| 1651 | Richard Taylor | William Clarke, Edward Sturgis. |
| 1652 | Richard Sears | William Lumpkin, John Joice. |
| 1653 | John Joice | Anthony Thatcher, John Hall. |
| 1654 | Anthony Thatcher | William Lumpkin, John Gorham. |
| 1655 | Edward Sturgis | William Lumpkin, Thomas Follan. |
| 1656 | Yelverton Crowe | Samuel Rider, Sr., Andrew Hallett. |
| 1657 | Samuel Rider, Sr. | William Chase, Sr., Richard Taylor. |
| 1658 | John Crow | Andrew Hallett, Thomas Gage. |
| 1659 | William Lumpkin | |
| 1660 | Samuel Rider, Andrew Hallett | |
| 1661 | John Whilden | |
| 1662 | Anthony Thatcher, Wm. Clarke | John Joice, William Eldred. |
| 1663 | James Mathews | John Joice, William Eldred. |
| 1664 | John Burgess | |
| 1665 | John Joice | |
| 1666 | John Thacher | Samuel Rider, Sr., Thomas Gage. |
| 1667 | John Bryant | Thomas Gage, Judah Thacher. |
| 1668 | William Clarke | Thomas Gage, Judah Thacher. |
| 1669 | John Whilden | Edward Sturgis, Jr., John Burgess. |
| 1670 | Judah Thacher | Edward Sturgis, Jr., John Burgess. |
| 1671 | John Bryant, Sr. | Edward Sturgis, Sr., Joseph Howes. |
| 1672 | John Miller | Edward Sturgis, Sr., Joseph Howes. |
| 1673 | Nathaniel Bassett | |
| 1674 | John Bryant, Sr. | William Eldred, John Whilden. |
| 1675 | Andrew Hallett | William Eldred, Jonn Whilden. |
| 1676 | John Bryant | John Bryant, Samuel Hall. |
| 1677 | John Whilden | William Eldred, John Rider. |
| 1678 | Nicholas Nickarson | Nathaniel Bassett, John Burgiss. |
| 1679 | Zachariah Ryder | Nathaniel Bassett, John Burgiss. |
| 1680 | John Burgiss | Joseph Severance, John Hawes. |
| 1681 | Thomas Fallon, Jr. | |
| 1682 | Joseph Howes | |
| 1683 | Shubael Dimmock | John Whilden, Samuel Howes. |
| 1684 | Thomas Sturgis | |
| 1685 | John Miller, Richard Taylor | Thomas Sturgis, Ananias Wing. |
| 1686 | | |
| 1687 | | |
| 1688 | | |
| 1689 | | |
| 1690 | | |
| 1691 | | |
| 1692 | | |

## PERSONS APPOINTED TO SOLEMNIZE MARRIAGES.

| Names. | Residences. | Date of Appointment. |
|---|---|---|
| John Doane | Eastham | June 1, 1663. |
| Josias Cooke | Eastham | June 8, 1664. |
| Stephen Skiff | Sandwich | October 2, 1689. |
| Anthony Thacher | Yarmouth | June 29, 1652. |

## INN KEEPERS.

| Name of Town. | Name of Person. | When Licensed. | When Cancelled. |
|---|---|---|---|
| Barnstable— | Thomas Lumbert | Dec. 3, 1639. | |
| | John Crocker | June 6, 1649. | |
| | Joseph Lothrop | June 9, 1653. | |
| | Thomas Huckins | June 1, 1663. | |
| Falmouth— | Isaac Robinson | Feb. 7, 1665. | |
| | Jonathan Hatch | June 2, 1685. | |
| Sandwich— | John Ellis | May 3, 1659. | |
| | William Swift | July 5, 1669. | |
| | Thomas Dexter | Sept. 28, 1680. | |
| Yarmouth— | John Miller | Oct. 30, 1667. | July 5, 1670. |
| | Edward Sturgis | July 5, 1670. | |

## PERSONS LICENSED TO RETAIL SPIRITUOUS LIQUORS.

| Name of Town. | Name of Person. | Kind of Liquor. | Date of License. |
|---|---|---|---|
| Barnstable— | Henry Cobb | Wine | June 5, 1644. |
| | Thomas Huckens | Wine and Strong Waters | March 1, 1653. |
| | Thos. Walley, Jr. | Strong Liquors | March 1, 1664. |
| | ...... Wright | Strong Liquors | March 1, 1664. |
| Eastham— | Josias Cooke | Wine | June 7, 1648. |
| | Edward Bangs | Wine and Strong Waters | Oct. 6, 1657. |
| | Daniel Cole | Wine and Strong Waters | June 10, 1661. |
| Falmouth— | Jonathan Hatch | Liquor | June 2, 1685. |
| Sandwich— | William Newland | Wine | June 5, 1644. |
| | William Bassett, Jr. | Wine and Strong Waters | March 1, 1659. |
| | John Ellis | Wine and Strong Waters | May 3, 1659. |
| Yarmouth— | Anthony Thacher | Wine | June 5, 1644. |
| | Edward Sturgis | Wine | July 7, 1646. |

## RECEIVERS OR COLLECTORS OF THE EXCISE.

| Name of Town. | Name of Collector. | Date of Appointment. |
|---|---|---|
| Barnstable— | Isaac Robinson | July 7, 1646. |
| | Henry Cobb | June 8, 1664. |
| | Nathaniel Bacon | June 8, 1664. |
| | Lieut. Joseph Lothrop | June 5, 1667. |
| | Thomas Huckens | June 5, 1667. |
| Eastham— | Nicholas Snow | June 7, 1648. |
| | John Doane, Jr. | June 8, 1664. |
| | William Walker | June 8, 1664. |
| | Ensign William Merrick | June 3, 1668. |
| Sandwich— | Peter Gaunt | July 7, 1646. |
| | James Skiff | June 8, 1664. |
| | Thomas Tobey | June 8, 1664. |
| | Thomas Tupper, Jr. | June 5, 1667. |
| Yarmouth— | Edmund Hawes | July 7, 1646. |
| | Richard Taylor | June 8, 1664. |
| | Robert Dennis | October 3, 1665. |
| | Anthony Thacher | October 3, 1685. |
| | John Miller | June 3, 1668. |
| | John Hawes | June 3, 1668. |

Under date of June 2, 1646, the General Court of Plymouth Colony enacted that the rates for excise should be as follows:—

That such strangers as have liberty to fish at the Cape to pay five shillings per share.

Upon every gallon of Spanish wine drawn by retail by such as are allowed, eight pence.

Upon every gallon of French wine drawn by retail by such as are allowed, four pence.

Upon every hogshead of beer, two shillings.

Upon every gallon of strong water, eighteen pence.

Upon every pound of tobacco retailed, one penny,

## COLLECTORS OF MINISTERS' RATES OR TAXES.

| Name of Town. | Name of Collector. | When Appointed. |
|---|---|---|
| Barnstable— | ...... Hinkley | June 7, 1670. |
| | Thomas Huckens | June 7, 1670. |
| Eastham— | Lieut. John Freeman | June 7, 1670. |
| | Jonathan Sparrow | June 7, 1670. |
| Sandwich— | Thomas Dexter | June 1, 1675. |
| | Thomas Tupper | June 1, 1675. |
| Yarmouth— | Thomas Howes | June 7, 1670. |
| | John Thacher | June 7, 1670. |
| | Samuel Rider | June 5, 1671. |
| | John Miller | June 5, 1671. |

# BRISTOL COUNTY.

INCORPORATED JUNE 2, 1685. SHIRE OR COUNTY TOWN. BRISTOL.

## COUNTY MAGISTRATES.

| Name. | Residence. | Term of Service. |
| --- | --- | --- |
| Nicholas Peck | Rehoboth | June 2, 1685, to 1690. |
| Thomas Leonard | Taunton | June 2, 1685, to June, 1690. July 7, 1691, to 1692. |
| Joseph Church | Little Compton | June 2, 1685, to 1692. |
| Nathaniel Byfield | Bristol | June 4, 1686, to June 5, 1690. |
| William Paybodie | Little Compton | June 4, 1686. to June 5, 1690. |
| George Macey | Taunton | May 20, 1690, to 1691. |
| Seth Pope | Dartmouth | May 20, 1690, to 1692. |

### CLERK OF COUNTY COURT AND REGISTER OF DEEDS.

| Name. | Residence. | Term of Service. |
| --- | --- | --- |
| Stephen Burton | Bristol | 1685, to 1693. |

### COUNTY TREASURER.

| Name. | Residence. | Term of Service. |
| --- | --- | --- |
| John Walley | Bristol | |

Act of Incorporation :—

"It is further Ordered; That Bristol, Taunton, Rehoboth. Dartmouth, Swanzey, Little Compton, Free Town. Sowammit, Pocasset, Punkatest and all such Places. Towns and Villages as are or may be settled on said Lands, shall be a County, Bristol the County Town, and the said County shall be called the County of Bristol; In which County shall be kept two County Courts annually at the County Town; one on the third Tuesday in May, and the other on the third Tuesday in November."

# TOWN OFFICERS.

## BRISTOL. INCORPORATED OCTOBER 28, 1681. Indian name—POKANOKET.

| Date. | SELECTMEN. | CONSTABLES. | REPRESENTATIVES. |
|---|---|---|---|
| 1681 | John Rogers, Jabez Howland | John Rogers | |
| 1682 | Capt. Benjamin Church, Jabez Howland, Ensign......Rogers | Increase Robinson | Capt. Benjamin Church. |
| 1683 | Benjamin Church, Jabez Howland, John Carey | Joseph Ford | Capt. Benjamin Church. |
| 1684 | Benjamin Church, Jabez Howland, John Carey | Thomas Doggett | Capt. Benjamin Church. |
| 1685 | John Carey, Jabez Howland, John Rogers | Capt. Nath'l Hayman | Stephen Burton, John Rogers. |
| 1686 | Capt. Benjamin Church, John Rogers, Thomas Walker | Nathan Hayman | Stephen Burton, John Rogers. |
| 1687 | Benjamin Church, John Rogers, Thomas Walker | Nathan Hayman | Stephen Burton, John Rogers. |
| 1688 | Benjamin Church, Nathaniel Byfield, Nathaniel Hayman | | |
| 1689 | Stephen Burton, John Rogers, William Throope | John Bletsoe, David Carey | John Rogers, Jabez Howland, John Saffin, Nathaniel Byfield. |
| 1690 | Stephen Burton, John Rogers, Jabez Howland | Elisha Adams, Sam'l Pullen | Stephen Burton, Jabez Howland. |
| 1691 | John Rogers Nathaniel Reynolds, John Saffic | | William Throope. |

TOWN CLERKS.—Jabez Howland, 1681; Richard Smith, 1682 to 1687; Samuel Corbett, 1687 to 1692; Richard Smith, 1692 to 1696 or 1697.

ACT OF INCORPORATION.—"Att the request of Capt. John Walley, Mr. Nathaniel Byfield, Mr. Nathaniel Olliur and Mr. Stephen Burton, purchasers of the lands on Mount Hope it is by this Court granted that together with such as they haue admitted inhabitants or shall hereafter orderly admitt shall from this time be a towne and enjoy all such liberties and haue all such power in all respects as is allowed to any other towne of this jurisdiction, and doe order the said grannt to be recorded and the towne to be called by the name of Bristol."

## DARTMOUTH. INCORPORATED JUNE 8, 1664. Indian names—APONAGANSET, ACUSHENA and COAKSET.

| Date. | SELECTMEN. | CONSTABLES. | REPRESENTATIVES. |
|---|---|---|---|
| 1664 | | James Shaw | John Russell. |
| 1665 | | Daniel Wilcox | John Cooke. |
| 1666 | John Russell, Samuel Hicks, Arther Hathewey | William Palmer | John Cooke. |
| 1667 | | Peleg Tripp | John Cooke. |
| 1668 | | John Briggs | John Russell. |
| 1669 | | John Cooke | John Russell. |
| 1670 | James Shaw, Samuel Hicks, John Cooke | Ralph Earle | |
| 1671 | | Thomas Cornell | John Russell. |
| 1672 | John Russell, John Cooke, Arther Hathewey | George Soule | John Russell. |
| 1673 | John Cooke, Arther Hathewey, James Shaw | Jacob Mitchell, William Hayward | John Cooke. |
| 1674 | John Russell, James Shaw, William Palmer | William Earle | John Cooke. |
| 1675 | John Cooke, Arther Hathewey, James Shaw | John Russell, Sr. | John Cooke. |
| 1676 | | | |
| 1677 | } Settlement broken up by King Philip's War. | | |
| 1678 | | | |
| 1679 | John Cooke, John Russell, Arther Hathewey | Joseph Kent, John Hathewey | John Cooke. |
| 1680 | John Cooke, John Russell, Arther Hathewey | Jonathan Delano | John Cooke. |
| 1681 | John Cooke, John Russell, Arther Hathewey | Jonathan Delano | John Cooke. |
| 1682 | John Cooke, John Russell, Arther Hathewey | Samuel Cornell | John Cooke. |
| 1683 | John Cooke, John Russell, Arther Hathewey | | John Russell. |
| 1684 | | | John Cooke. |
| 1685 | Seth Pope, Jonathan Russell, Thomas Taber | William Wood | |
| 1686 | Jonathan Delano, Seth Pope, Joseph Tripp | James Sisson | Joseph Tripp. |
| 1687 | } Government interrupted by Andros. | | John Cooke. |
| 1688 | | | |
| 1689 | Jonathan Delano, Seth Pope, James Sisson | | |
| 1690 | Jonathan Delano, Joseph Tripp, Thomas Taber | | Capt. Seth Pope, Jonathan Delano. |
| 1691 | | | Capt. Seth Pope. |

## FREETOWN. INCORPORATED JULY, 1683. Indian name—ASSONET.

[What afterward became Freetown was made a Constableric as early as Sept. 28, 1680, when John Hathwey, of Taunton, was sworn in Constable, and John Reed was summoned by the Colonial Court to appear as Grand Juryman at the next session of that court.]

| Date. | SELECTMEN. | CONSTABLES. | REPRESENTATIVES. |
|---|---|---|---|
| 1683 | Mr. Terry, Thomas King, John Bailey | Job Winslow | Joseph Bailey. |
| 1684 | Thomas Terry, Thomas King, Job Winslow | | Joseph Bailey. |
| 1686 | John Hathaway | William Makepeace | Job Winslow. |
| | | Benjamin Chase | |
| 1687 | John Hathaway, Samuel Gardiner | John Reed | |
| | | Joshua Tisdale | |
| 1688 | Lieut. Thomas Terry, Job Winslow, John Read | | Lieut. Thomas Terry. |
| 1689 | Lieut. Thomas Terry, Samuel Gardiner, Samuel Howland | Thomas King | Samuel Gardiner. |
| 1690 | | | |
| 1691 | | | |
| 1692 | Job Winslow, Samuel Gardiner, John Reed | Mathew Boomer | Job Winslow, Samuel Gardiner. |

TOWN CLERK.—Samuel Gardiner, 1688 to 1692. TREASURER.—Samuel Gardiner, June 24, 1690, probably to December, 1693.

ACT OF INCORPORATION.—"This Court orders that the inhabitants of the freemens land att the Fall River, shalbe a townshipp and haue a constable and grandjurymen and be henceforth called by the name of Freetown."

## LITTLE COMPTON. INCORPORATED JUNE 6, 1682. Indian name—SOGCONNET or SACONETT.

| Date. | SELECTMEN. | CONSTABLES. | REPRESENTATIVES. |
|---|---|---|---|
| 1682 | Capt. Edward Richmond, Joseph Church, William Southworth | William Brownell | Henry Head. |
| 1683 | Edward Richmond, William Peabody, William Southworth | Josiah Clauson | Henry Head. |
| 1684 | Capt. Edward Richmond, William Peabody, William Southworth | | Henry Head. |
| 1685 | Edward Richmond, William Peabody, Joseph Church | | Edward Richmond. |
| 1686 | | | |
| 1687 | | | |

| | | |
|---|---|---|
| 1688 | Capt. Edward Richmond, Lieut. Thomas Way, Robert Brownell | Henry Head. |
| 1689 | Capt. Edward Richmond, Henry Head | Joseph Church. |
| 1690 | | Simon Rouse. |
| 1691 | | |

ACT OF INCORPORATION.—Upon the petition of Mr. Joseph Church and the rest of the proprietors and inhabitants of Saconett, the Court haue granted that the said proprietors and inhabitants that are or shalbe there admitted orderly according to the lawes of this colonie shalbe from this time a towneship, and haue the liberties of a towne as other townes of this collonie, and shalbe called by the name of Little Compton."

ORDER OF OCT. 28, 1681.—" An Order directed to Joseph Church, of Saconett, as followeth.

"Whereas the Court are enformed that youer naighborhood is destitute of leading men either to call a meeting or otherwise to acte in youer publicke concernes, this Court impowers you the aboue named Joseph Church to call your naighborhood att Saconett together in convenient time, to make such necessary and wholesome orders as may be for your comon good & peace, and to choose and present some fitt p'son or p'sons to informe the Court of the p'sent state and condition of the said naighborhood respecting the p'mises to the Court of his ma'tie to be holden att Plymouth aforsaid in June next, and that they choose and send fitt persons to the said Court to serue in the offices of constable and grand jurymen."

## REHOBOTH. INCORPORATED JUNE 4, 1645. Indian name—SEEKONK.

| Date. | SELECTMEN. | CONSTABLES. | REPRESENTATIVES. |
|---|---|---|---|
| 1645 | | Stephen Paine | Walter Palmer. |
| 1646 | | Peter Hunt | |
| 1647 | | William Smith | Walter Palmer, Stephen Paine. |
| 1648 | | John Allin | Robert Titus, John Doggett. |
| 1649 | | William Duvoll | Stephen Paine, Robert Titus. |
| 1650 | None Chosen. | John Read | Stephen Paine, Robert Titus. |
| 1651 | | Thomas Cooper | Stephen Paine, Richard Bowen. |
| 1652 | | Walter Palmer | Stephen Paine, Thomas Cooper. |
| 1653 | | Robert Martin | Stephen Paine, Thomas Cooper. |
| 1654 | | William Carpenter | Stephen Paine, Peter Hunt. |
| 1655 | | Stephen Paine | Stephen Paine, Peter Hunt. |
| 1656 | | Stephen Paine | Stephen Paine, William Carpenter. |
| 1657 | | William Buckland | Stephen Paine, William Sabin. |
| 1658 | | Philip Walker | Stephen Paine, Thomas Cooper. |

## REHOBOTH (CONTINUED).

| Date. | SELECTMEN. | CONSTABLES. | REPRESENTATIVES. |
|---|---|---|---|
| 1659 | | Henry Smith | Stephen Paine, William Sabin. |
| 1660 | | John Butterworth | Peter Hunt, William Sabin. |
| 1661 | | Thomas Cooper | Peter Hunt, William Sabin. |
| 1662 | | Nathaniel Paine | Peter Hunt, Henry Smith. |
| 1663 | | William Carpenter | Peter Hunt, Stephen Paine. |
| 1664 | | Samuel Newman | Peter Hunt, Stephen Paine. |
| 1665 | | Anthony Perry | Peter Hunt, Stephen Paine. |
| 1666 | Stephen Paine, Sr., James Brown, John Allen | Samuel Carpenter, John Perram | Stephen Paine, James Brown. |
| 1667 | Stephen Paine, John Allin, James Browne | Nicholas Peck, John Titus | Peter Hunt, Henry Smith. |
| 1668 | | Robert Fuller, George Kendrick | Peter Hunt, Henry Smith. |
| 1669 | | John Peck, Sam'l Peck | Philip Walker, Nicholas Peck. |
| 1670 | Lieut. Peter Hunt, Stephen Paine, Ensign Henry Smith | John Fitch, Richard Bowen | Stephen Paine, William Sabin. |
| 1671 | Lieut. Peter Hunt, Stephen Paine, Sr., Ensign Henry Smith | Daniel Smith, Preserved Abell | Stephen Paine, William Sabin. |
| 1672 | Lieut. Peter Hunt, Stephen Paine, Sr., Ensign Henry Smith | William Sabin, Sr., John Miller, Sr. | Lieut. Peter Hunt, Daniel Smith. |
| 1673 | | Nathaniel Paine, Gilbert Brookes | Lieut. Peter Hunt, Anthony Perry. |
| 1674 | Lieut. Peter Hunt, Stephen Paine, Sr., Ensign Henry Smith | Jonathan Fuller, John Doggett | Ensign Henry Smith, Daniel Smith. |
| 1675 | Lieut. Peter Hunt, Stephen Paine, Sr., Ensign Henry Smith | Nathaniel Cooper, John Miller, Jr. | Ensign Henry Smith, Daniel Smith. |
| 1676 | Ensign Henry Smith, Daniel Smith, Nathaniel Paine | Nathaniel Cooper | Daniel Smith, Nathaniel Paine. |
| 1677 | Lieut. Peter Hunt, Daniel Smith, Nathaniel Paine | Thomas Cooper, Jr., Samuel Carpenter | Daniel Smith, Nathaniel Paine. |
| 1678 | Lieut. Peter Hunt, Daniel Smith, Ensign Nicholas Peck | Thomas Read, Abraham Perrin | Daniel Smith, Nicholas Peck. |

| Year | | | |
|---|---|---|---|
| 1679 | Lieut. Peter Hunt, Daniel Smith, Ensign Nicholas Peck | Samuel Peck, John Titus, Jr. | Nicholas Peck, Gilbert Brooks. |
| 1680 | Lieut. Peter Hunt, Ensign Nicholas Peck, Gilbert Brooks | Joseph Palmer, Moses Read | Lieut. Peter Hunt, Nicholas Peck. |
| 1681 | Lieut. Peter Hunt, Ensign Nicholas Peck, Gilbert Brooks | Stephen Paine, Nathaniel Chaffee | Ensign Nicholas Peck, Gilbert Brooks. |
| 1682 | Lieut. Peter Hunt, Ensign Nicholas Peck, Gilbert Brooks | Jonathan Bliss, Samuel Walker | Capt. Peter Hunt, Ensign Nicholas Peck. |
| 1683 | Capt. Peter Hunt, Lieut. Nicholas Peck, Gilbert Brooks | Nathaniel Paine | Capt. Peter Hunt, Lieut. Nicholas Peck. |
| 1684 | Capt. Peter Hunt, Lieut. Nicholas Peck, Gilbert Brooks | | Lieut. Nicholas Peck, Gilbert Brooks. |
| 1685 | Capt. Peter Hunt, Lieut. Nicholas Peck, Gilbert Brooks, John Peck, William Sabin | Thomas Cooper, Joseph Peck | Lieut. Nicholas Peck, Gilbert Brooks |
| 1686 | Capt. Peter Hunt, Lieut. Nicholas Peck, Gilbert Brooks, John Peck, William Sabin | John Ormsbee | Lieut. Nicholas Peck, Gilbert Brooks. |
| 1687 1688 | } Government interrupted by Andros. | | |
| 1689 | Lieut. Nicholas Peck, Gilbert Brooks, John Peck, Thomas Cooper, William Carpenter | | Nicholas Peck, Samuel Peck. |
| 1690 | Lieut. Nicholas Peck, Thomas Cooper, Christopher Saunders, John Fitch, Jonathan Fuller | | Gilbert Brooks, Christopher Saunders. |
| 1691 | Lieut. Nicholas Peck, William Carpenter, Jonathan Fuller, Sergt. Thomas Read, Christopher Saunders | | John Woodcock, Christopher Saunders. |
| 1692 | | | Christopher Saunders, Samuel Peck. |

Town Clerks.—William Carpenter, 1645 to 1649; Peter Hunt, 1649 to 1664; Richard Bowen, 1664 to 1658; Richard Bullock, 1659 to 1668; William Carpenter, May, 1668, to 1693.

## SWANSEA. INCORPORATED OCT. 30, 1667. Indian names—ASHUELOT, MATTAPOISET, WANNAMOISET.

| Date. | SELECTMEN. | CONSTABLES. | REPRESENTATIVES. |
|---|---|---|---|
| 1667 | | Nathaniel Peck | John Allen. |
| 1668 | | Jonathan Bosworth | James Browne. |
| 1669 | | Nathaniel Chafee | John Allen. |
| 1670 | James Browne, Mr. Tanner, John Allen | John Martin | James Browne. |
| 1671 | James Browne, Hugh Cole, Samuel Luther | Thomas Barnes | James Browne. |
| 1672 | James Browne, Hugh Cole, Thomas Lewis | John Cole | Hugh Cole. |
| 1673 | Hugh Cole, John Allen | | Hugh Cole. |
| 1674 | Francis Combe, Hugh Cole, Samuel Luther | Hezekiah Luther | Hugh Cole. |
| 1675 | John Allen, Sr., Hugh Cole, Samuel Luther | | |
| 1676 | | | |
| 1677 | John Allen, Sr., Nicholas Tanner, Lieut. John Browne | John Thurburrow | Samuel Luther. |
| 1678 | | Caleb Eddy | Samuel Luther. |
| 1679 | John Allen, Capt. John Browne, Samuel Luther | | Samuel Luther. |
| 1680 | | | Hugh Cole. |
| 1681 | Ensign Thomas Estabrook, Samuel Luther, Obadiah Bowen | | Obadiah Bowen. |
| 1682 | John Brown, Samuel Luther, Obadiah Bowen | Jas. Cole, John Allen | Obadiah Bowen. |
| 1683 | Capt. John Brown, Capt. Samuel Luther, Obadiah Bowen | James Brown, Jr. | Hugh Cole. |
| 1684 | Capt. Samuel Luther, Obadiah Bowen, John Allen | Capt. John Browne | Hugh Cole. |
| 1685 | Capt. John Brown, Obadiah Bowen, Hugh Cole | John Wheeden, Robert Stanford | Hugh Cole. |
| 1686 | John Browne, Hugh Cole, Nicholas Tanner | | Sergt. Hugh Cole. |
| 1687 | } Government interrupted by Andros. | | |
| 1688 | | | |
| 1689 | | | Hugh Cole, Timothy Brooks, William Hayward. |
| 1690 | | | Lieut. James Cole, Thomas Wood. |
| 1691 | | | |
| 1692 | | | |

TOWN CLERKS.—John Myles, Jr., 1671 to 1673; Nicholas Tanner, 1674 to 1676.

## TAUNTON. INCORPORATED SEPTEMBER 3, 1639. Indian names—COHANNET and TECTICUT.

| Date. | SELECTMEN. | CONSTABLES. | REPRESENTATIVES. |
|---|---|---|---|
| 1639 | | John Stronge | Capt. William Poole, John Gilbert, Henry [Andrews. |
| 1640 | | John Deane | |
| 1641 | | William Parker | Capt. William Poole, John Stronge. |
| 1642 | | William Parker | John Strong, John Parker. |
| 1643 | | | Henry Andrews, John Stronge. |
| 1644 | None Chosen. | James Wiat | Capt. William Poole. |
| 1645 | | | William Parker, Richard Williams. |
| 1646 | | Oliver Purchase | Richard Williams. |
| 1647 | | Oliver Purchase | Henry Andrews, Edward Case. |
| 1648 | | Thomas Gilbert | Richard Williams, Edward Case. |
| 1649 | | | Henry Andrews, Edward Case. |
| 1650 | | George Macy | Richard Williams, Oliver Purchase. |
| 1651 | | William Hodges | Richard Williams, Oliver Purchase. |
| 1652 | | James Walker | Thomas Gilbert, Lieut. James Wyat. |
| 1653 | | William Parker | Richard Williams, Lieut. James Wyat. |
| 1654 | | John Deane | Richard Williams, James Walker. |
| 1655 | | John Tisdall | Richard Williams, Lieut. James Wyat. |
| 1656 | | Francis Smith | Richard Williams, Lieut. James Wyat. |
| 1657 | Capt. Wm. Poole, Geo. Hall, Wm. Parker, Lt. Jas. Wyatt, John Dean | Hezekiah Hoare | Richard Williams, Lieut. James Wyat. |
| 1658 | | Peter Pitts | William Parker, James Walker. |
| 1659 | | John Tisdall | Richard Williams, James Walker. |
| 1660 | Records destroyed by fire in 1838. | Henry Andrews | Lieut. James Wyatt, James Walker. |
| 1661 | | William Harvey | Lieut. James Wyatt, James Walker. |
| 1662 | | William Witherell | Lieut. James Wyatt, James Walker. |
| 1663 | | Hezekiah Hoare | Lieut. James Wyatt. |
| 1664 | | Francis Smith | Richard Williams, Lieut. James Wyatt. |
| 1665 | | Joseph Wilbore | Richard Williams, William Harvey. |
| 1666 | Geo. Hall, Rich'd Williams, Walter Dean, Jas. Walker, Wm. Harvey | John Hall | James Walker, William Harvey. |
| 1667 | Geo. Hall, Rich'd Williams, Walter Dean, Jas. Walker, Wm. Harvey | Richard Burt | James Walker, William Harvey. |
| 1668 | Geo. Hall, Rich'd Williams, Walter Dean, Jas. Walker, Wm. Harvey | Samuel Smith | James Walker, William Harvey. |
| 1669 | Geo. Hall, Rich'd Williams, Walter Dean, Wm. Harvey, Jas. Walker | Israel Dean | James Walker, William Harvey. |
| 1670 | James Walker, William Harvey | Nathaniel Williams | James Walker, William Harvey. |

## TAUNTON (CONTINUED).

| Year | | | |
|---|---|---|---|
| 1671 | Lieut. George Macey, Richard Williams, Walter Dean, William Harvey, James Walker | Joseph Wilbore | William Harvey, William Witherell. |
| 1672 | Lieut. George Macey, Richard Williams, Walter Dean, William Harvey, John Tisdale, Sr. | Richard Stevens Hezekiah Hoar | William Harvey, Lieut. George Macey. |
| 1673 | Lieut. George Macey, Richard Williams, Walter Dean, William Harvey, John Tisdale | Aaron Knap, Sr., John Deane | William Harvey, Lieut. George Macey. |
| 1674 | Lieut. George Macey, Richard Williams, Walter Dean, William Harvey, John Tisdale | John Richmond, Shadrach Wilbore | Lieut. George Macey, John Tisdale. |
| 1675 | Lieut. George Macey, Richard Williams, Walter Dean, William Harvey, John Tisdale, Sr. | James Tisdale, Thomas Dean | Lieut. George Macey, William Harvey. |
| 1676 | Lieut. George Macey, Richard Williams, Walter Dean, William Harvey, Samuel Smith | John Hathwey, Wm. Witherell | Lieut. George Macey, William Harvey. |
| 1677 | Lieut. George Macey, Richard Williams, Walter Dean, William Harvey, Samuel Smith | Thomas Gilbert, Jos. Hall | Lieut. George Macey, William Harvey. |
| 1678 | Lieut. George Macey, Walter Dean, William Harvey, James Walker, Samuel Smith | Samuel Williams, Thos. Harvey, Sr. | James Walker, Samuel Smith. |
| 1679 | Lt. Geo. Macey, Wm. Harvey, Walter Dean, Jas. Walker, Sam'l Smith | Jos. Willis, Isaac Dean | James Walker, Samuel Smith. |
| 1680 | George Macy, William Harvey, Walter Deane, Thomas Leonard | Giles Gilbert, Thomas Williams | John Hathwey, Ensign Thomas Leonard. |
| 1681 | Lieut. George Macy, William Harvey, Walter Dean, Thomas Leonard, John Hathwey | Henry Hodges, Ezra Deane | John Hathwey, Ensign Thomas Leonard. |
| 1682 | Lieut. George Macy, William Harvey, Walter Dean, Ensign | John White, James Walker, Jr. | John Hathwey, Ensign Thomas Leonard. |
| 1683 | Geo. Macy, Wm. Harvey, Walter Dean, Thos. Leonard, John Hathwey | | John Hathwey, Ensign Thomas Leonard. |
| 1684 | Lieut. George Macy, Walter Dean, Ensign Thomas Leonard, John Hathway, Sr., John Hall | Joseph Wilbur, John Hodges | John Hathwey, Ensign Thomas Leonard. |
| 1685 | George Macy, Walter Deane, Thomas Leonard, John Hall, William Wetherell | John Richmond, James Walker, Sr. | Ensign Thomas Leonard, Sergt. William Wetherell, Sr. |
| 1686 | Lt. Geo. Macy, Wm. Harvey, Walter Deane, Ens. Thos. Leonard, [John Hall | James Leonard, Joseph [Tilden | Lt. George Macy, Ensign Thomas Leonard. |
| 1687 1688 | } Government interrupted by Andros. | | |
| 1689 | Wm. Harvey, Thos. Leonard, Henry Hodges, Nath'l Williams, Jas. [Leonard, Jr. | | Thos. Leonard, Nath'l Williams, John Hall. |
| 1690 | William Harvey, Thomas Leonard, Henry Hodges, Nathaniel Williams, James Leonard, Jr. | | Thomas Leonard, William Harvey. |
| 1691 | | | John Hathwey, John Hall. |

TOWN CLERK.—Shadrach Wilbur, from 1665 to 1683, and perhaps longer.

# BRISTOL.

| Date. | GRAND JURYMEN. | SURVEYORS OF HIGHWAYS. |
|---|---|---|
| 1681 | John Carey | Jabez Gorham. |
| 1682 | John Carey | Jabez Gorham, John Walker. |
| 1683 | Jabez Gorham | William Ingraham, Solomon Curtis. |
| 1684 | Thomas Walker | Hugh Woodbury, Robert Taft. |
| 1685 | Increase Robinson, Nathaniel Byfield | John Smith, Nicholas Mead. |
| 1686 | Christopher Saunders, Benjamin Jones, Nathaniel Paine | Joseph Ford, Thomas Lewis. |
| 1687 | Nathaniel Bosworth, Nathaniel Reynolds, Thomas Lewis | Joseph Ford, Thomas Lewis. |
| 1688 | | John Saffin, William Throop. |
| 1689 | | Ussell Wardell, George Waldron. |
| 1690 | Nathaniel Reynolds, William Throop, John Rogers | Nathaniel Bosworth, William Stoer. |
| 1691 | Hugh Woodbury, Thomas Walker | John Saffin, Nathaniel Blagrove. |
| 1692 | Nathaniel Reynolds, Nathaniel Paine, Samuel Corbett | Bellamy Bosworth, Eliashil Adams. |

# DARTMOUTH.

| Date. | GRAND JURYMEN. | SURVEYORS OF HIGHWAYS. |
|---|---|---|
| 1664 | Arthur Hathewey | |
| 1665 | Samuel Hix | |
| 1666 | William Spooner | |
| 1667 | Richard Sisson | |
| 1668 | Arthur Hathewey | |
| 1669 | Daniel Wilcox | |
| 1670 | Peleg Sherman | |
| 1671 | George Sisson | William Palmer, Henry Tucker, Richard Sisson. |
| 1672 | Thomas Pope | John Smith, Peleg Tripp, William Palmer. |
| 1673 | William Palmer | Peleg Tripp, John Smith, Thomas Taber. |
| 1674 | Arthur Hathewey | William Bartrum, John Thurburrow. |
| 1675 1676 1677 | [Settlement broken up by King Philip's War.] | |
| 1678 | Arthur Hathewey | |
| 1679 | | Thomas Pope, Nicholas Sisson, Henry Tucker. |
| 1680 | William Bartrum, Seth Pope | |
| 1681 | John Smith, Jr. | |
| 1682 | John Briggs | |
| 1683 | William Earle | |
| 1684 | John Briggs, James Sampson | |
| 1685 | Thomas Briggs | James Sisson, John Russell, Jr., Josiah Smith. |

## FREETOWN.

| Date. | GRAND JURYMEN. | SURVEYORS OF HIGHWAYS. |
|---|---|---|
| 1683 | | |
| 1684 | John Hatheway, Jr. | |
| 1685 | Joshua Tisdale | John Simmons, Benjamin Chase. |
| 1686 | [Government interrupted | |
| 1687 | by Sir Edmund Andros.] | |
| 1688 | | Samuel Gardiner, Job Winslow. * |
| 1689 | | |
| 1690 | Job Winslow | Benjamin Chase, Ralph Earle. |
| 1691 | | |
| 1692 | Benjamin Chase, John Simmons | Ralph Earle, Thomas Makepeace. |

## LITTLE COMPTON.

| Date. | GRAND JURYMEN. | SURVEYORS OF HIGHWAYS. |
|---|---|---|
| 1682 | | |
| 1683 | Simon Rouse | John Irish, William Brownell. |
| 1684 | Jonathan Thurston | |
| 1685 | Simon Rouse | Jonathan Thurston, William Briggs. |

## REHOBOTH.

| Date. | GRAND JURYMEN. | SURVEYORS OF HIGHWAYS. |
|---|---|---|
| 1645 | | Robert Martin, Thomas Cooper. |
| 1646 | William Carpenter | |
| 1647 | Thomas Cooper, Thomas Clifton | Robert Titus, Thomas Bliss. |
| 1648 | Robert Sharp, Joseph Tocry | John Miller, John Pellum. |
| 1649 | Obadiah Holmes | Richard Bowen, Robert Sharp. |
| 1650 | Robert Sharp, Thomas Cooper | Walter Palmer, Peter Hunt. |
| 1651 | Walter Palmer, Peter Hunt | John Read, William Smith. |
| 1652 | Henry Smith | Joseph Peck, Jr., Jonathan Bliss. |
| 1653 | Joseph Peck | Richard Bowen, James Redway. |
| 1654 | James Walker | William Carpenter, George Kendrick. |
| 1655 | Philip Walker, Jonathan Bliss | Richard Ingraham, John Fitch. |
| 1656 | Peter Hunt | |
| 1657 | Nicholas Peck | Philip Walker, Obadiah Bowen. |
| 1658 | Richard Bowen | |
| 1659 | Stephen Paine | |
| 1660 | Nathaniel Paine | |
| 1661 | Samuel Carpenter, John Fitch | |
| 1662 | Daniel Smith, Samuel Newman | Nicholas Ide, John Peck. |
| 1663 | James Brown | John Perrin, Sr., Gilbert Brooks. |
| 1664 | William Sabine | |
| 1665 | John Woodcock | |
| 1666 | Samuel Peck | George Kendrick, Richard Bowen. |
| 1667 | Daniel Smith, Samuel Newman | |
| 1668 | Philip Walker, Jonathan Bliss | |
| 1669 | Stephen Paine, Jr. | Richard Martin, Nicholas Ide. |
| 1670 | Nathaniel Paine | Preserved Abel, John Butterworth. |
| 1671 | John Read | James Readway, John Perren. |

## REHOBOTH (Continued).

| Date. | GRAND JURYMEN. | SURVEYORS OF HIGHWAYS. |
|---|---|---|
| 1672 | John Perrin | Gilbert Brooks, John Doggett. |
| 1673 | Thomas Read | John Miller, Sr., Benjamin Sabine. |
| 1674 | Peter Hunt, Jr. | Nicholas Ide, John Perren, Jr. |
| 1675 | William Sabine, John Butterworth | George Kendrick, William Carpenter. |
| 1676 | William Sabine | Gilbert Brooks, Robert Fuller. |
| 1677 | John Titus, Sr. | Stephen Paine, Jr., John Butterworth. |
| 1678 | Philip Walker, Obadiah Bowen | Richard Bowen, John Perrin. |
| 1679 | Samuel Newman | Anthony Perry, John Wilmott. |
| 1680 | Joseph Peck | Samuel Carpenter, John Fitch. |
| 1681 | John Titus, Sr., Jonathan Bliss | Thomas Cooper, Jr., Samuel Perry. |
| 1682 | John Peck | William Sabine, John Carpenter. |
| 1683 | Samuel Newman | John Titus, Sr., John Pagett, Thomas Mann. |
| 1684 | Samuel Peck, Preserved Abel | |
| 1685 | William Sabine, John Titus, Sr. | Richard Bowen, Sr., John Doggett. |
| 1686 | | |
| 1687 | [Government interrupted | |
| 1688 | by Sir Edmund Andros.] | |
| 1689 | | |
| 1690 | | |
| 1691 | | |
| 1692 | | |

## SWANSEA.

| Date. | GRAND JURYMEN. | SURVEYORS OF HIGHWAYS. |
|---|---|---|
| 1667 | | |
| 1668 | James Browne | |
| 1669 | Nicholas Tanner | John Allen, Sr. |
| 1670 | Samuel Luther | |
| 1671 | Hugh Cole | Nathaniel Peck, Joseph Carpenter, Zachariah Eddy, |
| 1672 | | Nathaniel Chaffee, Jonathan Bosworth, Hezekiah Luther. |
| 1673 | Joseph Carpenter | John Martin, Jos. Chaffee, Caleb Eddy. |
| 1674 | | |
| 1675 | John Butterworth | Robert Jones, John Thurburrow. |
| 1676 | | |
| 1677 | Zachariah Eddy | Israel Peck, John Crabtree. |
| 1678 | John Butterworth | |
| 1679 | Thomas Eastabrooks | Israel Peck, William Hayward, Nathaniel Lewis. |
| 1680 | | |
| 1681 | John Butterworth | Hugh Cole, Wm. Ingraham, Jos. Chaffey. |
| 1682 | Timothy Brooks | |
| 1683 | | John Wheaton, John West, Geo. Webb. |
| 1684 | | |
| 1685 | Capt. John Brown | William Salisbury, John Martin, John Paddock. |
| 1686 | | |
| 1687 | [Government interrupted | |
| 1688 | by Sir Edmund Andros.] | |
| 1689 | | |
| 1690 | | |
| 1691 | | |
| 1692 | | |

## TAUNTON.

| Date. | GRAND JURYMEN. | SURVEYORS OF HIGHWAYS. |
|---|---|---|
| 1639 | | |
| 1640 | Henry Andrews | |
| 1641 | Henry Andrews | |
| 1642 | Walter, Deane, Edward Case | |
| 1643 | Edward Case, Thomas Gilbert | |
| 1644 | John Tisdale | James Wyatt. |
| 1645 | | James Burt. |
| 1646 | John Strong | |
| 1647 | John Tisdale | Edward Slocum, Edward Rew. |
| 1648 | James Walker, James Wyatt | John Dean, Richard Stacy. |
| 1649 | | James Wyatt, George Macy. |
| 1650 | Edward Case | Thomas Lincoln, Edward Case. |
| 1651 | George Macy | Hezekiah Hoar, John Gallop. |
| 1652 | William Hodges | Richard Paul, Clement Mayfield. |
| 1653 | John Bryant | John Cobb, William Phillips. |
| 1654 | Hezekiah Hoar, James Walker | Anthony Slocum, James Burt. |
| 1655 | William Harvey, Peter Pitts | James Wyatt, Richard Williams. |
| 1656 | George Macy, James Walker | Henry Andrews, Robert Thornton. |
| 1657 | John Tisdale, John Dean | Richard Stacy, Jonas Austin. |
| 1658 | William Wetherill | John Cobb, Richard Burt. |
| 1659 | Anthony Slocum | |
| 1660 | Joseph Wilbur | |
| 1661 | Francis Smith | |
| 1662 | George Macy | Anthony Slocum, William Harvey. |
| 1663 | Peter Pitts, John Bryant | James Leonard, Samuel Smith. |
| 1664 | John Dean | |
| 1665 | Hezekiah Hoar | |
| 1666 | Thomas Leonard | John Cobb, Samuel Williams. |
| 1667 | Joseph Wilbur | |
| 1668 | Edward Babbett | George Macy, Peter Pitts. |
| 1669 | Joseph Wilbur | Edward Rew, James Leonard, Jr. |
| 1670 | William Wetherill | |
| 1671 | Thomas Leonard | John Macomber, Increase Robinson. |
| 1672 | John Richmond | James Walker, Thomas Leonard. |
| 1673 | Peter Pitts | John Cobb, Joseph Wilbur. |
| 1674 | John Bryant, Sr. | Edward Rew, Israel Dean. |
| 1675 | Joseph Wilbur | John Turner, John Bryant. |
| 1676 | Isreal Dean | |
| 1677 | William Wetherill | Thomas Lincoln, Isaac Dean. |
| 1678 | Nathaniel Williams | James Tisdale, James Leonard, Jr. |
| 1679 | William Wetherill,John Richmond | Robert Crossman, Thomas Gilbert. |
| 1680 | James Tisdale, James Leonard, Jr. | Joseph Hall, Joseph Wilbur. |
| 1681 | Joseph Wilbur | Thomas Harvey, Joseph Willis. |
| 1682 | Nathaniel Williams | Robert Crossman, Sr., Samuel Thrasher. |
| 1683 | Henry Hodges | Miles Gilbert, John Lincoln, Sr. |
| 1684 | Isaac Dean | |
| 1685 | James Leonard, Jr., Malachi Holloway | John Bryant, Joseph Tisdale. |
| 1686 | | |
| 1687 | [Government interrupted | |
| 1688 | by Sir Edmund Andros.] | |
| 1689 | | |
| 1690 | | |
| 1691 | | |
| 1692 | | |

## PERSONS APPOINTED TO SOLEMNIZE MARRIAGES.

| Names. | Residences. | Date of Appointment. |
|---|---|---|
| Benjamin Church | Bristol | July 7, 1682. |
| John Carey | Bristol | July 7, 1682. |
| John Cooke | Dartmouth | June 5, 1667. |
| Joseph Church | Little Compton | Oct. 2, 1689. |
| Stephen Paine | Rehoboth | June 8, 1664. |
| Daniel Smith | Rehoboth | March 9, 1677. |
| Thomas Leonard | Taunton | June 5, 1684. |

## INN KEEPERS.

| Name of Town. | Name of Person. | When Licensed. | When Cancelled. |
|---|---|---|---|
| Bristol— | John Rogers | Oct. 28, 1681. | |
| | Jabez Howland | Oct. 28, 1681. | |
| | Uzall Wardell | June 5, 1684. | |
| Freetown— | John Hathway, Jr. | June 5, 1684. | |
| Little Compton— | John Simmons | July 7, 1674. | July 7, 1682. |
| Rehoboth— | John Read | June 6, 1649. | |
| | Robert Abel | July 3, 1656. | |
| | Daniel Smith | July 2, 1667. | |
| | John Woodcock* | July 5, 1670. | |
| Swansea— | Thomas Purdaine | June 6, 1682. | |
| Taunton— | James Leonard | | March 1, 1664. |
| | Richard Paul | Aug. 3, 1640. | |
| | Edward Rew† | March 6, 1670. | July 16, 1678. |
| | James Walker | June 3, 1679. | |

## PERSONS LICENSED TO RETAIL SPIRITUOUS LIQUORS.

| Name of Town. | Name of Person. | Kind of Liquor. | Date of License. |
|---|---|---|---|
| Bristol— | John Rogers | Cider, Beer, Wine and Rum | Oct. 28, 1681. |
| | Jabez Howland | Wine, Beer, Strong Liquors, Cider | Oct. 28, 1681. |
| | Uzal Wardell | Beer and Liquor | June 5, 1684. |
| Rehoboth— | John Read | Wine and Strong Waters | June 6, 1649. |
| | Daniel Smith | Liquors | July 2, 1667. |
| Swansea— | Thomas Purdaine | Beer and Cider | June 6, 1682. |
| Taunton— | William Parker | Wine | June 5, 1644. |
| | Thomas Leonard | Strong Liquors and Wine | Aug. 4, 1663. |
| | William Wetherill | Cider, Beer and Strong Liquors | June 2, 1685. |
| | Shadrach Wilbur | Strong Liquors | Oct. 27, 1685. |

* John Woodcock's inn was in what, in 1694, became Attleborough, and a public house was kept on the spot about 170 years.
† Edward Rew, of Taunton, died July 16, 1678, and Sarah his widow married James Walker, Sr., Nov. 4, 1678. She was a daughter of John Richmond, of Taunton.

### RECEIVERS OR COLLECTORS OF THE EXCISE.

| Name of Town. | Name of Collector. | Date of Appointment. |
|---|---|---|
| Dartmouth— | Samuel Hix | June 5, 1657. |
| | Sergt. James Shaw | June 3, 1668. |
| Rehoboth— | John Doggett | July 7, 1648. |
| | Lieut. Peter Hunt | June 8, 1664. |
| | Richard Bullock | June 8, 1664. |
| | Daniel Smith | June 5, 1667. |
| Taunton— | James Wyatt | July 7, 1646. |
| | James Walker | June 8, 1664. |
| | Francis Smith | June 8, 1664. |
| | Richard Burt | June 5, 1667. |
| | William Harvey | June 3, 1668. |

### COLLECTORS OF MINISTERS' RATES OR TAXES.

| Name of Town. | Name of Collector. | When Appointed. |
|---|---|---|
| Rehoboth— | Lieut. Peter Hunt | June 5, 1671. |
| | William Carpenter | June 5, 1671. |
| Taunton— | William Harvey | June 7, 1670. |
| | James Walker | June 7, 1670. |
| | William Wetherill | June 5, 1671. |
| | Samuel Smith | June 5, 1671. |

### PERSONS APPOINTED TO ENFORCE THE ORDERS RELATING TO LIQUORS.

| Town. | Name of Person. | Date of Appointment. |
|---|---|---|
| Rehoboth— | Samuel Newman | June 5, 1677. |
| Swansea— | John Butterworth, Sr. | June 5, 1677. |
| Taunton— | James Walker | June 5, 1677. |
| | Joseph Wilbur | |

# PLYMOUTH COUNTY.

INCORPORATED JUNE 2, 1685.   SHIRE OR COUNTY TOWN, PLYMOUTH.

## COUNTY MAGISTRATES.

| Name. | Residence. | Term of Service. |
| --- | --- | --- |
| Nathaniel Thomas | Marshfield | June 2, 1685, to 1692. |
| John Cushing | Scituate | June 2, 1685, to 1690. |
| Ephraim Morton | Plymouth | June 2, 1685, to 1692. |
| Thomas Hayward | Bridgewater | May 20, 1690, to 1692. |

### CLERKS OF COUNTY COURT.

| Name. | Residence. | Term of Service. |
| --- | --- | --- |
| Nathaniel Thomas, Sr. | Marshfield | 1685 to 1686. |
| Nathaniel Thomas, Jr. | Marshfield | 1686 to 1689. |
| Samuel Sprague | Marshfield | 1689 to 1692. |

### REGISTER OF DEEDS.

| Name. | Residence. | Term of Service. |
| --- | --- | --- |
| Nathaniel Thomas, Sr. | Marshfield | 1685 to |

### UNDER MARSHAL AND GAOL KEEPER.

| Name. | Residence. | Term of Service. |
| --- | --- | --- |
| Samuel Dunham | Plymouth | June, 1686, to |

Act of Incorporation :—

"It is Ordered That Plimouth, Duxbury, Scituate, Marshfield, Bridgewater and Middleborough, together with all such places and Villages, that do or may lye between the said Towns and the Patent Line, be a County, Plymouth the County Town, and the said County called the County of Plimouth; in which County shall be kept two County Courts annually at the Town of Plymouth; one on the third Tuesday in March; and the other on the third Tuesday in September."

# TOWN OFFICERS.

## BRIDGEWATER. INCORPORATED JUNE 3, 1656. Indian name—NUNKETEST.

| Date. | SELECTMEN. | CONSTABLES. | REPRESENTATIVES. |
|---|---|---|---|
| 1656 | None Chosen. | John Carey | John Willis. |
| 1657 | | Samuel Tompkins | John Willis. |
| 1658 | | Mark Lothrop | John Willis. |
| 1659 | | | John Willis. |
| 1660 | | Samuel Allen | John Willis. |
| 1661 | | John Hayward, Jr. | William Brett. |
| 1662 | | John Eames | William Brett. |
| 1663 | | Samuel Edson | William Brett. |
| 1664 | | Samuel Packer | John Willis, William Brett. |
| 1665 | | Nathaniel Willis | William Brett. |
| 1666 | Nicholas Byram, ...... Hayward, John Willis | Daniel Bacon | John Willis. |
| 1667 | Nicholas Byram, John Willis, John Carey | John Willis, Jr. | John Willis. |
| 1668 | Nicholas Byram, John Willis, John Carey | Nicholas Byram | |
| 1669 | | | |
| 1670 | John Willis, Sr., John Carey, Lieut. Thomas Hayward | Joseph Bassett | John Willis. |
| 1671 | John Willis, John Carey, Lieut. Thomas Hayward | Thomas Snell | John Willis. |
| 1672 | John Willis, John Carey, Lieut. Thomas Hayward | Robert Latham | John Willis. |
| 1673 | John Willis, Sr., Lieut. Thomas Hayward, John Carey | Samuel Edson, Jr. | John Willis. |
| 1674 | John Willis, Sr., Lieut. Thomas Hayward, John Carey | Samuel Packer | John Willis. |
| 1675 | John Willis, Lieut. Thomas Hayward, John Carey | William Brett, Jr. | John Willis. |
| 1676 | John Willis, Sr., John Carey, Samuel Edson | John Aimes, Jr., | John Willis. |
| 1677 | John Willis, Sr., John Carey, Sr., Samuel Edson | John Field | John Willis. |
| 1678 | John Carey, Sr., Samuel Edson, Ensign John Hayward | Zacheus Packer | John Willis. |
| 1679 | John Carey, Sr., John Willis, Sr., Samuel Edson, Sr. | Mark Lothrop | John Willis, Sr. |
| 1680 | | Thomas Snell | John Willis, Sr. |
| 1681 | Dea. John Willis, John Carey, Samuel Edson, Sr. | Edward Vinton | Lieut. Thomas Hayward. |
| 1682 | John Willis, Samuel Edson, Lieut. Thomas Hayward | Joseph Hayward | Lieut. Thomas Hayward |

| Date | Selectmen | Constables | Representatives |
|---|---|---|---|
| 1683 | Dea. John Willis, Samuel Edson, Lieut. Thomas Hayward | Nicholas Byram, Jr. | Lieut. Thomas Hayward. |
| 1684 | Dea. John Willis, Samuel Edson, Lieut. Thomas Hayward | Thomas Washburn | Lieut. Thomas Hayward. |
| 1685 | Dea. John Willis, Samuel Edson, Lieut. Thomas Hayward | | Lieut. Thomas Hayward. |
| 1686 | Dea. John Willis, Samuel Edson, Sr., Lieut. Thomas Hayward | | |
| 1687 | } Government interrupted by Andros. | | |
| 6 1688 | | | |
| 1689 | | | Capt. Thomas Hayward, William Brett. |
| 1690 | John Willis, Capt. Thomas Hayward, Lieut. John Hayward, John Field, John King | | William Brett. |
| 1691 | | | Josiah Edson. |

TOWN CLERKS.—John Carey, 1656 to 1681; Thomas Hayward, 1681 or 1682 to 1683; Samuel Allen, 1683 to 1702.

ACT OF INCORPORATION, PASSED JUNE 3, 1656.—"Ordered that henceforth Duxburrow New Plantation bee allowed to be a townshipe of yᵗ selfe, destinct from Duxburrow, and to bee called by the name of Bridgwater, provided that all publicke rates bee borne by them with Duxburrow vpon equall proportions."—*Old Colony Records*, vol. iii.

## DUXBURY. INCORPORATED JUNE 7, 1637. Indian name—MATTAKEESET.

| Date | Selectmen | Constables | Representatives |
|---|---|---|---|
| 1637 | | Edmund Chandler | Jonathan Brewster, Edmund Chandler. |
| 1638 | | Chr'pher Wadsworth | William Bassett, Christopher Wadsworth. |
| 1639 | | Stephen Tracy | John Alden, Jonathan Brewster. |
| 1640 | None Chosen. | Joseph Rogers | John Alden, Jonathan Brewster. |
| 1641 | | Constant Southworth | William Bassett, Edmund Chandler, Thomas Beebeech. |
| 1642 | | Edmund Hewes | |
| 1643 | | Thomas Bonney | Capt. Miles Standish, John Alden, Jonathan Brewster, William Bassett. |
| 1644 | | Thomas Bonney | John Alden, George Soule, William Bassett, Edmund Chandler. |
| 1645 | | John Tisdale | |
| 1646 | | George Partridge | John Alden, George Soule. |

## DUXBURY (CONTINUED).

| Date. | SELECTMEN. | CONSTABLES. | REPRESENTATIVES. |
|---|---|---|---|
| 1647 | None Chosen. | William Merrick | John Alden, Constant Southworth. |
| 1648 | | Thomas Hayward | John Alden, William Bassett. |
| 1649 | | Francis Sprague | John Alden, Constant Southworth. |
| 1650 | | | George Soule, Constant Southworth. |
| 1651 | | John Vobes | George Soule, Constant Southworth. |
| 1652 | | William Bassett | Constant Southworth, John Bradford. |
| 1653 | | Abram Sampson, Thos. Hayward, Jr. | Constant Southworth, George Soule. |
| 1654 | | Stephen Bryant, John Aimes | Constant Southworth, George Soule, Christopher Wadsworth, W. Paybody. |
| 1655 | | William Clark | Constant Southworth, William Paybody. |
| 1656 | | Edward Hunt | Constant Southworth, William Paybody. |
| 1657 | | Constant Southworth | William Paybody, John Rogers. |
| 1658 | | John Tracy | Constant Southworth, William Paybody. |
| 1659 | | John Washburn | Constant Southworth, William Paybody. |
| 1660 | | Francis West | Constant Southworth, William Paybody. |
| 1661 | | Henry Sampson | Constant Southworth, William Paybody. |
| 1662 | | Benjamin Bartlett | Constant Southworth, William Paybody. |
| 1663 | | John Sprague | Constant Southworth, William Paybody. |
| 1664 | | Joseph Andrews | Constant Southworth. |
| 1665 | | Samuel Seabury, Walter Briggs | Constant Southworth, Lt. Josiah Standish. |
| 1666 | Christopher Wadsworth, Josiah Standish, Benjamin Bartlett | John Rogers | Constant Southworth, Christ'r Wadsworth. |
| 1667 | Christopher Wadsworth, Josiah Standish, Benjamin Bartlett | Samuel Hunt | Constant Southworth, Christ'r Wadsworth. |
| 1668 | Christopher Wadsworth, Benjamin Bartlett, William Paybody | Joseph Wadsworth | Constant Southworth, Josiah Standish. |
| 1669 | Christopher Wadsworth, Benjamin Bartlett, Samuel Seabury | Alexander Standish | Constant Southworth. |
| 1670 | Christopher Wadsworth, Benjamin Bartlett, Samuel Seabury | John Rogers, Jr. | William Paybody. |
| 1671 | Christopher Wadsworth, Benjamin Bartlett, Samuel Seabury | Benjamin Church | Josias Standish, William Paybody. |
| 1672 | William Pabodie, Samuel Seabury, Josiah Standish | John Wadsworth | Josias Standish, William Paybody. |
| 1673 | William Pabodie, Samuel Seabury, Benjamin Bartlett | Ralph Thacher | Josias Standish, William Paybody. |
| 1674 | William Pabodie, Samuel Seabury, Benjamin Bartlett | Samuel West | Josias Standish, William Paybody. |

| Year | | | |
|---|---|---|---|
| 1675 | William Pabodie, Samuel Seabury, Benjamin Bartlett | William Brewster | Josias Standish, William Paybody. |
| 1676 | | David Alden | Josias Standish, William Paybody. |
| 1677 | Josias Standish, Samuel Seabury, John Tracy | Edward Southworth | Josias Standish, William Paybody. |
| 1678 | Benjamin Bartlett, John Tracy, John Wadsworth | John Simmons | Josiah Standish, William Paybody. |
| 1679 | | Joseph Chandler | Josiah Standish, William Paybody. |
| 1680 | Samuel Seabury, William Paybody, John Tracy | Wrestling Brewster | Josiah Standish, William Paybody. |
| 1681 | Samuel Seabury, Benjamin Bartlett, John Tracy | Benjamin Bartlett, Jr. | Josiah Standish, William Paybody. |
| 1682 | Josiah Standish, Benjamin Bartlett, John Tracy | John Partridge | Josiah Standish, William Paybody. |
| 1683 | Josiah Standish, Benjamin Bartlett, John Tracy | Josiah Holmes | Josiah Standish, John Tracy. |
| 1684 | John Wadsworth, Benjamin Bartlett, John Tracy | William Vobes | Josiah Standish, John Tracy. |
| 1685 | Francis Barker, Benjamin Bartlett, John Tracy | Robert Barker, Samuel Bartlett | Josiah Standish, Benjamin Bartlett. |
| 1686 | Francis Barker, Benjamin Bartlett, John Tracy | | F. Barker, J. Tracy. |
| 1687 | John Tracy, John Alden, Dea. J. Wadsworth | Isaac Barker, Joseph Harlow | Edward Southworth, Seth Arnold. |
| 1688 | John Alden, F. Barker, E. Southworth | | Edward Southworth, Seth Arnold. |
| 1689 | John Tracy, John Alden, Dea. J. Wadsworth | Roger Glass, Francis Barker | Edward Southworth, Seth Arnold. |
| 1690 | Benjamin Bartlett, John Tracy, Dea. J. Wadsworth | Stephen Sampson, John Russell | Dea. J. Wadsworth, David Alden. |
| 1691 | Benjamin Bartlett, John Tracy, Francis Barker | Thomas Oldham, Thomas Delano | Edward Southworth, Dea. J. Wadsworth. |
| 1692 | John Tracy, William Brewster, John Alden | James Partridge, William Tubbs | Edward Southworth, Dea. J. Wadsworth. |

TOWN CLERKS.—William Pabodie, 1666 to 1684; Rodolphus Thacher, 1685 to 1694. TREASURERS.—William Brewster; David Alden, 1701.

ACT OF INCORPORATION, PASSED JUNE 7, 1637.—"It is enacted by the Court that Ducksborrow shall become a township and unite together for their better securitie and to haue the priveledges of a towne; onely their bounds & limmits shalbe sett and appoynted by the next Court."

## MARSHFIELD. INCORPORATED MARCH 2, 1640.

| Date. | SELECTMEN. | CONSTABLES. | REPRESENTATIVES. |
|---|---|---|---|
| 1640 | | Josias Winslow | William Thomas, Thomas Bourne. |
| 1641 | | | Thomas Bourne, Kenelm Winslow, Nathaniel Thomas. |
| 1642 | | Francis West | Josias Winslow, Kenelm Winslow, Robert Waterman. |
| 1643 | | John Russell | Kenelm Winslow, Robert Waterman. |
| 1644 | | John Dingley | |
| 1645 | | John Rowae, Gilbert Brooke | William Thomas, Thomas Bourne. |
| 1646 | None Chosen. | Thos. Chillingsworth, Robert Barker | Josias Winslow, Robert Waterman. |
| 1647 | | Kenelm Winslow, Peter Collamore | Josias Winslow, Robert Waterman. |
| 1648 | | John Gorham, Thomas Tilden | Robert Waterman, Thos. Chillingsworth. |
| 1649 | | | Kanelm Winslow, Robert Waterman. |
| 1650 | | Joseph Bedle, Morris Trouant | Kanelm Winslow, Robert Waterman. |
| 1651 | | John Burne, Jeremiah Burrows | Kanelm Winslow, Josiah Winslow. |
| 1652 | | Anthony Snow, Lieut. Peregrine White | Kanelm Winslow, Thos. Chillingsworth. |
| 1653 | | Robert Latham, Richard Beaae | Kanelm Winslow, Anthony Eames. |
| 1654 | | Georg. Russell, John Rogers | Anthony Eames, Josias Winslow. |
| 1655 | | John Bradford, Richard Silvester | Anthony Eames, Josias Winslow. |
| 1656 | | Timothy Williamson, George Vaughn | Anthony Eames, Anthony Snow. |

| Year | | | |
|------|---|---|---|
| 1657 | | John Howland, John Phillips | Anthony Eames. |
| 1658 | | William Foard, James Doughey | Anthony Eames, Anthony Snow. |
| 1659 | | Elisha Bisbee, Christopher Winter | Josias Winslow, Sr., Anthony Snow. |
| 1660 | | William Macomber, John Adams | Josias Winslow, Sr., Anthony Snow. |
| 1661 | | John Rogers, John Carner | Anthony Eames, Anthony Snow. |
| 1662 | | Capt. Nath. Thomas, Thomas Little | Lt. Peregrine White, Ensign Mark Eames. |
| 1663 | | William Holmes, Justice Eames | Ensign Mark Eames. |
| 1664 | | John Thomas, Francis Crocker | Anthony Snow, Mark Eames. |
| 1665 | | Nathaniel Thomas, Joseph Silvester | Anthony Snow, Mark Eames. |
| 1666 | Peregrine White, Mark Eames, Anthony Snow, John Bourne, William Foard, Sr. | William Foard, Jr., Jonathan Winslow | Ensign Mark Eames, John Bourne. |
| 1667 | Anthony Snow, Mark Eames, John Bourne | Nathaniel Winslow, Josias Keine | Mark Eames, John Bourne. |
| 1668 | Peregrine White, Mark Eames, Anthony Snow | Clement King, Samuel Sprague | Anthony Snow, Mark Eames. |
| 1669 | | John Foster, Joseph Bent | Ensign Mark Eames, Anthony Snow. |
| 1670 | Ensign Mark Eames, John Bourne, William Foard, Sr. | Jacob Dingley | Ensign Mark Eames, Anthony Snow. |
| 1671 | Ensign Mark Eames, Anthony Snow, John Bourne | Wm. Thomas, Arther Howland, Jr., | Ensign Mark Eames, Anthony Snow. |
| 1672 | Lieut. Peregrine White, Ensign Mark Eames, John Bourne | John Sawyer, Josias Snow | Ensign Mark Eames, Nathaniel Thomas. |
| 1673 | | Wm. Sherman, Jr., John Branch | Ensign Mark Eames, Anthony Snow. |
| 1674 | Josias Winslow, Sr., Anthony Snow, Nathaniel Thomas | Michael Foard, John Hewitt | Ensign Mark Eames, Anthony Snow. |
| 1675 | John Bourne, William Foard, Sr., Nathaniel Thomas | John Rouse, Jr., Thos. Doggett | Ensign Mark Eames, Anthony Snow. |
| 1676 | | | Ensign Mark Eames, Anthony Snow. |

## MARSHFIELD (CONTINUED).

| Date. | SELECTMEN. | CONSTABLES. | REPRESENTATIVES. |
|---|---|---|---|
| 1676 | Ensign Mark Eames, William Foard, Sr., Anthony Snow | John Bourne, Samuel Sherman | Ensign Mark Eames, Anthony Snow. |
| 1677 | Anthony Snow, Nathaniel Thomas, Samuel Sprague | Isaac Little, Ralph Powell | Anthony Snow, Nathaniel Thomas. |
| 1678 | | Samuel Arnold, Thos. Macomber | Ensign Mark Eames, Anthony Snow. |
| 1679 | Anthony Snow, Ensign Mark Eames, John Bourne | Ephraim Little, John Thomas, Jr. | Ensign Mark Eames, Anthony Snow. |
| 1680 | Anthony Snow, Ensign Mark Eames, John Bourne | Joseph Waterman, Joseph Bumpus | Ensign Mark Eames, Anthony Snow. |
| 1681 | Anthony Snow, Ensign Mark Eames, Samuel Sprague | | Ensign Mark Eames, Anthony Snow. |
| 1682 | Anthony Snow, John Bourne, Capt. Nathaniel Thomas | Isaac Holmes, John Doggett | Capt. Nath. Thomas, Ser. Samuel Sprague. |
| 1683 | Lieut. Mark Eames, John Bourne, Capt. Nathaniel Thomas | Hopestill Bisbee | Capt. Nath. Thomas, Ser. Samuel Sprague. |
| 1684 | Lieut. Isaac Little, John Bourne, Nathaniel Winslow | Israel Holmes | Capt. Nath. Thomas, Ser. Samuel Sprague. |
| 1685 | Capt. Nathaniel Thomas, Ens. Wm. Ford, Sr., Serg. Nath. Winslow | Samuel Doggett, Jonathan Crucker | Capt. Nath. Thomas, Lieut. Isaac Little. |
| 1686 | Capt. Nathaniel Thomas, Sergt. Nathaniel Winslow, Sergt. Sprague | Samuel Little | Lieut. Isaac Little, Sergt. Samuel Sprague. |
| 1687 1688 | } Government interrupted by Andros. | | |
| 1689 | Nathaniel Winslow, Josiah Snow | | Nathaniel Winslow, John Bourne, Isaac Little. |
| 1690 1691 1692 | Ephraim Little, John Foster, Joseph Waterman | | Capt. Nathaniel Thomas, Lieut. Isaac Little. Capt. Nathaniel Thomas, Lieut. Isaac Little. |

MIDDLEBOROUGH. INCORPORATED JUNE, 1669. Indian names—ASSAWOMSET, NEMASKET.

| Date. | SELECTMEN. | CONSTABLES. | REPRESENTATIVES. |
|---|---|---|---|
| 1669 | | John Nelson | |
| 1670 | | | |
| 1671 | | | |
| 1672 | | | |
| 1673 | | | |
| 1674 | John Thompson, Jonathan Dunham, Francis Combs | John Irish | John Morton. |
| 1675 | John Thompson, Jonathan Dunham, Francis Combs | John Dunham | John Morton. |
| 1676 | | Isaac Howland | John Thompson. |
| 1677 | [Settlement broken up by King Philip's War.] | George Vaughn | John Thompson. |
| 1678 | | | |
| 1679 | | | |
| 1680 | John Thompson, Francis Combs, Samuel Fuller | Ebenezer Tinkham | John Thompson. |
| 1681 | John Thompson, Francis Combs, John Nelson | Daniel Thomas, Jr. | John Thompson. |
| 1682 | John Thompson, Francis Combs, John Nelson | Ephraim Tinkham, Jr. | John Thompson. |
| 1683 | John Thompson, Isaac Howland, John Nelson | Samuel Wood | John Thompson. |
| 1684 | John Thompson, Isaac Howland, Samuel Wood | David Wood | John Thompson. |
| 1685 | John Thompson, John Nelson, Isaac Howland | John Nelson | John Thompson. |
| 1686 | John Thompson, John Nelson, Isaac Howland | John Allen | John Thompson. |
| 1687 | John Thompson, Isaac Howland, John Allyn | John Miller | |
| 1688 | [Government interrupted by Andros.] | Abiel Wood | |
| 1689 | Samuel Wood, Joseph Vaughn, Nathaniel Warren | William Nelson | Isaac Howland. |
| 1690 | Joseph Vaughn, Ebenezer Tinkham, John Allyn | John Cobb | Isaac Howland. |
| 1691 | | Peter Tinkham | Isaac Howland. |
| 1692 | Isaac Howland, Joseph Vaughn, John Bennett | | Isaac Howland. |

William Hoskins was by a unanimous vote chosen Town Clerk of Middleborough, May 24, 1681; he was succeeded in that office, March 28, 1693, by John Bennett. The town voted to give William Hoskins a load of fish, taken at the herring weir and delivered at his house, for one year's service as town clerk.

PLYMOUTH. INCORPORATED DEC. 11, 1620. Indian names—ACCOMAC, APAUM and PATUXET.

| Date. | SELECTMEN. | CONSTABLES. | REPRESENTATIVES. |
|---|---|---|---|
| 1633 | | Joshua Pratt* | |
| 1634 | | | |
| 1635 | | | |
| 1636 | | | |
| 1637 | | Joshua Pratt | |
| 1638 | | Joshua Pratt | |
| 1639 | None Chosen. | George Bower | John Dome, William Paddy, Manasseh Kempton, John Cook, Jr., John Dunham. |
| 1640 | | Richard Sparrow | William Paddy, Manasseh Kempton, John Cooke, John Dunham. |
| 1641 | | Josiah Cooke | William Paddy, John Jenney, John Atwood, John Howland. |
| 1642 | | Giles Rickett | William Paddy, John Dome, John Cooke, John Atwood. |
| 1643 | | John Finney | John Dome, William Paddy, John Atwood, John Cooke, Jr. |
| 1644 | | James Cole, John Jenkins, Sr. | Wm. Paddy, John Dome, Manasseh Kempton, John Cooke, John Winslowe. |
| 1645 | | Thomas Pope, Robert Finney | Manasseh Kempton, John Howland, John Cooke, Jr., John Dunham, Sr. |
| 1646 | | Robert Paddock, Thomas Whitney | John Howland, Manasseh Kempton, John Dunham, Sr, Thomas Willet. |
| 1647 | | Andrew Ring, Robert Wickson | William Paddy, John Dunham, John Howland, James Hust. |
| 1648 | | Ephraim Morton | William Paddy, John Howland, John Cooke, Manasseh Kempton. |
| 1649 | | | Mr. Paddy, Mr. Howland, Manasseh Kempton, John Dunham, Sr. |
| 1650 | | John Thompson | Mr. Paddy, Mr. Howland, Manasseh Kempton, John Dunham, Sr. |

| Year | | | |
|------|------|------|------|
| 1651 | | John Lettice | John Howland, Manasseh Kempton, Lieut. Southworth, Thomas Clark. |
| 1652 | | Richard Wright | John Howland, John Winslow, John Dunham, Lieut. Thomas Southworth. |
| 1653 (7) | | John Keith | John Howland, Thomas Southworth, John Dunham, Sr., John Cooke. |
| 1654 | | John Morton, Samuel Hicks | John Howland, John Winslow, John Dunham, John Cooke. |
| 1655 | | Thomas Whitney | John Howland, John Dunham, Sr., John Cooke, Thomas Clarke. |
| 1656 | | John Rickard | John Howland, John Dunham, Sr., John Cooke, Thomas Clarke. |
| 1657 | | Gyles Richard | John Howland, Robert Finney, Nathaniel Warren. |
| 1658 | None Chosen. | Gyles Richard, Sr. | John Howland, Robert Finney, Nathaniel Warren. |
| 1659 | | William Shurley | John Dunham, Sr., Robert Finney, Nath'l Warren, Ephraim Morton. |
| 1660 | | George Watson | John Dunham, Sr., Robert Finney, Ephraim Morton, Manasseh Kempton. |
| 1661 | | William Marlow | John Dunham, Sr., John Howland, Nathaniel Warren, E. Morton. |
| 1662 | | Abraham Jackson | John Dunham, Sr., Robert Finney, Ephraim Morton, John Morton. |
| 1663 | | Stephen Bryant | John Howland, Robert Finney, Nathaniel Warren, Ephraim Morton. |
| 1664 | | Samuel Sturtevant | John Dunham, Sr., Robert Finney, Nathaniel Warren, Ephraim Morton. |
| 1665 | John Howland, George Watson, Lt. Ephraim Morton, Robert Finney | William Crow | Nathaniel Warren, Ephraim Morton. |
| 1666 | Lieut. Ephraim Morton, Nathaniel Warren, William Harlow, William Clarke, William Crow | Edward Gray | John Howland, Lieut. Ephraim Morton. |
| 1667 | | Francis Comb | John Howland, Lieut. Ephraim Morton. |
| 1668 | Lieut. Ephraim Morton, Sergt. William Harlow, William Crow | John Wood | Lieut. Ephraim Morton, Samuel Dunham. |
| 1669 | Lieut. Ephraim Morton, Sergt. William Harlow, William Crow | William Clarke | Lieut. Ephraim Morton, Robert Finney. |
| 1670 | Lieut. Ephraim Morton, Sergt. William Harlow, William Crow | Joseph Warren | John Howland, Lieut. Ephraim Morton. |
| 1671 | Lieut. Ephraim Morton, Sergt. William Harlow, William Crow | Jacob Cooke | Lieut. Ephraim Morton, Robert Finney. |
| 1672 | Lieut. Ephraim Morton, Sergt. William Harlow, William Crow | George Watson | Lieut. Ephraim Morton, Robert Finney. |
| 1673 | Lieut. Ephraim Morton, Sergt. William Harlow, William Crow | John Fallowell | Lieut. Ephraim Morton, William Crow. |

## PLYMOUTH (CONTINUED).

| Date. | SELECTMEN. | CONSTABLES. | REPRESENTATIVES. |
|---|---|---|---|
| 1674 | Lieut. Ephraim Morton, Sergt. William Harlow, William Crow | Samuel Dunham | Lieut. Ephraim Morton, William Clarke. |
| 1675 | Lieut. Ephraim Morton, Sergt. William Harlow, William Crow, William Clarke, Ephraim Tinkham | Jabez Howland | Lt. Ephraim Morton, Sergt. Wm. Harlow. |
| 1676 | Lt. Ephraim Morton, William Crow, William Clarke, Joseph Howland | George Morton | Lieut. Ephraim Morton, Edward Gray. |
| 1677 | Lieut. Ephraim Morton, Sergt. William Harlow, William Crow | Jonathan Barnes | Edward Gray, Lieut. Joseph Howland. |
| 1678 | Lieut. Ephraim Morton, William Crow, William Clarke | Nathaniel Southworth | Lt. Ephraim Morton, Lt. Joseph Howland. |
| 1679 | Lieut. Ephraim Morton, Lieut. Joseph Howland, William Crow | John Bartlett | Lieut. Ephraim Morton, Edward Gray. |
| 1680 | Lieut. Ephraim Morton, William Crow, Edward Gray | John Doten | Lieut. Ephraim Morton, William Clarke. |
| 1681 | Lieut. Ephraim Morton, William Crow, William Clarke | Abraham Jackson | Lieut. Ephraim Morton, Joseph Warren. |
| 1682 | Lieut. Ephraim Morton, William Crow, William Clarke | Elkanah Watson | Lieut. Ephraim Morton, Joseph Warren. |
| 1683 | Lieut. Ephraim Morton, William Crow, William Harlow | | Lieut. Ephraim Morton, Joseph Warren. |
| 1684 | Lieut. Ephraim Morton, Lieut. Joseph Howland, Sergt. William Harlow, William Clarke, Joseph Warren | John Bryant, Jr. | Lieut. Ephraim Morton, Joseph Warren. |
| 1685 | William Harlow, Lieut. Joseph Howland, Isaac Cushman | John Rickard | Lieut. Ephraim Morton, Joseph Warren. |
| 1686 | Lieut. Ephraim Morton, Sergt. William Harlow, Joseph Warren, Sr. | John Churchell | Lieut. Ephraim Morton, Joseph Warren. |
| 1687 | Joseph Warren, Sr, Joseph Howland, Isaac Cushman | | |
| 1688 | Joseph Warren, Sr., William Harlow, John Bradford | John Sturtevant | |
| 1689 | | | |
| 1690 | Lieut. E. Morton, Sergt. W. Harlow, Thomas Faunce | | John Bradford, Isaac Cushman. |
| 1691 | | | John Bradford, Isaac Cushman. |
| 1692 | Isaac Cushman, Thomas Faunce, William Shurtliff | Samuel Lucas, Eleazer Ring | John Bradford, Lieut. Ephraim Morton. |

* Constable Joshua Pratt also held the office of Messenger, not only for the town of Plymouth but for the whole colony.

## SCITUATE. INCORPORATED OCT. 5, 1636. Indian name—SATUIT.

| Date. | SELECTMEN. | CONSTABLES. | REPRESENTATIVES. |
|---|---|---|---|
| 1636 | None Chosen. | Humphrey Turner | Anthony Annable, Edward Foster. |
| 1637 | | James Cudworth | Edward Foster, Humphrey Turner, Richard Sillis, John Williams. |
| 1638 | | Anthony Annable | |
| 1639 | | Humphrey Turner | Edward Foster, Humphrey Turner, Edmund Eddenden. |
| 1640 | | George Kennerick | Humphrey Turner, Edmund Eddenden, George Kennerick. |
| 1641 | | Samuel Fuller | Edmund Eddenden, Thomas Chambers, George Kennerick, John Williams, Thomas Robinson, Thomas Rawlins. |
| 1642 | | Josias Checkett | John Williams, Humphrey Turner. |
| 1643 | | John Stockbridge, Robert Stetson | Humphrey Turner, William Hatch. |
| 1644 | | William Reade, Gowen White | Humphrey Turner, John Lewes. |
| 1645 | | Thomas Clapp, John Allen | Humphrey Turner, John Williams. |
| 1646 | | Ephraim Kempton, John Hollett | John Williams, Thomas Chambers. |
| 1647 | | Edward Jenkins, George Sutton | Wm. Hatch, James Cudworth, Thos. Clapp. |
| 1648 | | Isaac Stedman | James Cudworth, Humphrey Turner. |
| 1649 | | | James Cudworth, Humphrey Turner. |
| 1650 | | George Russell, John Williams | James Cudworth, Humphrey Turner. |
| 1651 | | Peter Collamore, George Petcock | Humphrey Turner, Thomas Byrd. |
| 1652 | | John Whetcom, William Parker | |
| 1653 | | Joseph Coleman | Capt. James Cudworth, Robert Stetson. |
| 1654 | | Thomas Robinson, Walter Hatch | Capt. James Cudworth, Robert Stetson. |
| 1655 | | Thomas Pinchen, John Turner | Capt. James Cudworth, Robert Stetson. |
| 1656 | | Abraham Sattley | John Bryant. |
| 1657 | | Joseph Wormall, Henry Ewell | Robert Stetson, Isaac Chittenden. |
| 1658 | | Humphrey Johnson, Isaac Buck | Robert Stetson. |
| 1659 | | John Hews, Richard Curtis | Cornet Robert Stetson, Lieut. Jas. Torrey. |
| 1660 | | Joen Turner, Jr., John Merritt | Robert Stetson, Lieut. James Torrey. |
| 1661 | | Matthias Briggs, Rodolphus Elmes | Robert Stetson, Lieut. James Torrey. |
| 1662 | | John Bryant, John Damon | |

## SCITUATE (CONTINUED).

| Date. | SELECTMEN. | CONSTABLES. | REPRESENTATIVES. |
|---|---|---|---|
| 1663 | | John Sutton | Lieut. James Torrey, Isaac Buck. |
| 1664 | Thomas King, Cornet Robert Stetson, Isaac Chittenden | Isaac Chittenden, William Curtis | Lieut. James Torrey, Isaac Buck. |
| 1665 | Robert Stetson, Thomas King, Isaac Chittenden | George Russell | Lieut. James Torrey, Isaac Buck. |
| 1666 | Thomas King, John Sutton, Isaac Buck | William Peakes | Robert Stetson, Isaac Chittenden. |
| 1667 | | Michael Peirse, William Brooks | Robert Stetson, Isaac Chittenden. |
| 1668 | | Matthew Gannett, Benj. Stetson | Robert Stetson, Isaac Chittenden. |
| 1669 | | Charles Stockbridge, John Vinall | Thomas King. |
| 1670 | | Samuel Clapp, Timothy White | Robert Stetson, Isaac Chittenden. |
| 1671 | | Anthony Collimore, John Ensign | Robert Stetson, Isaac Chittenden. |
| 1672 | Michael Peirse, Jeremiah Hatch, John Cushing | | Robert Stetson, Isaac Chittenden. |
| 1673 | Michael Peirse, Jeremiah Hatch, John Cushing | Nath'l Turner, Henry Chittenden | Robert Stetson, Isaac Chittenden. |
| 1674 | John Cushing, Robert Stetson, Isaac Chittenden | | Robert Stetson, Isaac Chittenden. |
| 1675 | John Cushing, Jeremiah Hatch, John Damon | | John Damon, Jeremiah Hatch. |
| 1676 | | | John Damon, John Cushing. |
| 1677 | John Cushing, John Bryant, Sr., Lieut. Isaac Buck | Joseph Silvester, Joseph White | Robert Stetson, John Bryant, Sr. |
| 1678 | John Cushing, John Bryant, Isaac Buck | Nathaniel Tilden, James Briggs | Robert Stetson, John Bryant. |
| 1679 | John Cushing, Jeremiah Hatch, Lieut. Isaac Buck | John Turner, Jr., Thomas Jenkins | John Cushing, Jeremiah Hatch. |
| 1680 | John Cushing, Jeremiah Hatch, Isaac Buck | John Turner, Jr., Thomas Wade | John Cushing, Jeremiah Hatch. |
| 1681 | John Cushing, Jeremiah Hatch, Capt. John Williams | John Otis, Sr., Thos. Stetson, Sr. | Jeremiah Hatch, Samuel Clapp. |
| 1682 | John Cushing, Jeremiah Hatch, Samuel Clapp | Thomas Nichols, Thomas Perry | Samuel Clapp, Capt. John Williams. |
| 1683 | John Cushing, Jeremiah Hatch, Samuel Clapp | Thomas Pincen, Benjamin Peirse | John Cushing, Samuel Clapp. |
| 1684 | John Cushing, Jeremiah Hatch, Samuel Clapp | William Barrett, John Bryant | John Cushing, Samuel Clapp. |
| 1685 | John Cushing, Jeremiah Hatch, Samuel Clapp | | John Cushing, Samuel Clapp. |
| 1686 | John Cushing, Samuel Clapp | Samuel Stetson, Wm. Ticknor, Sr. | John Cushing, Samuel Clapp. |
| 1687 | } Government interrupted by Andros. | Nathan'l Church. Sam'l Holbrook | John Cushing, Samuel Clapp. |
| 1688 | | John Allen, William Barstow | |
| 1689 | Samuel Clapp, James Briggs, Thomas Jenkins | | Joseph Silvester, Jeremiah Hatch. |
| 1690 | Jeremiah Hatch, Thomas King, Israel Chittenden | | Capt. Joseph Silvester, Samuel Clapp. |
| 1691 | Samuel Clapp, Thomas Jenkins, Nathaniel Tilden. | | |

Scituate was a Constablerick as early as Jan. 1, 1634, when Anthony Annable was "chosen constable for the ward of Scituate, and to serue the King in that office for the space of one whole yeare." Jan. 1, 1636, it was agreed that he should continue in that office another year.

TOWN CLERK.—Lieut. James Torrey, July 18, 1663, and for many years after; Isaac Buck appears to have been clerk from 1674 to 1677.

## BRIDGEWATER.

| Date. | GRAND JURYMEN. | SURVEYORS OF HIGHWAYS. |
|---|---|---|
| 1656 | | |
| 1657 | Joseph Alden | Arthur Harris, John Hayward. |
| 1658 | Thomas Hayward, Jr. | John Aimes |
| 1659 | Arthur Harris | |
| 1660 | Joseph Alden | |
| 1661 | | |
| 1662 | John Carey | |
| 1663 | John Willis | John Willis, Jr., Samuel Allen. |
| 1664 | Nicholas Byram | |
| 1665 | Thomas Hayward | |
| 1666 | Joseph Alden | |
| 1667 | Josias Standish | |
| 1668 | John Hayward | |
| 1669 | | Samuel Allen, Joseph Alden. |
| 1670 | John Hayward | Joseph Bassett, Robert Latham. |
| 1671 | Samuel Allen | John Eames, Sr., John Hayward, Sr. |
| 1672 | John Carey | Samuel Edson, Samuel Packer. |
| 1673 | John Eames | Mark Lothrop, Giles Leach. |
| 1674 | | |
| 1675 | | |
| 1676 | | |
| 1677 | John Carey | Mark Lothrop, John Hayward. |
| 1678 | John Eames | Thomas Turner, John Hayward. |
| 1679 | Samuel Allen, John Hayward, Jr. | Joseph Alden, Joseph Bassett. |
| 1680 | Joseph Alden | |
| 1681 | William Brett, John Carey | |
| 1682 | John Hayward | Elihu Brett, Nicholas Byram, Jr. |
| 1683 | Edward Vobes | |
| 1684 | Joseph Willis | |
| 1685 | Edward Mitchell | Joseph Alden, Comfort Willis. |

## DUXBURY.

| Date. | GRAND JURYMEN. | SURVEYORS OF HIGHWAYS. |
|---|---|---|
| 1637 | Christopher Wadsworth | |
| 1638 | Jonathan Brewster | |
| 1639 | Christopher Wadsworth | |
| 1640 | Jonathan Brewster | Experience Mitchell, Constant Southworth. |
| 1641 | Samuel Nash | Joseph Biddle, Samuel Nash. |
| 1642 | Samuel Nash | Edmund Hawes. |
| 1643 | Love Brewster | |
| 1644 | Constant Southworth | John Rogers, William Sherman. |
| 1645 | John Washburn | John Maynard, Edmund Hunt. |
| 1646 | Joseph Biddle | William Merrick, Morris Trouant. |
| 1647 | Richard Church | Edward Hall, John Brown. |
| 1648 | Love Brewster | Francis Sprague, Abram Sampson. |
| 1649 | Henry Sampson | John Starr, John Washburn. |
| 1650 | Henry Howland | John Starr, John Washburn, Jr. |
| 1651 | John Bradford | Thomas Ganett, John Aimes. |
| 1652 | Christopher Wadsworth | |
| 1653 | John Washburn, Jr. | Edmund Weston, Thomas Bonney. |
| 1654 | George Partridge | Thomas Andrews, Robert Barker. |
| 1655 | Joseph Andrews | Thurston Clarke, Zachariah Soule. |

## DUXBURY (Continued).

| Date. | GRAND JURYMEN. | SURVEYORS OF HIGHWAYS. |
|---|---|---|
| 1656 | Christopher Wadsworth | Henry Howland, John Tracy, Thomas Ensign. |
| 1657 | William Sherman | Moses Simmons, Francis Sprague. |
| 1658 | William Merrick | Experience Mitchell, Francis West. |
| 1659 | Experience Mitchell | Jonathan Shaw, William Clarke. |
| 1660 | Christopher Wadsworth | |
| 1661 | George Partridge | |
| 1662 | William Clarke, Francis West | Christ'r Wadsworth, Moses Simmons. |
| 1663 | Henry Sampson | Samuel Seabury, Samuel Hunt. |
| 1664 | John Tracy | |
| 1665 | Philip Delano | |
| 1666 | Alexander Standish | Joseph Wadsworth, Samuel Chandler, John Williams, Jr. |
| 1667 | Philip Delano | |
| 1668 | Samuel Seabury | George Partridge, Henry Howland. |
| 1669 | Francis West | John Rogers, Sr., Roger Glass. |
| 1670 | John Tracy | |
| 1671 | John Rogers, Sr. | John Wadsworth, Samuel West. |
| 1672 | Jonathan Alden | Robert Barker, John Soule, Joseph Howland. |
| 1673 | Philip Delano | Joseph Wadsworth, Josias Wormall, John Hudson. |
| 1674 | John Rogers, Sr. | John Rogers, Jr., Peter West, Isaac Barker. |
| 1675 | John Wadsworth, Joseph Howland | John Rogers, Sr., Joseph Wadsworth, Joseph Rogers. |
| 1676 | William Peabody | John Rogers, Jr., Thomas Delano. |
| 1677 | Experience Mitchell | George Partridge, Peter West, Robert Barker, Sr. |
| 1678 | Francis West | John Rogers, Abraham Sampson, William Tubbs. |
| 1679 | Philip Delano, Sr. | Robert Barker, Sr., John Tracy, Wrestling Brewster. |
| 1680 | John Rogers | John Wadsworth, Peter West, John Hudson. |
| 1681 | Alexander Standish | George Partridge, Joseph Wadsworth, Josiah Holmes. |
| 1682 | John Wadsworth | John Rogers, Edmund Weston, Abraham Peirce. |
| 1683 | Seth Arnold | |
| 1684 | John Washburn, Jr. | |
| 1685 | Robert Barker, Sr., Josiah Wormall | John Simmons, Joseph Howland, William Tubbs. |
| 1686 | | |
| 1687 | | Wrestling Brewster, Robert Barker, Jr., Elnathan Weston. |
| 1688 | | |
| 1689 | | Joseph Wadsworth, John Russell, John Simmons. |
| 1690 | | James Partridge, James Bishop, John Tracy. |
| 1691 | | Philip Delano, John Bonney, James Partridge. |
| 1692 | | Elnathan Weston, John Russell. |

## MARSHFIELD.

| Date. | GRAND JURYMEN. | SURVEYORS OF HIGHWAYS. |
|---|---|---|
| 1640 | | |
| 1641 | Kanelm Winslow | |
| 1642 | Francis West | |
| 1643 | Robert Waterman | |
| 1644 | William Brooks | |
| 1645 | John Dingley | Thos. Chillingworth, Robert Barker. |
| 1646 | John Bourne | John Dingley, William Brooks. |
| 1647 | Anthony Snow | Thomas Bourne, Thomas Tilden. |
| 1648 | Thomas Bourne | John Russell, Robert Barker. |
| 1649 | | Josias Winslow, William Brooks. |
| 1650 | John Dingley | John Bourne, Richard Beare. |
| 1651 | Elisha Bisbee | Anthony Snow, Peregrine White. |
| 1652 | Robert Carver | Joseph Bedle, William Sherman. |
| 1653 | Thomas Tilden | Robert Carver, William Macomber. |
| 1654 | Kanelm Winslow | John Rouse, Richard Silvester. |
| 1655 | John Dingley | John Phillips, Timothy Williamson. |
| 1656 | Resolved White | |
| 1657 | John Russell | William Foard, Thomas Tilden. |
| 1658 | William Macomber | |
| 1659 | Anthony Snow | |
| 1660 | Peregrine White | |
| 1661 | John Russell | |
| 1662 | William Macomber | John Rouse, William Foard, Jr. |
| 1663 | John Dingley | Thomas Doggett, Anthony Snow. |
| 1664 | Thomas Little | |
| 1665 | John Dingley | |
| 1666 | Anthony Snow | John Dingley, Josias Keane. |
| 1667 | John Dingley | |
| 1668 | Nathaniel Thomas | Joseph Bedle, Resolved White. |
| 1669 | Robert Barker | Joseph Bedle, William Macomber. |
| 1670 | Nathaniel Thomas | |
| 1671 | Nathaniel Winslow | Nathaniel Thomas, Michael Foard. |
| 1672 | John Dingley | Joseph Bedle, Samuel Sprague. |
| 1673 | John Carver | Thomas Doggett, Timothy Williamson. |
| 1674 | Thomas Doggett | John Carver, William Foard, Jr. |
| 1675 | William Brooks | Jonathan Winslow, Samuel Sprague. |
| 1676 | Kanelm Winslow | Jonathan Winslow, Samuel Sprague. |
| 1677 | Nathaniel Winslow | John Foster, John Bourne. |
| 1678 | Francis West | |
| 1679 | Isaac Little | William Foard, John Thomas, Sr. |
| 1680 | William Foard | Nathaniel Winslow, Thos. Macomber. |
| 1681 | Francis West | Josiah Snow, Francis Crocker. |
| 1682 | Thomas Macomber | Ralph Powell, Thomas Doggett. |
| 1683 | Michael Foard | |
| 1684 | Joseph Waterman | |
| 1685 | John Foster, John Rouse | Joseph Waterman, Ralph Powell. |

## MIDDLEBOROUGH.

| Date. | GRAND JURYMEN. | SURVEYORS OF HIGHWAYS. |
|---|---|---|
| 1669 | | ...... Nelson. |
| 1670 | | |
| 1671 | | |
| 1672 | John Miller | Isaac Howland. |
| 1673 | Obadiah Eddy | Samuel Wood. |
| 1674 | | Samuel Wood. |
| 1675 | John Nelson | Obadiah Eddy, John Morton. |
| 1676 | [Settlement broken up by | |
| 1677 | King Philip's War.]* | |
| 1678 | | |
| 1679 | Obadiah Eddy | |
| 1680 | John Thompson | |
| 1681 | Obadiah Eddy | William Nelson, John Miller. |
| 1682 | Isaac Howland | |
| 1683 | Obadiah Eddy | David Thomas, Jr., Joseph Vaughn. |
| 1684 | | |
| 1685 | Obadiah Eddy | John Nelson, David Wood. |

* The town records of Middleborough were lost (probably burned) in King Philip's War.

## PLYMOUTH.

| Date. | GRAND JURYMEN. | SURVEYORS OF HIGHWAYS. |
|---|---|---|
| 1637 | | . |
| 1638 | Thos. Willett, Wm. Paddy | |
| 1639 | Geo. Watson, Nath'l Morton | |
| 1640 | Francis Cooke, James Hurst | Nicholas Snow, Richard Sparrow, Josiah Cooke, Thomas Cushman. |
| 1641 | John Dunham | |
| 1642 | John Winslow, John Dunham, Sr., Edw'd Bangs, Rich'd Church | Giles Rickett. |
| 1643 | John Dunham | |
| 1644 | Thomas Southworth | John Barnes, Thomas Southworth, Thos. Clarke, John Shaw, Sr. |
| 1645 | Gabriel Fallowell | |
| 1646 | Nathaniel Morton | Robert Wixon, Robert Finney, John Finney. |
| 1647 | Giles Ricard, John Morton | |
| 1648 | John Dunham, Sr., Rob't Finney | Richard Sparrow, John Barnes, Thos. Clarke, Jacob Cooke. |
| 1649 | | ...... Howland, Wm. Paddy, Thos. Willett. |
| 1650 | Giles Ricard | Thomas Willett, ...... Howland, William Paddy. |
| 1651 | John Bradford | James Cole, Thos. Pope, Sam'l Sturtevant, Joseph Warren. |
| 1652 | Robert Finney | James Cole, Thos. Pope, Sam'l Sturtevant, Joseph Warren. |
| 1653 | Richard Sparrow | John Moses, Christopher Winter, Thos. Morton. |
| 1654 | Ephraim Morton | Andrew Ringe, Nathaniel Warren, Edward Gray. |
| 1655 | Andrew Ringe | Robert Finney, Henry Wood, William Spooner. |
| 1656 | Henry Wood | Ephraim Tinkham, Wm. Harlow, Jas. Cole, Jr., William Shurtliff. |

## PLYMOUTH (Continued).

| Date. | GRAND JURYMEN. | SURVEYORS OF HIGHWAYS. |
|---|---|---|
| 1657 | John Finney | Samuel Jenney, Thos. Morton, . . . . . . Shaw. |
| 1658 | Joseph Warren | Stephen Bryant, Sam'l Rider, Benajah Pratt. |
| 1659 | Richard Sparrow | Stephen Bryant, Sam'l Rider, Benjamin Pratt. |
| 1660 | Samuel Rider | |
| 1661 | Robert Finney | Robert Bartlett, Andrew Ringe, John Dunham, Sr. |
| 1662 | Jacob Cooke | Joseph Warren, Thos. Lettice, Francis Comb. |
| 1663 | John Morton | James Cole, Sr., Joseph Warren, Sam'l Sturtevant. |
| 1664 | William Harlow | John Barnes, Jacob Cooke, Thomas Morton. |
| 1665 | John Morton | |
| 1666 | | Jacob Cooke, Robert Finney, Thomas Lettice. |
| 1667 | Joseph Warren | John Barnes, . . . . . . Bradford, Hugh Cole. |
| 1668 | Henry Wood | George Bonum, Joseph Howland, Jonathan Morey. |
| 1669 | Andrew Ringe | George Morton, Thomas Cushman, Jr., Benajah Pratt. |
| 1670 | John Finney | George Bonum, Stephen Bryant, Abraham Jackson. |
| 1671 | Edward Gray | Joseph Warren, Daniel Dunham, John Dotey. |
| 1672 | John Finney | John Holmes, Joseph Bartlett, Benajah Pratt. |
| 1673 | William Harlow | Joseph Warren, Andrew Ringe, Jonathan Shaw, Nathaniel Southworth. |
| 1674 | John Finney, Sr. | Stephen Bryant, Andrew Ringe, Thos. Faunce, Ephraim Tillson. |
| 1675 | Andrew Ringe | Joseph Warren, Samuel Dunham, John Doten, Robert Ransom. |
| 1676 | William Harlow | Stephen Bryant, Isaac Cushman, Ephraim Tillson, Moredcai Ellis. |
| 1677 | Benajah Pratt | Ephraim Morton, Wm. Harlow, . . . . . . Crow. |
| 1678 | Wm. Harlow, Joseph Warren | Joseph Howland, James Cole, Jr., Ephraim Morton, Jr. |
| 1679 | Andrew Ringe | |
| 1680 | William Harlow | James Clarke, Abraham Jackson, Ephraim Tillson, Elkanah Watson. |
| 1681 | Benajah Pratt | George Bonum, Jonathan Shaw, John Bryant, Jr., Ephraim Morton, Jr. |
| 1682 | William Harlow | Nathaniel Holmes. |
| 1683 | Andrew Ringe | Thos. Faunce, Jonathan Pratt, Elkanah Watson, . . . . . . Tinkham. |
| 1684 | Thomas Faunce, Geo. Morton, Jr. | |
| 1685 | Wm. Harlow, Sr., Baruch Jordan | Joseph Warren, James Cole. |

## SCITUATE.

| Date. | GRAND JURYMEN. | SURVEYORS OF HIGHWAYS. |
|---|---|---|
| 1636 | | |
| 1637 | Edward Foster | |
| 1638 | Thomas Bisbee, Henry Bourne | |
| 1639 | Isaac Robinson | |
| 1640 | John Lewis | Richard Sillis, John Lewis. |
| 1641 | Richard Sillis | Thomas Chambers, John Williams. |
| 1642 | Thos. Raulins, Thos. Ensign | |
| 1643 | Humphrey Turner, Thomas King | |
| 1644 | William Brooks | Henry Merritt, Thomas Raulins. |
| 1645 | Thomas Ensign | John Stockbridge, Walter Woodward. |
| 1646 | Thomas Raulins | John Stockbridge, Walter Woodward. |
| 1647 | John Damon | John Williams, Thos. Chambers, Humphrey Turner, Isaac Stockman. |
| 1648 | John Stockbridge | John Willis, Humphrey Turner, Thos. Bird, Thomas Chambers. |
| 1649 | | Walter Briggs, Edward Jenkins. |
| 1650 | Edward Jenkins | Peter Collamore, Richard Curtis. |
| 1651 | Joseph Tilden | Thomas Pynchon, John Turner, Sr. |
| 1652 | Robert Stetson | John Hews, Sr., Ephraim Kempton. |
| 1653 | John Williams, Jr. | John Hews, Sr., Ephraim Kempton. |
| 1654 | Humphrey Johnson | John Hallett, Peter Collamore. |
| 1655 | Matthias Briggs | James Cudworth, Robert Stetson. |
| 1656 | Henry Bourne | Walter Woodward. |
| 1657 | Matthew Gannett | George Pitcock, William Randall. |
| 1658 | Edward Jenkins | John Hallett, William Randall. |
| 1659 | Walter Briggs | |
| 1660 | John Bryant | |
| 1661 | Edward Jenkins | Joseph Tilden, Humphrey Johnson. |
| 1662 | Joseph Tilden | James Doughtey, Stephen Vinall. |
| 1663 | John Williams | John Cushing, William Brooks. |
| 1664 | John Hallett | |
| 1665 | Joseph Tilden, Edward Jenkins | |
| 1666 | John Cushing | John Williams, Jr., William Barstow, Thomas Pynchon. |
| 1667 | Joseph Tilden | William Barstow, John Ensign. |
| 1668 | John Damon | Rob't Stetson, Wm. Tickner, Wm. Peaks. |
| 1669 | Joseph Tilden | Rodolphus Elms, James Doughtey. |
| 1670 | Walter Briggs | Michael Peirce, John Turner, Jr., Joseph Barstow. |
| 1671 | Michael Peirce | Richard Curtis, James Cudworth, Jr., Joseph Silvester. |
| 1672 | John Damon | Robert Stetson, Edward Jenkins, Charles Stockbridge. |
| 1673 | Michael Peirce | John Bryant, Sr., Stephen Vinall. |
| 1674 | John Bryant, Sr. | Joseph Barker, James Cudworth, Jr., John Turner, Jr. |
| 1675 | William Brooks | Moses Simmons, Charles Stockbridge, Richard Dwelly. |
| 1676 | John Bryant | |
| 1677 | Richard Curtis | Chas. Stockbridge, John Wetherell. |
| 1678 | John Cushing | John Bryant, Jr., John Vinall. |
| 1679 | Stephen Vinall | Robert Stetson, Edward Jenkins, William Hutch. |
| 1680 | Thomas King, Jr. | Richard Dwelly, Peter Collamore, John Vinall. |
| 1681 | Samuel Stetson | |
| 1682 | Stephen Vinall | Peter Collamore, Jas. Briggs, Benj. Peirce. |
| 1683 | Joseph Silvester | William Randall, Sr., Thomas King, Jr., John Sutton, Sr. |
| 1684 | Joseph Barstow | |
| 1685 | Benj. Stetson, William Perry | John Booth, Edward Jenkins. |

## INN KEEPERS.

| Name of Town. | Name of Person. | When Licensed. | When Cancelled. |
|---|---|---|---|
| Bridgewater— | Samuel Packard<br>John Hayward | March 8, 1671.<br>Oct. 29, 1672. | |
| Duxbury— | Francis Sprague<br>John Sprague | Oct. 1, 1638.<br>Oct. 29, 1669. | June 5, 1666.*<br>March 26, 1676.† |
| Marshfield— | Robert Barker<br>Timothy Williamson<br>Mary Williamson | July 7, 1646.<br>March 4, 1674.<br>Oct. 30, 1678. | June 5, 1666. |
| Middleborough— | George Vaughn<br>Francis Combs<br>Isaac Howland<br>Mrs. Mary Combs | July 5, 1669.<br>Oct. 30, 1678.<br>June 5, 1684.<br>July 1, 1684. | [1682.<br>He died Dec. 31, |
| Plymouth— | John Morton<br>James Cole<br>Giles Rickard, Sr. | March 6, 1649.<br>June 9, 1653.<br>March 7, 1660. | |
| Scituate— | Edward Jenkins<br>Nicholas Wade<br>Isaac Chittenden<br>Joseph Barstow<br>Mathew Gannett<br>Joseph Silvester | July 7, 1646.<br>Oct. 6, 1657.<br>March 6, 1666.<br>March 4, 1673.<br>March 4, 1673.<br>March 5, 1684. | March 5, 1684. |

### PERSONS LICENSED TO RETAIL SPIRITUOUS LIQUORS.

| Name of Town. | Name of Person. | Kind of Liquor. | Date of License. |
|---|---|---|---|
| Duxbury— | Thomas Sprague<br>Constant Southworth<br>William Collier | Wine<br>Wine<br>Wine and Strong Waters | July 7, 1646.<br>June 7, 1648.<br>June 13, 1660. |
| Marshfield— | Robert Barker<br>Timothy Williamson<br>Mary Williamson<br>Nathaniel Thomas | Wine<br>Beer<br>Beer, Wine and Liquors<br>Strong Liquors | July 7, 1646.<br>March 4, 1674.<br>Oct. 20, 1681.<br>July 7, 1682. |
| Middleboro'— | Francis Combs | Beer, Wine and Liquors | Oct. 30, 1678. |
| Plymouth— | John Doane<br>John Barnes<br>John Morton | Wine<br>Beer<br>Wine | Jan. 7, 1645.<br>May 3, 1648.<br>March 6, 1649. |
| Scituate— | William Eddenden<br>Edward Jenkins<br>Richard Sillis<br>William Barstow<br>Isaac Chittenden<br>Edward Jenkins<br>William Barrell<br>Margaret Murphy | Wine<br>Wine<br><br><br>Wine and Liquors<br>Beer<br>Brandy and Rum<br>Strong Liquors | June 5, 1644.<br>July 7, 1646.<br>June 7, 1648.<br><br>March 6, 1666.<br>July 3, 1677.<br>Oct. 27, 1685.<br>June, 1686. |

* His license was revoked or cancelled in 1639, and renewed not long after.
† He was a soldier under Capt. Michael Peirce, and slain in battle near Pawtucket, March 26, 1676.

## PERSONS APPOINTED TO SOLEMNIZE MARRIAGES.

| Names. | Residences. | Date of Appointment. |
|---|---|---|
| John Willis | Bridgewater | June 7, 1659. |
| Timothy Hatherly | Scituate | June 7, 1659. |
| James Torrey | Scituate | June 8, 1664. |
| John Cushing | Scituate | June 3, 1673. |
| James Cudworth | Scituate | July 4, 1673. |

## RECEIVERS OR COLLECTORS OF THE EXCISE.

| Name of Town. | Name of Collector. | Date of Appointment. |
|---|---|---|
| Bridgewater— | John Willis | June 8, 1664. |
| | Arthur Harris | June 5, 1667. |
| | John Eames | June 3, 1668. |
| Duxbury— | John Willis | July 7, 1646. |
| | William Paybody | June 4, 1650. |
| | Benjamin Bartlett | June 8, 1664. |
| | Henry Sampson | June 5, 1667. |
| Marshfield— | Robert Waterman | July 7, 1646. |
| | Joseph Beedle | June 1, 1647. |
| | John Bourne | June 8, 1664. |
| | William Macomber, Sr. | June 5, 1667. |
| | Anthony Snow | June 3, 1668. |
| Plymouth— | John Finney | July 7, 1646. |
| | Richard Sparrow | June 1, 1647. |
| | John Morton | June 8, 1664. |
| | William Harlow | June 8, 1664. |
| | Benajah Pratt | June 5, 1667. |
| Scituate— | Samuel House | July 7, 1646. |
| | Samuel Jackson | June 1, 1647. |
| | Henry Merritt | June 4, 1650. |
| | Edward Jenkins | June 8, 1664. |
| | John Damon | June 8, 1664. |
| | John Cushing | June 5, 1667. |
| | Isaac Chittenden | June 3, 1668. |

## COLLECTORS OF MINISTERS' RATES OR TAXES.

| Name of Town. | Name of Collector. | When Appointed. |
|---|---|---|
| Bridgewater— | Lieut. Thomas Hayward | June 7, 1670. |
| | Samuel Parker, Sr. | June 7, 1670. |
| | John Willis | June 7, 1670. |
| Marshfield— | Elisha Bisbee | June 7, 1670. |
| | John Bourne | June 7, 1670. |
| | Josias Winslow | June 5, 1671. |
| | Thomas Doggett | June 5, 1671. |
| Scituate— | Edward Jenkins | June 7, 1670. |
| | John Turner, Sr. | June 7, 1670. |

## DUTIES OF CIVIL OFFICERS AS DEFINED IN THE LAWS OF PLYMOUTH COLONY.

### SELECTMEN.

**1662.**

It is enacted by the Court, That in every Towne of this jurisdiction there be three or five Celectmen chosen by the Townsmen out of the freemen such as shalbee approved by the Court; for the better managing of the afaires of the respective Townshipes; and that the Celectmen in every towne or the major p'te of them are heerby impowered to heare and determine all debtes, and differences arising between p'son and p'son within theire respective Townshipes not exceeding forty shillings; as alsoe they are heerby impowered to heare and determine all differences arising betwixt any Indians and the English of theire respective townshipes about damage done in Corne by the Cowes, Swine, or any other beastes belonging to the Inhabitants of the said respective townshipes; and the determination of the abovesaid differences not being satisfyed as was agreed, the p'ty wronged to repaire to some Majestrate for a warrant to receive such award by distraint.

It is further enacted by the Court, That the said Celectmen in every Township approved by the Court, or any of them, shall have power to give forth sumons in his Ma'ties name, to require any p'sons complained of to attend the hearing of the case, and to sumon witnesses to give testimony upon that account, and to determine of the Controversyes according to legal evidence; and that the p'sons complaining shall serve the summons themselves upon the p'sons complained against, and in case of theire non-appeerance to proceed on, notwithstanding in the hearing and determination of such controversy as comes before them; and to have twelve pence apeece for every award they agree upon.

**1666.**

That one or two of the selectmen whom the Court shall appoint in each Township of this Jurisdiction, bee heerby impowered to administer an oath in all cases committed to them, as alsoe to grant an execution for such p'sons as neglect or refuse to pay theire just dues according to the verdicte of the said p'sons; and that the said Selectmen in every towne bee under oath for the true p'r formance of theire office; and if any p'son finds himselfe agreived with the verdict of said Selectmen, Then they have theire liberty to appeale to the next Court of his Ma'tie holden att Plymouth, provided that forwith they put in Cecuritie to prosecute the appeale to effect and alsoe enter the grounds of theire apeales; and in case any towne doe neglect to chose and p'sent such yearly unto the Courts of Election, That every such Towne shalbee lyable to pay a fine of five pounds to the Countrey's use.

It is enacted by the Court, That the Celectmen in every Township of this Gov'ment shall take notice of all such p'sons that are or shall come into any of the Townships without the approbation of the Gov' and two of the Assistants according to order of the Court, and the said Celectmen shall warne the said p'sons to aply themselves for approbation according to order; which if they shall refuse or neglect, the said Celectmen are heerby impowered to require the p'son or p'sons to appeer att the next Court to bee holden att Plymouth, and to require Cecuritie for theire appeerance, which if any refuse to doe the Celectmen shall informe the Constable of the Towne where hee liveth, which said Constable shall forthwith carry the said p'son or p'sons before the Gov' or some one of the Assistants of this Gov'ment.

Whereas the Court takes notice of great neglect of frequenting the publicke worship of God upon the Lord's day; it is enacted by the Court and the authoritie thereof, That the Celectmen of each Township of this Gov'ment shall take notice of such in there Townshipps as neglect through prophannes and slothfulnes to come to the publicke worship of God; and shall require an account of them, and if they give them not satisfaction, that they returne theire names to the Court,

**1681.**

It shalbe lawfull for either plaintiffe or defendant to require a subpena of any Celectman of the same Towne where the witnesses live to require any p'son to appeer before some one of the Celectmen of the same Towne to give evidence, before some

one or more, whoe shall convey it to the Celect Court of that Towne where the case is
depending.

It is ordered by the Court and the authoritie thereof that the choice of Celectmen
be specified in the warrants that are sent downe to the several Townes for the choice
of his Ma'ties officers; and theire names to be returned into the Court under the
Constables hand, and to be called in Court to take theire oath as is in such case provided; and if in case any providence prevent theire appearance then to appeer before
some Majestrate of this Gov'ment within one month after the said Court, to take
oath under the penalty of twenty shillings.

1683.

That the Poor May be provided for as necessity requireth; This Court ordereth that
the Celectmen in each Towne shall take care and see that the poor in theire respective
Townes be provided for, and are heerby Impowered to relieve and provide for them according as necessitie in theire descretion doth require, and the Towne shall defray the
charge thereof.

And the Select Men of the several Towns are hereby required to give in a list of
the names of such as mispend their time whether House holders or others; and all
single persons that live from under Family Government or will not be governed by
their Parents or Masters where they live, that so the Court may proceed with them
as the case may require.

## CONSTABLES.

1639, March 3d.

That the Constables that live remote hence [i. e. remote from Plymouth] in the
further plantacons, shalbe freed from attendance at the general Courts after they are
sworne except there be speciall cause, and that if the Constable of any towne do goe
from hoame he shall depute some other man in his roome until his returne, provided
it bee such person as hath borne the same place, & for default to forfeit ten shillings.

1640, Sept. 1.

That the Constables of every Towne within the Gov't shall warne the Townsmen
whereof they are to come together as they doe for other townes businesse, when the
Committees shall think it fitt, as well to acquaint them with what is propounded or
enacted at the Court, as to receive instruccions for any other businesse they would have
done.

1654.

In regard that divers that were chosen to the office of Cunstable doe not appear to
take oath: It is enacted by the Court, that any that have been this yeare chosen by
any towne to serve in the office or for the future shalbee, and shall refuse to the take
oath of the Constable being thereunto required by any one Majestrate, shall pay for a
fine fifty shillings.

1657.

That all fines under forty shillings that shall fall in any of the remote Townes of
this Gov'ment, shalbee levied by the Cunstable of that Towne by warrant from the
Treasurer, without sending the Marshall.

1659.

It is enacted by the Court, that every Cunstable of this Jurisdiction shall have a
Cunstable staffe wherby to distinguish them in theire office from others, and to bee
provided by the Treasurer, and to bee delivered by the foregoing Cunstable to him that
succeeds yearly.

1662.

It is enacted by the Court, that the Cunstable in each Township in this Gov'ment
shall gather in all fines that shall fall within his liberties, not exceeding five pounds,
and to have two shillings on the pound for gathering of them.

## DEPUTIES OR REPRESENTATIVES.

1638.

Wheras complaint was made that the freemen were put to many inconveniences and
great expense by their continual attendance at the Courts. It is therefore enacted by
the Court, for the ease of the several Colonies and Townes within the Government,

That every Towne shall make choyce of two of their freemen, and the Town of Plymouth of foure, to be Committees or deputies to joyne with the Bench, to enact and make all such lawes and ordinances as shall be judged to be good and wholesome for the whole, provided that the lawes they doe enact shalbee propounded one Court, to be considered upon till the next Court, and then to be confirmed, if they shal be approved of except the case require present confirmation. And if any act shall be confirmed by the Bench and Committees, which upon further deliberacon shall prove prejudiciall to the whole, That the freemen at the next eleccon Court after meeting together may repeale the same and enact any other usefull for the whole.

And that every Township shall beare their Committees charges, and that such as are not freemen but have taken the oath of fidelitie and are masters of famylies, and Inhabitants of the same Townes as they, are to beare theire p't in the charges of their Committees so as to have a vote in the choyce of them, provided they choose them onely of the freemen of the said Towne whereof they are; but if any such Committees shalbe insufficient or troublesome, that then the Bench and t'other Committees may dismisse them, and the Towne to choose other freemen in their place.

#### 1646.
It is enacted by the Court, That the Ma'trates and committees do constantly meete in Court during the Court tyme, and at the hower of seaven of the clock in the morning in the summer tyme, and at eight in the winter, upon the penalty of VId, for every default made by any, and so continue untill eleven and then to rise to dinner, and after dinner to returne againe, and to continue until a convenyent hower in the evening as the Governour shall think meete, and for every hower any of them shalbe absent after they are called, to pay VId pr hower, except there be sufficient reason shewed for their absence that the Court doth allow of, Provided that the first day of the Court, nine of the clock shalbe the hower to meete at in the morneing.

### TOWN CLERKS.
#### 1646.
It is enacted by the Court, That there shalbe in every Towne within this Government a Clark or some one appoynted and ordained to keep a Register of the day and yeare of the marriage byrth and buriall of every man, weoman, and child within their Township.

#### 1671.
And the Town Clerk or Register keeper of every Town shall exhibit a true and perfect copy into March Court, annually, of all the Marriages, Births and Burials of the year past. And lastly That the Town Clerk shall publish all Contracts of Marriages in the Town.

### GRAND JURY MEN.
#### 1636.
That a great Quest be pannelled by the Gov' and Assistants or the major part of them, & warned to serve the king by enquiring into the abuses & breaches of such wholesome lawes & ordinances, as tend to the preservacon of the peace and good of the subject.

And that they present such to the Court as they either finde guilty or probably suspect, that so they may be prosecuted by the Gov't by all due meanes.

#### 1640, March 2d.
It is enacted, That no presentment hereafter shalbe exhibited to the Grand enquest to be brought to the Bench except it be down upon oath, and that it shalbe lawfull for any of the Assistants to administer an oath in such case.

#### 1644.
That if any man be warned to serve on the Grand Inquest and shall fayle to come and do the service, and take the oath of fidellyty, if he have not taken it already, shall forfaite XXs to the Colonies use.

#### 1646.
It is ordered that the grand jurymen in every Towneshipp once in the yeare, annually doe view all the measures, weights, and tolle dishes in their several towneshipps, & see that they be lawfull according to order, & that every householder have ladders sufficient according to order, & present the defects.

**1659, June.**

It is enacted by the Court, that the severall townes of this Jurisdiction shall pay theire grand jurymen, towards theire expense of time and charge at three Courts, two shillings and sixpence a day, and nothinge att election Courts.

**1686, June.**

Ordered that the Grand Jurymen who are chosen for this next year appear at their severall County Towns upon the third Tuesday of this Instant, to take the oaths and and receive their charge.

## SURVEYORS OF HIGHWAYS.

**1633, July 2d.**

That at such convenient time as shall seeme meet to the Gov^r and Councill upon warning given all men meet together for the mending of the highwaies with such tooles and instruments as shall be appointed.

And for default every person to forfeit three shillings.

**1639.**

It is enacted by the Court, that if an highway bee wanting in any township of this Govern^t upon due complaint, that then the Gov^r or any of the Assistants impanell a Jury, and upon oath charge them to lay out such waies, both for horse and foot, as in Concience they shall find most beneficiall for the Comonwealth, and as little preju- diciall as may bee to the particulares, and that all old pathes shalbee still alowed except other procesion bee orderly made, and that where there are allowed foot pathes over any man's ground which is fenced up the owners of such fences shall make convenient stiles or gates.

**1644.**

That the surveyors of the heigh wayes shall give three days warening to the Teames and other particular persons when they are to amend the heigh wayes as often as need shall require, provided that they warne not one teame nor one person twice before they have gone over all the teames and persons in their towneship.

And he that shall refuse to come being so warned, shalbe brought to the Court to answer his contempt. And that every Surveyor that shall neglect his duty in re- paireing the heigh wayes shall forfaite Xs to the Colonies use.

**1649.**

That if any bee orderly warned to work at the hiewayes & shall neglect, shall be fined for his said neglect 3s per day, & for every teame so warned y^t shall neglect eight shillings per day, & y^t the Surveyors of such Townes wherein such neglect is shall returne theire names to the next Majestraite, y^t by warrant the said fines may bee required by the Cunstable of said Towne for the Townes use, and if it so fale out y^t in the yeare all the teames and persons in the same Towne have not been warned unto the work aforesaid, y^t thay bee all warned over before thay begin again.

**1667, July 2d.**

It is enacted by the Court, That whoesoever are or shalbee chosen to be surveyors of the highwaies shall att the expiration of the yeare give an account of theire actinges about the highwaies to the Selectmen of that Towne.

**1668.**

It is enacted by the Court, That all the Kinge's highwaies within this Gov^rment shalbe forty foot in breadth att least.

## WHO AUTHORIZED TO SOLEMNIZE MARRIAGES.

**1671, June.**

And as the Ordinance of Marriage is honourable amongst all, so should it be ac- cordingly solemized.

It is therefore Ordered, That no person in this Jurisdiction shall joyn any persons together in Marriage but the Magistrate, or such other person as the Court shall authorize in such place where no Magistrate is near, nor shall any joyn themselves in Marriage but before some Magistrate or person authorized as aforesaid, nor shall any Magistrate or other person to be authorised, joyne or suffer any to joyne together in Marriage in their presence, before such persons Publication according to Law.

## INNS AND INN KEEPERS.

**1638.**

Forasmuch as greate inconveniences have beene occationed by young men and other labourers that have dyeted in Inns and Ale houses especially who have had other houses to repaire unto in the same Towne, It is therefore enacted by the Court, That none shall dyett in Inns or Alehouses, nor haunt them which are in the Townes they live in, nor make them the ordinary place of their abode.

**1663.**

It is enacted by the Court and the authority thereof, that noe ordinary keeper in any towne in this Gov'ment shall permit any single persons, either children or servants, under the Gov'ment of parents or masters, or any that are not housekeepers, to buy any strong liquors or wine in theire houses or where they have to doe without libertie from their parents or masters, upon the penaltie of paying a fine of five shillings for every default.

It is enacted by the Court and the authoritie thereof, that all ordinary keepers or retaylers of strong waters doe pay an exise of six pence a gallon for all such liquors as are made in the Collonie and drawn forth and retailed by them, and twelve pence a gallon for all such as they bring in or have brought in unto them from other p'tes, and eight pence a gallon for all wine that shalbe brought in and retailled as aforsaid, and that those that are appointed in each towne to look after the law concerning excessive bringing liquors into the Gov'ment, shall also take up the excise and to have two pence a gallon for all liquors distilled in the Gov'ment, and four pence a gallon for all such as shalbee brought into the Gov'ment, and two pence a gallon for all wine that is brought in and retailled as aforesaid, and that all·such retaillers or ordinary keepers shall make payment of the said Excise unto those that are appointed to receive it; att the same time that they bring in such wine or liquors, or that it is brought in unto them, or give a bill under theirs hand for the payment therof in some short time after upon the penaltie of paying a fine of five pounds for any that shalbee brought in and not excised or securitie given for the payment thereof as aforesaid.

**1671, June.**

For the prevention of great abuse by the excessive drinking of Liquors in ordinaries; This Court doth order that every ordinary keeper in this Gov'ment shall be heerby impowered and required, That in case any p'son or p'sons doe not attend order but carry themselves uncivilly by being importunately desirous of drink when denyed, and doe not leave the house when required, such ordinary keeper shall returne theire names to the next Court; that soe they may be prosecuted according to the nature of the offence; and in case any ordinary keepers shall neglect soe to doe he shalbee fined five shillings for every default.

**1674, June 4th.**

It is enacted by the Court, That as to the restraining of abuses in ordinaries.

That noe ordinary keeper shall sell or give any kind of drinks to Inhabitants of the Towne upon the Lord's day, and alsoe that all ordinary keepers be required to cleare theire houses of all Towne dwellers and strangers that are there on a drinking accoumpt, except such as lodge in the house, by the shutting in of the day light upon the forfeture of five shillings, the one halfe to the Informer and the other halfe to the Townes use.

**1682, June 7th.**

It is enacted by the Court and the authoritie therof, that none shalbe allowed to keepe an Ordinary or publicke house of entertainment, but such as first be approved soe to doe by the Townes wherein they live.

It is enacted that in every place wher week day lectures are kept all victuallers and ordinary keepers shall cleare theire houses of all p'sons able to goe to meeting during the time of the exercise, except in extreordinary cases for the necessary relieffe of strangers unexpected repairing to them, on penalty of five shillings for every such offence.

And that whosever is Licensed to keep such publick house of Entertainment shall be well provided of Bedding to entertaine Strangers and Travellers, and shall also have convenient Pasturing for Horses, and Hay and Provender for their entertainment in the Winter, and shall not be without good Beer, and if any Ordinary keeper do frequently fail in any or all of these upon complaint he shall lose his License.

9

## LICENSED LIQUOR SELLERS.

**1646.**

It is enacted & by the Corte ordered that whosoever shall draw out and sell a lesser quantity or Caske of wine than 10 gallons to any shall be accounted a retayler.

That whosoever retailes beere or wine or strong water & not licensed by order of Courte shalbe fined & pay for the first default double the value of what is so sould and retayled.

**1659, June 7th.**

It is enacted by the Court that no strong liquors shalbee sould in any place within this Government to exceed in prise three shillings a quart.

**1663.**

It is enacted by the Court that noe liquors bee sold in any p'te of this Gov'ment that shall exceed in prise six shillings the gallon, except it bee English speritts.

It is enacted by the Court that whosoever shall sell any wine or stronge waters in any towne of this Government being not alowed by the Court shalbee fined five pounds to the use of the Collonie.

**1669.**

It is enacted by the Court and the authoritie thereof that none shall sell wine, liquors, Cyder or beere by retaile in this Collonie except they have a license and to pay for theire lycense according to the Capacitie of the place where they live.

## COLLECTORS OF EXCISE.

**1650, June 5th.**

Whereas complaint is justly made y' due course is not provided or att least performed and executed for the defraying of such nessesary charges as are expended by the Magestrates of the Government in attending att Courts and uppon other publick ocations for the adminestration of Justice:

It is therefore Ordered by the Generall Court assembled, That forthwith due care bee had y' the order extant concerning the excise bee duely executed and that fit persons bee appointed to receive it and in case of neglect of none payment That then forthwith uppon such neglect warrants be required and graunted out to destraine uppon the goods of such persons as doe neglect to pay it, and y' it be payed in good merchantable pay such as may conduce to the ends aforesaid.

**1661, June 4th.**

It is enacted by the Court that a sufficient man in every town bee appointed to take up what excise shalbee due to the Countrey whether Iron, Tarr, boards, oysters &c., and that the said men bee under oath, and that they shall have power to make serch, and what forfeites they find they shall have the one halfe thereof, and out of the said excise evidenced to have three shillings upon the pound, and that they give a just account to the Treasurer the first of November and the first of May annually.

## COLLECTORS OF MINISTER'S RATES.

The Court proposeth it as a thing they judge would be very comendable and beneficiall to the townes where God's Providence shall cast any whales; if they should agree to sett apart some p'te of every such fish or oyle for the Incouragement of an able Godly Minister amongst them.

**1670.**

Forasmuch as it appeareth to be greatly inconvenient that the minnesters should be troubled to gather in rates for theire maintainance; and may be an occation to prejudice some p'ons against them or theire minnestry, It is enacted by this Court that att June Courts yearly two meet p'sons in each Towne be appointed by the said Court unlesse the townes have already provided whoe shall take care for the gathering in of theire minnester's maintainance for that yeare by inciting of the people to theire duty in that respect, demanding it when due, and if need be by procuring distraint upon the estate of any that shall neglect or refuse to pay theire rates or proportions towards his support according to the order of Court in that case provided. And in case any minnester shall scruple to receive what is soe raised, it shall nevertheless be gathered as abovesaid and be disposed as the Court shall order or advise for the good of the place.

# MILITARY LISTS.

Roster and Rolls of Plymouth Colony Militia,

1621—1692.

## MILITIA COMPANIES.

### BARNSTABLE COUNTY.

| Where Located. | Rank of Officers. | Names of Officers. | Date of Commission. | Date of Discharge. | Cause of Discharge. |
|---|---|---|---|---|---|
| Barnstable— | Captains— | Mathew Fuller | ...... 1668 | ...... 1668 | Promotion. |
| | | Joseph Lothrop | ...... 1682 | ...... 1682 | Promotion. |
| | Lieutenants— | Thomas Dimmock | October 10, 1643 | | |
| | | Mathew Fuller | October 15, 1652 | | |
| | | Joseph Lothrop | ...... 1668 | | |
| | | John Howland | March 8, 1683 | | |
| | Ensigns— | Thomas Dimmock | June, 1638 | | |
| | | Barnard Lumbert | October 15, 1652 | October 10, 1643 | Promotion. |
| | | John Howland | July 7, 1674 | March 8, 1683 | Promotion. |
| | | Shubael Dimmock | ...... 1683 | | |
| Eastham— | Captain— | Jonathan Sparrow | June, 1680 | | |
| | Lieutenants— | Joseph Rogers | June 1, 1647 | | |
| | | Joseph Snow | June, 1680 | | |
| | Ensigns— | John Freeman | March, 1655 | October 2, 1669 | Promotion. |
| | | Jonathan Higgins | June 1, 1675 | July 4, 1679 | Resignation. |
| | | Jonathan Bangs | June, 1680 | | |
| Falmouth— | Ensign— | Jonathan Hatch, Jr. | October 2, 1689 | | |
| Rochester— | Lieutenant— | John Hammond | May 20, 1690 | | |
| | Ensign— | Joseph Doty | May 20, 1690 | | |
| Sandwich— | Captain— | Thomas Tupper | ...... 1690 | ...... 1690 | Promotion. |
| | Lieutenants— | John Blackmore | June, 1638 | | |
| | | William Newland | June 1, 1647 | | |
| | | John Ellis | June 9, 1653 | | |
| | | Thomas Tupper | October 27, 1680 | | |

| Where Located | Rank of Officers | Names of Officers | Date of Commission | Date of Discharge | Cause of Discharge |
|---|---|---|---|---|---|
| Yarmouth— | Ensigns— | Thomas Dexter, Jr. | June 8, 1665 | ...... 167. | Death. |
|  |  | John Gibbs | October 27, 1680 | ...... 16.. | Death. |
|  | Captains— | William Hedge | August 2, 1659 | ...... 169. | Promotion. |
|  |  | Thomas Howes | June 3, 1674 |  |  |
|  |  | John Thacher | ......16.. |  |  |
|  | Lieutenants— | William Palmer | October 10, 1643 |  |  |
|  |  | Samuel Ryder | June 9, 1653 |  |  |
|  |  | John Marchant | Aug. 11, 1670 |  |  |
|  |  | ......Dillingham | July 7, 1674 | ...... 16.. | Promotion. |
|  |  | John Thacher | June 7, 1681 |  |  |
|  |  | Silas Sears | July 7, 1682 |  |  |
|  | Ensigns— | William Palmer | June, 1638 | October 10, 1643 | Promotion. |
|  |  | William Hedge | June 9, 1653 | August 2, 1659 | Promotion. |
|  |  | John Marchant | June 8, 1664 | Aug. 11, 1670 | Promotion. |
|  |  | Thomas Howes | Aug. 11, 1670 | June 3, 1674 | Promotion. |
|  |  | John Thacher | July 7, 1674 | June 7, 1681 | Promotion. |
|  |  | Silas Sears | October 28, 1681 | July 7, 1681 | Promotion. |
|  |  | John Hawes | July 7, 1682 | July 7, 1682 | Promotion. |

JUNE 2, 1686, the Companies at Barnstable, Eastham, Sandwich and Yarmouth, were organized into a Regiment, called the Third Regiment, of which JOHN FREEMAN, of Eastham, was commissioned Major Commandant. The Company at Falmouth was added in 1689, and the Company at Rochester in 1690. A Company at Harwich was probably added in 1694, and one at Chatham in 1712.

## BRISTOL COUNTY.

| Where Located | Rank of Officers | Names of Officers | Date of Commission | Date of Discharge | Cause of Discharge |
|---|---|---|---|---|---|
| Bristol— | Captains— | John Walley | June 6, 1684 | ...... 1702 | Promotion. |
|  |  | Nathaniel Byfield |  |  | Promotion. |
|  | Lieutenant— | Nathaniel Reynolds | June 6, 1684 |  |  |
|  | Ensign— | Jabez Howland | June 6, 1684 |  |  |
| Dartmouth— | Captain— | Thomas Taber | May 20, 1690 |  |  |

## BRISTOL COUNTY (CONTINUED).

| Where Located. | Rank of Officers. | Names of Officers. | Date of Commission. | Date of Discharge. | Cause of Discharge. |
|---|---|---|---|---|---|
| Dartmouth— | Lieutenants— | John Smith | March 4, 1674 | | |
| | | Seth Pope | June 4, 1686 | | |
| | | Jonathan Delano | May 20, 1690 | | |
| | Ensigns— | Jacob Mitchell | March 4, 1674 | 1675 | Slain by Indians. |
| | | James Tripp | May 20, 1690 | | |
| Freetown— | Lieutenant— | Thomas Terry | June 4, 1686 | | |
| Little Compton— | Captain— | Edward Richmond | May 20, 1690 | | |
| | Lieutenants— | Edward Richmond | June 4, 1686 | May 20, 1690 | Promotion. |
| | | William Southworth | May 20, 1690 | | |
| | Ensigns— | Joseph Church | June 4, 1686 | | |
| | | Robert Brownell | May 20, 1690 | | |
| Rehoboth— | Captain— | Peter Hunt | July 7, 1682 | | |
| | Lieutenants— | Peter Hunt | August 1, 1654 | July 7, 1682 | Promotion. |
| | | Nicholas Peck | July 7, 1682 | | |
| | Ensigns— | John Brown, Jr. | August 1, 1654 | November, 1676 | Died. |
| | | Henry Smith | July 8, 1664 | July 7, 1682 | Promotion. |
| | | Nicholas Peck | June 5, 1678 | | |
| | | Thomas Wilmarth | July, 1683 | | |
| Swansea— | Captains— | Samuel Luther | July 7, 1682 | | |
| | | John Brown | June 4, 1686 | | |
| | Lieutenants— | Timothy Brooks | May 20, 1690 | | |
| | | Timothy Brooks | June 4, 1686 | May 20, 1690 | Promotion. |
| | | James Cole | May 20, 1690 | | |
| | Ensigns— | James Cole | June 4, 1686 | May 20, 1690 | Promotion. |
| | | Robert Sanford | May 20, 1690 | | |
| Taunton— | Captains— | William Poole | June, 1638 | | |
| | | George Macy | April 2, 1690 | | |

| Rank of Officers. | Names of Officers. | Date of Commission. | Date of Discharge. | Cause of Discharge. |
|---|---|---|---|---|
| Lieutenants— | James Wyatt | October 7, 1651 | July 5, 1664 | Death. |
| | George Macy | June 7, 1665 | April 2, 1690 | Promotion. |
| Ensigns— | Oliver Purchase | June 5, 1651 | | |
| | George Macy | | | |
| | Thomas Leonard | June 7, 1665 | June 7, 1664½ | Promotion. |
| Captain— | Thomas Leonard (2d Company) | April 2, 1690 | April 2, 1690 | Promotion. |

JUNE 2, 1685, the Companies at Bristol, Dartmouth, Freetown, Little Compton, Rehoboth, Swansea and Taunton, were organized into a Regiment, called the Second Regiment, of which JOHN WALLEY, of Bristol, was commissioned Major Commandant. A Company at Taunton was added in 1690, and probably a Company at Attleborough in 1694—thus making nine Companies. The increase of Companies was so slow that the Militia in Bristol Co. was not divided into two Regiments until about 1740.

## PLYMOUTH COUNTY.

| Where Located. | Rank of Officers. | Names of Officers. | Date of Commission. | Date of Discharge. | Cause of Discharge. |
|---|---|---|---|---|---|
| Bridgewater— | Captain— | Thomas Hayward | October 2, 1689 | August 16, 1698 | Death. |
| | Lieutenants— | Josias Standish | June 6, 1660 | | |
| | | Thomas Hayward, Jr. | September 27, 1664 | October 2, 1689 | Promotion. |
| | Ensigns— | John Hayward, Sr. | October 2, 1689 | October 2, 1689 | Promotion. |
| | | John Hayward, Sr. | September 27, 1664 | | |
| | | Samuel Packard | October 2, 1689 | | |
| Duxbury— | Captain— | Jonathan Alden | October 2, 1689 | February, 1697 | Death. |
| | Lieutenants— | Samuel Nash | June 4, 1646 | | |
| | | Samuel Hunt | ......1681 | | |
| | | John Tracy | October 2, 1689 | | |
| | | Seth Arnold | ......1692 | | |
| | Ensigns— | Constant Southworth | July 7, 1646 | | |
| | | Josiah Standish | October 3, 1664 | April 6, 1653 | Promotion. |
| | | Jonathan Alden | June 1, 1658 | October 2, 1689 | Promotion. |
| | | Francis Baker | October 2, 1689 | ......1691 | |
| | | Benjamin Bartlett | ......1691 | | |
| Marshfield— | Captains— | Nathaniel Thomas | March 5, 1644 | | |
| | | Josias Winslow | June 8, 1655 | June 3, 1673 | Promotion. |

## PLYMOUTH COUNTY (CONTINUED).

| Where Located. | Rank of Officers. | Names of Officers. | Date of Commission. | Date of Discharge. | Cause of Discharge. |
|---|---|---|---|---|---|
| Marshfield— | Captain— | Nathaniel Thomas | July 7, 1681 | ...... 169 . | Promotion. |
| | Lieutenants— | Peregrine White | June 8, 1666 | | |
| | | Isaac Little | July 7, 1681 | | |
| | Ensigns— | Nathaniel Thomas | June, 1638 | | |
| | | Jonas Winslow | June 7, 1648 | August 29, 1643 | Promotion. |
| | | Mark Eames | June 8, 1655 | June 8, 1655 | Promotion. |
| | | William Foard | July 7, 1681 | | |
| Plymouth— | Captains— | Miles Standish | February 27, 1621 | | |
| | | Thomas Willett | March 7, 1648 | December 18, 1669 | Death. |
| | | Thomas Southworth | August, 1659 | | |
| | Lieutenants— | William Holmes | ...... 1636 | | |
| | | Nathaniel Thomas | August 29, 1643 | March 5, 1644 | Promotion. |
| | | Thomas Southworth | March 7, 1648 | August, 1659 | Promotion. |
| | | Ephraim Morton | June 8, 1644 | | |
| | Ensigns— | William Bradford, Jr. | March 7, 1648 | October 2, 1659 | Promotion. |
| | | Joseph Bradford | June 8, 1664 | | |
| Scituate— | Captains— | James Cudworth | June 29, 1652 | | |
| | | Joseph Silvester | October 2, 1689 | | |
| | Lieutenants— | John Vassell | June 29, 1652 | ...... 1690 | Death. |
| | | James Torrey | June 8, 1655 | | |
| | | Isaac Buck | March 1, 1670 | | |
| | Ensigns— | Joseph Tilden | June 29, 1662 | | |
| | | John Williams, Jr. | June 8, 1655 | March 6, 1666 | |
| | | John Sutton | March 1, 1670 | | |
| | | Israel Chittenden | October 2, 1689 | | |

OCTOBER 2, 1658, all the Militia of Plymouth Colony was organized into a Regiment, of which JOSIAS WINSLOW, of Marshfield, was commissioned Major Commandant; he held the office till June 3, 1673, when, being made Governor of the Colony, he was succeeded by WILLIAM BRADFORD, of Plymouth. The Colonial Regiment continued till June 2, 1686, when the Colony was divided into three Counties, and the Militia of each County was made to constitute a Regiment of itself; from that time the Militia of Plymouth County was called the First Regiment.

### Officers of Cavalry Company, Raised at Large in the Colony.

William Bradford, of Plymouth, Captain; John Freeman, of Eastham, Lieutenant; Robert Stetson, of Scituate, Cornet; all commissioned Oct. 2, 1659.

This Company having neglected or refused to procure carbines, according to directions from the Colonial Court, by orders bearing date of June 1, 1675, it was directed that the company should be disbanded.

---

## COMPANY ROLLS.

Containing the names of all male persons residing in Plymouth Colony, between the ages of sixteen and sixty years, who were able to perform military duty, in August, 1643, as shown by the official returns of an actual examination and inspection made at that time.

### BARNSTABLE COMPANY.

COMMISSIONED OFFICER.—Thomas Dimmock, *Lieutenant.*

NON-COMMISSIONED OFFICERS AND PRIVATES.

| | | |
|---|---|---|
| John Lothrop | William Casley | Robert Shelley |
| John Mayo | John Bursley | William Pearse |
| Richard Foxwell | Thomas Allen | William Beetes |
| Nathaniel Bacon | Samuel Jackson | John Crocker |
| Samuel Mayo | William Tilly | Abraham Blush |
| John Scudder | Samuel Hinckley | Henry Ewell |
| Roger Goodspeed | Thomas Hinckley | Dolar Davis |
| Henry Cobb | John Smyth | Lawrence Litchfield |
| Barnard Lumbert | James Cudworth | Thomas Boreman |
| Thomas Huckens | Nicholas Symkins | Anthony Annable |
| Edward Fitzrandle | James Hamblin | John Casley |
| George Lewis | Henry Coggen | John Russell |
| Isaac Wells | Henry Bourne | John Foxwell |
| Henry Rowley | William Crocker | Thomas Blossom |
| Thomas Lothrop | Austin Bearse | Samuel Lothrop |
| John Hall | Thomas Shaw | Joseph Lothrop |
| Thomas Lumbert | John Cooper | David Linnett |
| Robert Linnett | Thomas Hatch | |

### SANDWICH COMPANY.

COMMISSIONED OFFICER.—John Blackmer, *Lieutenant.*

NON-COMMISSIONED OFFICERS AND PRIVATES.

| | | |
|---|---|---|
| Henry Feake | Nathaniel Willis | John Presbury |
| Daniel Wing | Anthony Wright | John Freeman |
| Peter Gaunt | Richard Chadwell | Edmund Clarke |
| Thomas Johnson | Jonathan Fish | William Swift |
| Miles Black | Samuel Arnold | Michael Turner |
| Nicholas Wright | George Allen | Peter Wright |
| Edward Dillingham | Richard Burges | Stephen Wing |
| John Fish | Henry Cole | Thomas Bordman |
| Richard Kerby | Joseph Holly | Ralph Allen |
| Thomas Launder | Thomas Burges | Francis Allen |
| Henry Saunderson | Thomas Burges, Jr. | Thomas Gibbs |
| John Wing | Thomas Tupper | Edmund Freeman, Jr. |
| William Wood | Henry Dillingham | Nathaniel Fish |
| John Ellis | Henry Stephen | Robert Bodfish |
| Thomas Nichols | Thomas Butler | Thomas Greenfield |
| Anthony Bessy | James Skiff | Mathew Allen |
| Joseph Winsor | Lawrence Willis | John Johnson |

10

## YARMOUTH COMPANY.

COMMISSIONED OFFICER.—William Palmer, *Lieutenant.*

NON-COMMISSIONED OFFICERS AND PRIVATES.

Robert Dennis
Thomas Flaune
Nicholas Sympkins
William Chase
William Chase, Jr.
Anthony Thacher
Andrew Hallett, Jr.
Samuel Williams
John Derby
Thomas Paine
William Twining
James Mathews
Yelverton Crowe
John Crowe
Tristham Hull
Edward Sturges
Anthony Berry

Thomas Howe
Thomas Falland
Nicholas Wadiloue
Samuel Hallett
Richard Taylor
William Lumpkin
William Grause
Henry Wheildon
Samuel Rider
Richard Prichett
Richard Temple
Thomas Starr
Benjamin Hammond
James Bursell
William Edge
Robert Davis
Richard Sears

Hugh Norman
Peter Worden
William Nicholson
John Burstall
Emanuel White
William Norcutt
Marmaduke Mathews
Richard Hoar
Roger Else
John Gray
Andrew Hallett, Sr.
Job Cole
Daniel Cole
Hugh Tilly
John Joice
William Pearse
. . . . . . Boreman

## SCITUATE COMPANY.

NON-COMMISSIONED OFFICERS AND PRIVATES.

Charles Chauncey
Thomas Hanford
Robert Hayward
Ralph Clemes
Nathaniel Mote
Henry Advard
William Parker
John Hallett
Gowen White
William Perry
William Holmes
Thomas Ensign
George Willard
Richard . . . . . .
Walter Briggs
John Hoar
John Wadfield
Thomas Allen
John Hewes
James Cudworth
John Whistons
Nicholas Wade
John Tilton
Thomas Symons
Edward Foster
Thomas Rawlins
Thomas Rawlins, Jr.
Robert Brelles
John Witherden
John Beamont
Richard Toute
George . . . . . .
Thomas Tarte
John Dammon
John Hammon

Christopher Winter
Henry Merritt
John Merritt
Isaac Chittenden
Joseph Coleman
John Whitcomb
Thomas Lapham
Edmund Eddenden
Thomas Hyland
John Rogers
Thomas Chambers
Richard Curtis
William Curtis
Joseph Tilden
Thomas Tilden
Edward Tarte
George Sutton
Simon Sutton
Thomas Pynson
Richard Gannett
William Randall
William Hatch
John Lewis
Thomas Wyborne
John Winter
Humphrey Turner
John Turner
John Turner
John Hews
John Williams
John Williams, Jr.
Edward Williams
James Cushman
James Till
Jeremie . . . . . .

Peter Collamore
William Wills
Samuel Fuller
Isaac Buck
William Hatch
Walter Hatch
Harke Luse
Thomas Clay
Goodman Read
Thomas Robinson
Edward . . . . . .
Ephraim Kempton
Ephraim Kempton, Jr.
Walter Woodworth
Isaac Stedman
George Russell
George Moore
William Vassell
John Vassell
Resolved White
William Pakes
Jacob . . . . . .
Thomas King
. . . . . . Wetherell
Thomas Byrd
Edward Jenkins
George Kendrick
. . . . . . Garratt
Henry Mason
Elisha Bisbee
John Bryant
John Hatch
John Stockbridge
Robert Stetson
. . . . . . Glass

## TAUNTON COMPANY.

COMMISSIONED OFFICER.—William Poole, *Captain.*

NON-COMMISSIONED OFFICERS AND PRIVATES.

| | | |
|---|---|---|
| John Browne | Edward Rew | John Stronge |
| John Browne | Thomas Harvey | Thomas Caswell |
| James Browne | James Chichester | John Deane |
| James Walker | William Seward | Edward Abbott |
| ·Oliver Purchase | Aaron Knapp | Walter Deane |
| Thomas Gilbert | John Barrett | William Wetherell |
| Richard Stacye | Richard Williams | Hezekiah Hoar |
| William Holloway | Nicholas Hart | George Macey |
| Timothy Holloway | William Powell | George Hall |
| William Parker | Edward Bobbett | John Perry |
| Peter Pitts | Richard Paule | Benjamin Wilson |
| John Parker | Anthony Slocum | Nicholas Street |
| William Hailstowe | Edward Case | Richard Williams |
| William Hodges | Thomas Farwell | William Evans |
| William Phillips | Tobias Saunders | Christopher Thrasher |
| John Macomber | Henry Andrews | Thomas Cooke |
| Thomas Coggin | John Gallop | Thomas Cooke, Jr. |
| James Wyatt | John Gilbert, Jr. | John Gingell |

## DUXBURY COMPANY.

COMMISSIONED OFFICER.—Miles Standish, *Captain.*

NON-COMMISSIONED OFFICERS AND PRIVATES.

| | | |
|---|---|---|
| Moses Simmons | Henry Sampson | Robert Hussey |
| Samuel Tompkins | John Brown | Richard Wilson |
| James Lindall | Edmund Hunt | Thomas Hayward |
| Thomas Oldham | William Brett | Thomas Hayward, Jr. |
| Edmund Weston | John Phillips | Thomas Robbins |
| William Ford | Thomas Gannet | Arthur Harris |
| Francis West | William Mullins | Edward Hall |
| Francis Godfrey | John Tisdale | Christopher Wadsworth |
| Solomon Lenner | Nathaniel Chandler | William Clark |
| John Irish | John Harding | Comfort Starr |
| Philip Delano | John Ames | John Starr |
| John Alden | Francis Goole | Daniel Turner |
| John Alden, Jr. | John Washburn | George Partridge |
| Moris Trouant | John Washburn, Jr. | John Maynard |
| John Vobes | Philip Washburn | Stephen Bryan |
| William Sherman | William Bassett | John Rogers |
| Samuel Nash | ·William Bassett, Jr. | Joseph Rogers |
| Abraham Sampson | Francis Sprague | Joseph Prior |
| George Soule | William Lawrence | Benjamin Read |
| Zachery Soule | John Willis | Abraham Peirce |
| William Macomber | Jonathan Brewster | William Merrick |
| William Tubbs | William Brewster | William Hartub |
| William Peabody | Love Brewster | ...... Hayden |
| William Hillier | Constant Southworth | Samuel Chandler |
| Experience Mitchell | John Hayward | Joseph Alden |
| Henry Howland | John Farneseed | Alexander Standish |
| | Thomas Bonney | |

## MARSHFIELD COMPANY.

COMMISSIONED OFFICER.—Nathaniel Thomas, *Lieutenant.*

NON-COMMISSIONED OFFICERS AND PRIVATES.

| | | |
|---|---|---|
| Edward Winslow | John Rowse | Alexander Williams |
| John Thomas | Robert Carver | James Pittney |
| Robert Chambers | Anthony Waters | John Dingley |
| Arthur Hadaway | Thomas Roberts | Thomas Chillingsworth |
| Twyford West | Henry Draton | Edward Buckley |
| Edward Bumpus | Ralph Trumble | William Haile |

76        PLYMOUTH COLONY.

Timothy Williams
John Bourne
William Launder
Roger Cooke
Robert Waterman
Josias Winslow
...... Lillye
...... Russell
Kenelme Winslow
James Adams
Arthur Howland

William Holloway
Edward Brough
John Barker
Thomas Howell
Ralph Chapman
Robert Barker
William Barden
William Brooks
Gilbert Brooks
Nathaniel Biel
Richard Beare

Jos. Winslow
Anthony Snow
John Gorham
Joseph Biddle
...... Putle
...... Sherman
John Walker
...... Winman
William Latham
...... Lawrence

## PLYMOUTH COMPANY.

### NON-COMMISSIONED OFFICERS AND PRIVATES.

William Hanbury
Ralph Jones
John Jenkins
Charles Thurston
Robert Eldred
Robert Wixon
George Crips
John Howland
John Howland, Jr.
Francis Cooke
Jacob Cooke
Jacob Cooke, Jr.
Samuel Eaton
William Spooner
Phineas Pratt
George Clarke
Francis Billington
Benjamin Eaton
Abraham Pearse
Mathew Fuller
John Bundy
Thurston Clarke, Jr.
Gregory Armstrong
Robert Lee
Nicholas Hodges
Thomas Gray
John Shaw
James Shaw
John Shaw, Jr.
Stephen Bryan
John Harman
John Winslow
Samuel King
Edward Dotey
William Snow
John Holmes
William Hoskins
James Hurst
George Lewis
John Atwood
William Crowe
Thomas Southwood
John Done
James Cole
James Cole, Jr.
Hugh Cole
Thomas Lettis
John Grome
...... Brick

Thomas Willet
John Cooke
Samuel Hicks
Ephraim Hicks
Richard Knowles
James Renell
James Adams
John Young
Edward Holman
Caleb Hopkins
John Hayward
William Baker
Richard Bishop
John Gorham
William Paddy
Henry Atkins
...... Bradford
John Bradford
Samuel Stertevant
Samuel Cutbert
Thomas Prence
Thomas Roberts
William Nelson
John Smith
Nathaniel Souther
John Reynor
Samuel Fuller
Samuel Eddy
Richard Sparrow
John Kerby
John Jenney
Samuel Jenney
John Jenney, Jr.
Richard Smith
Josias Cooke
John Wood
Henry Wood
Stephen Wood
Robert Paddock
Joshua Pratt
Richard Wright
Andrew Ringe
Gabriell Fallowell
Thomas Cushman
Thomas Savery
John Finney
Webb Addey
Thomas Pope
Giles Rickett
John Rickett

Giles Rickett, Jr.
George Watson
John Barnes
Edward Edwards
John Jordon
John Dunham
Thomas Dunham
Samuel Dunham
Edmund Tilson
John Smalley
Francis Goulder
Thomas Whitney
Ezra Covell
Anthony Snow
Richard Higgens
John Jenkine
Nathaniel Morton
Manasseh Kempton
John Morton
Ephraim Morton
James Glass
Edward Bangs
Joseph Ramsden
Jeremiah Whitney
Nicholas Snow
Mark Snow
William Fallowell
Robert Finney
John Smith, Sr.
Thomas Clarke
George Bonum
William Shercliffe
John Churchill
Joseph Greene
Thomas Morton
Thomas Williams
John Faunce
Richard Church
Gabriell Royle
Nathaniel Warren
Joseph Warren
Robert Bartlett
Thomas Shreeve
Thomas Little
John Thompson
Ephraim Tinkham
William Browne
Thomas Tiley
William Hartopp

## MILITIA LAWS OF PLYMOUTH COLONY, AND DATES OF THE SEVERAL ENACTMENTS.

**1632.**

In regard to our dispersion so far asunder and the inconvenience that may befall, it is further ordered that every freeman or other inhabitant of this colony provide for himselfe and each under him able to beare armes, a sufficient musket and other serviceable peece for war with bandeleroes and other apurtenances, with what speede may be; and that for each able person aforesaid, he be at all times after the last of May next ensuing, furnished with two pounds of powder and ten pounds of bullets, and for each default in himselfe or serv$^t$ to forfiet ten shillings.

**1633, July 1st.**

That all and every person within the colony be subject to such military order for trayning and exercese of arms as shallbe thought meet agreed on and prescribed by the Gov$^r$ and Assistants.

That no servant coming out of his time or other single person be suffered to keep house or be for him or themselves till such time as he or they be competently provided of arms and municon according to the orders of the Colony. And that if any such be yet wanting they be provided as aforesaid, or else provide themselves such masters as may provide for them. And this to be done within the space of one month ensuing.

**1636.**

That in case necessity require to send forces abroade and there be not volunteers sufficient offered for the service, then it be lawfull for the Gov'r and assistants to presse in his Ma$^{ties}$ name by their warrant directed to the Constables.

Provided if any that shall goe returne maymed & hurt he shall be mayntayned competently by the colony duringe his life.

And also that if there shalbe need of horses for the Countreys service, it shalbe lawfull for the Gov$^r$ and assistants likewise to presse horses, paying them for them, for said service by the               , or taking order for their payment.

That concerning misdemanors as any shall be convicted in court of any particular, to be sensured by the bench according to the nature of the offence as God shall direct them.

**1640.**

That the inhabitants of every Towne within the Government fitt and able to beare armes, be trayned at least six tymes in the yeare.

**1641.**

That every Township in the Govern$^t$ shall provide a barrell of powder and leade or bulletts answerable, to be kept by some trusty man or men in every towne, that it may be ready for defence in tyme of neede and danger.

**1642, Sept. 6th.**

It is enacted That those that are appoynted in every Towne to exercise men in Armes, shall have power to set a fyne on such as shall absent themselves upon the days appoynted for exercise, if there be not sufficient reason given for their absence, provided the fyne be with the consent of the company so exercised, or the major part of them, and such fynes to be gathered by the Constable of the place and to be for the benefitt of that Company where such fyne shall happen.

That the Courts doth give power to the Townes to propound two or three persons to the Court to be in any cheefe place above the degree of Serjeants, to exercise their men in armes and to present them to the Court, and such as are approved by the Court to be established and such Officers to choose their under officers with consent of the Body.

That the cheefe millitary comanders of every Towne have power to call forth men & to exercise men in their armes, and to appoynt dayes and the Serjeants to give warning thereof, and to be donn as often as the Court hath appoynted.

That in tyme of feare and danger or suddaine assault of an enemie, the Millitary Commander in every Towne shall have power to call the soldiers of that Towne together, and putt them into a posture of warr, whose commands every souldier shall obey for the defence of the Towneship, and that they follow the directions of the millitary commander of that towne in keeping watch and ward, provided that the ordinary watch be set and appoynted with the Ma$^{trats}$ approbacon of that towne if there be any.

That the millitary company have power together with their cheife comanders to make orders for fineing all such as shall not have their armes compleat and shalbe defective in their appearance & exercise of armes, and to make such orders for furnishing the company with such necessaries as shalbe needful for the exercise.

That all such military fines and forfaitures be levyed & gathered by the Clark of the Company and constable, or one of them, and to bee ymployed to the benefitt of that company.

That all Smyths within the Government be compelled to amend and repaire all defective armes brought unto them speedyly and to take Corne for their pay at reasonable rates ; and the smyth refusing to answer at his p'ill.

#### 1643.

The guns and peeces allowed for service are these viz. Musketts, firelocks and matchcocks, so that they have four fathome of match at all tymes for every matchcock, Caliver, Carbines and fouleing-peeces, so that they be not above foure foot & a half long, and not under bastard muskett or caliver bore.

#### 1645, June 4th.

That the military Officers in every Towne shall see that the Armes of that Towne be fix & compleat, and such as are allowed for length & bore, and to present such as are defective.

#### 1646.

It is enacted by the Court, That in case any cheefe Military Officer as Captaine. Leeftenant or Ensigne be wanting in any Towne within this Government, such Township shall present two or three persons of the fittest they have for that place to the Court, and such person or persons as shall be approved of the Court shalbe established in such place and office.   And such cheefe officer to choose their under officers with consent of the Body.

It is enacted by the Court, That as the Captaine, Leiftenant & Ensign of a Company are established into their places by the authoryty and approbation of the Court, so such Captaine, Leiftenant and Ensigne shall not lay downe their places, but by the consent and approbacon of the Court upon penalty of five pounds for every Captaine, fifty shillings for every Leiftenant and fifty shillings for Ensigne, so laying downe his place without the leave and liking of the Court.   And if any Captaine, Leeftenn[t] or Ensigne shall neglect to trayne their men on the dayes appoynted or shalbe negligent in his or their places, upon proofe therof made shalbe fyned x s. for every such defalt.

It is enacted by the Court, That every Township within this Government before the next October Court, eich Township shall provide two sufficient snaphaumes or firelock peeces, two swords and two pouches for every thirty men they have in their Towneship, and so proportionably for their number they are to set forth be the greater or lesser which shalbe ready at all tymes for service upon any occasion, upon such penalty for every delinquent as the Court shall judg meete according to the nature of the offence.

#### 1657, June 3d.

It is ordered by the Court, That the Millitary companie of every Township in this government shall bring their armes by course every Lord's day to the meeting, viz., that the fourth p[le] of every such companie shall bring theire armes as aforesaid with powder and bullett to improve if occation shall require, and whosoever shall neglect to carry his armes as aforesaid shalbee fined twelve pence for every default to be levied by the Cun. of the towne for the companies use ; and the time of carring of armes to begin on the first of Aprill untill the last of November annually.

#### 1658.

Enacted that every towne that shalbee defective in the want of a drum att any time for the space of two monthes shall forfeit the sume of forty shillings to the Collonies use ; that shalbe defective in Coulbers the space of six months, four pounds.

That every Towne provide halberts for theire sergeants of theire milletary Companie.

That a considerable Companie of half pikes be provided in every towne att the charge of the township, viz.: where 80 men are able to beare armes there twenty to bee provided, and soe proportionable to theire number bee they greater or lesser.

Enacted that such as are chosen Clarke of any Milletary Companie shalbee sworne, and any that shall refuse to serve as Clarke for one yeare, being chosen, shalbee fined twenty shillings ; and he that is next chosen and serves to have the said sume.

It is enacted by the Court and the authority thereof that a fourth part of each Militery Companie in this Jurisdiction shall every Lords day carry theire armes to the publicke meeting in the Township where they dwell, viz., some servicable peece and sword and three charges of powder and bullets, on paine of the forfeiture of 2 shillings and six pence for each daies neglect; and this to bee observed from the first of March to the last of November yearly; these defects to bee gathered by the Milletary Clarke and the Cunstable to the use of the Companie.

It is further enacted by the Court, that the chiefe Milletary Comander in each towne shall take care that a list bee drawne and sett up in the meeting house by which every man may know to what Squadron he belongs and when he is to carry armes, and alsoe to appoint some over every Squadron to take notice and give an account of the severall defects on the penaltie of the forfeiture of five pounds to the Countreys use for such neglect; and that this order take place and begine from the seventeenth of this Instant October, 1658, except men be sick or abroad and have none att home to carry theire armes.

It is enacted by the Court and the authoritie therof, that a troop of horse well appointed with furniture, viz., a Saddle and a case of Petternells for every horse, shalbee raised out of the severall Townshipps to bee reddy for service when required and maintained for that purpose to bee raised as followeth, viz., Plymouth 3, Duxborrow 3, Scituate 4, Sandwich 3, Taunton 3, Yarmouth 3, Barnstable 3, Marshfield 3, Rehoboth 4, Eastham 3, Bridgwater 1. In all thirty and three, and that all such shalbee freed from foot service and from watching & warding and theire horses rate free; and to bee reddy by June next ensueing the date heerof, on the penaltie of the forfeiture of ten pounds for every towne that shall neglect.

1660.

Whereas the Milletary Companies of this Jurisdiction are entered into a Regementall Posture, and therefore that the use of Pikes is nessasary and some alreddy provided for that end; It is enacted by the Court that the charge of the said pikes shalbee borne by the townes respectively and that notwithstanding this order that such as exercised with the said pikes shall keep theire other armes, viz., Muskett &c. fix and fit for service.

In reference unto the Order of Court conserning carrying of armes to the meetings on the Lords day it is enacted by the Court and the authoritie therof, that if any overseer of any Squadron in any milletary Companie of this Jurisdiction that shall neglect to take notice of and p'sent a true list of such as are defective in bringing theire armes to the meeting on the Lords day shalbee fined the sume of three pounds to the Colonies use.

1662.

It is ordered by the Court, that the Generall training shalbee one yeare at Duxborrow and another yeare att Yarmouth, that is to say every other yeare for the future att one of those townes; onely this p'sent yeare for speciall cause it is ordered to bee att Plymouth on the third Wednesday in September next.

It is enacted by the Court that if any one of the foot souldiers of any milletary Companie of this Jurisdiction shall unnessesarily exempt himselfe from appearance att the generall trainings att the time and place appointed except in case of sickness, lameness, Countery business or the like, shalbee fined five shill. a day for every day they shall soe neglect in case they cannot give satisfactory reason therof unto the milletary Comander in cheife of that Companie, and that all such fines shalbee to the use of the Companie to which the delinquents doe belong; and these fines to bee as well for the daies of marching out and home as for the daies of exercise in training.

It is enacted by the Court that the whole troop of horse both they and the voulenteers aded to them shall have the same libertie that was graunted to those that were first Troopers, viz., to be freed from foot service, watching and warding; and likewise theire horses to bee rate free.

Liberty is granted unto the major to admitt soe many volunteers into the troop of horse as will make up the number of forty eight; the Commission officers excepted and all such as continew three years att the least.

1664, June 8th.

This Court takeing notice that there is a great defect of appearance att the Generall trainings, and that hitherto nothing hath bine done effectually in reference unto the troopers for the gathering of theire fines; This Court doth order that such fines as are by the troop settled for defect of appearance att any Generall Training, that upon an order from the Major or the Captaine of the Troope the Constables of such Townes where any such defects are shall forthwith collect the fine in some good and current pay and soe much besides as may transport it unto the Clarke or some place that hee shall appoint for the receiving of it.

It is alsoe enacted by the Court, that noe Trooper whilest hee stands listed in the Troope shall att any time put away or dispose of his Trooping horse unlesse hee have some other horse that is approved by some of the Comission officers of the Troop on penaltie of double the fine for non appeerance. Moreover it is. enacted by the Court, That sufficient warning being given of a generall muster, noe busines or occations by sea or land if in the Countrey shall excuse non appeerance theratt; nor any thinge but sicknes, lamnes or Countrey service.

Wheras the Clarke of each milletary Companie of this Jurisdiction is required to gather in all fines which are or shalbee belong to theire Companie. It is enacted by the Court and the authoritie therof, That in case any shall refuse to pay any such as are or shalbe orderly amersed, That the said Clarke is heerby authorized by destresse to levy all such fines by vertue of his said office without any further order.

1667.

In reference to milletary concernments it is enacted by the Court, that noe single p'sons under twenty yeares of age either children or servants shall voate as to that accompt or any that are not settled Inhabitants of that place and have taken the oath of fidelitie.

1668.

It is ordered by the Court, that there shalbe a Generall Training of both horse and foot att the Towne of Plymouth in the second weeke of October, 1669, and once in three yeare for the future the places to bee att Plymouth, Taunton and Yarmouth successively, that is to say this first att Plymouth as aforsaid, the second att Taunton and the third att Yarmouth att the time of the yeare above mensioned, and that every freman be provided with two pound of powder against the time appointed to be improved in the said expeditions and exercises att the Townes charge.

1669.

It is enacted by the Court, that whosoever hath three sonnes in his family that beare armes in the Milletary Companie; theire father shalbe freed from that service if the Councill of warr or any three of them shall see cause.

Wheras by order of the Councell of warr the Townes of this Jurisdiction respectively are to find drumes, pikes, halberts and Coullers att theire own charge; It is thought meet and accordingly ordered by the Court that all such troopers as find and maintaine theire owne armes be excused from bearing any charge in such drums, pikes, halberts and Coullers.

1672.

For the regulating of the troope, It is ordered by the Court that they be devided into three Squadrons, viz.: To the Captaine, Leiftenant and Cornett to exercise each Squadron twise in the yeare; And that they take a list of the troop and see that they keep horses with armes, amunition and acoutrements fitt for that service. As alsoe that every trooper shall provide himself with a fix Carbine or horsmans peece, betwixt this and the next election Court; or return unto the foot Companie where they dwell.

1673.

It is enacted by the Court, That the Comission officers of each Township of this Jurisdiction as often as they see cause shall make serch and take notice of the defects in armes and amunition in each Township; which defects being delivered to the Constable by the above said officers the Constable with the Clarke of that Companie shall levy the fines by distresse for the use of the Companie according to order of Court, and that the said Milletary Officers have the like power: to make serch and levy fines for defect on ancient p'sons and all Inhabitants altho not of the traine band and the fine of such to be to the poor of the Towne or other Towne use.

1674.

It is enacted by the Court, that it be signifyed to the Townes that the Court expects that the troopers in each towne be as many in number as before, and that they be provided with armes and other acueterments fitt for that service; and that theire names be sent in to the July Court.

1675.

It is ordered by the Court, that foure halberteers be in a reddiness to attend the Gov^r and Assistants on dayes of election yeerly, and two after the election is over all the time which that Court contineweth.

Whereas it was ordered by the Court that the Troope were required to procure Carbines; and serve as a troop of Dragoneers, understanding that they have generally declined it; the Court have ordered that they returne againe to theire foot Companies and doe service therin and be subject to such orders as are requisite in that behalfe in the severall Townshipes wherunto they belonge.

It is ordered by the Court, that it shall and may be lawfull to and for any of the comission officers and souldiers in any of our Townshipes, with the advice of theire Towne councell if opportunitie serve to consult them; or without if the p'sent exegency of an advantage against an enimie present to prosecute the warr against them tho it should be without the respective Townshipps, as if such officers had a p'ticulare comission therunto.

It is ordered by the Court, That during the time of publicke danger every one that comes to the meeting on the Lords day bring his Armes with him, and furnished with att least six charges of powder and shott untill further order shall be given; under the penaltie of 2s. for every such defect to be levied by destresse by the Constable by order of any of the comission officers for the Townes use.

1676.

It is ordered by the Court and the authoritie therof, that the Gov' or in his absence the deputie Gov' with any two more of the Assistants upon any suddain exegent or emergent occation falling out wherin more of the councell can not speedily be convened shall have as full power and authoritie to presse and send forth men, horses, armes, amunitions and provissions and all other Nessesaries Needfull for the countries service as if the whole councell of warr were convened.

It is ordered by the Court and the authoritie therof, That every such p'son or p'sons as refuse or neglect to attend the countreyes service wherto they are or shalbe pressed by any pressmaster or theire deputies by order from any legal authoritie heer established or Impowered shall forfeit five pound; or in want therof be compelled to run the Gantlett or both as the Transgression shalbe cercomstanced for every such defalt; and where there is or may be opportunity for such delinquents timely to declare theire resolution not to attend the said service that soe another may be pressed in theire sted and shall neglect the same shall forfit the sume of five pounds more to be levied by destresse on theire goods, the said forfeitures to be the one halfe therof to the countrey and the other halfe to the Townes where such delinquents doe belong; the said forfeitures being to be levied in such case as aforsaid in case a satisfactory reason be not Given by such delinquents to the court and councell for such neglect being forthwith to be brought up by the Constable or his order to theire tryall.

It is ordered by this Court, That the comission officers of every towne together with the Towne councell or the Major pte of the whole shall have full power and authoritie to appoint and require any p'ty or p'ties of theire men as a scout for the descovery or surprisall of the enemie within or neare theire respective townes as alsoe for the reliefe of any of theire Naighbour townes or plantations as occation May require, also that the comission officer or officers in every towne are Impowered in case of any suddaine exegent wherin hee or they cannot have opportunitie to advise with the towne councell to command and lead forth such a p'ty of men as hath bine before agreed on or to him shall seeme nessesary for the present reliefe of any p'te of theire owne towne; or Naighbour towne assaulted or repelling the enimie in his advance therunto, and that every such souldier as shall not obey in any of the cases appointed or comaunded as aforsaid shall forfeite five shillings a day for such his defalt to be levied by warrant from any of the Majestrates or celectmen of the towne or be layed necke and heeles where noe estate can be found unlesse such delinquent give a satisfactory reason to the Comaunder and towne councell for such his neglect.

It is ordered by this Court and the authoritie therof, That where the comission officers and Towne Councell of divers Townes are or shalbe in a consosiation or vicinity for theire mutuall defence and preservation; and have and shall agree to keep out a standing scout att any place for the comon Good of the whole vicinitie aforsaid if any of those Townes shall fayle in sending and keeping out the whole or any p'te of theire men agreed to be on the said scoute shall forfeite to the other Townes in vicinitie as aforsaid five shillings for every day for every such man wanting to be levied by destresse by warrant from any one Majestrate on the Goods of such delinquents or on the Goods of any of the comission officers or towne councell of such defective Townes; and by them to be recovered by destresse or otherwise on the proper delinquents the said fines to be Improved by the comission officers and Towne councell of any the said Townes to promote the said scoute or other publicke service of those townes.

11

It is further ordered that where the comission officers and Towne councell of such Townes in viciety as aforsaid have or shall agree to have such a p'te of theire men in a reddines to march forth to the relieffe of any of those townes assaulted or in eminent danger to be assaulted, or to surprise or repell any p'ty of the enemie which may be discovered to lye lurking about any places neare any of those townes; wherby they may have oppertunitie suddainly to assault them if not prevented, if any such Townes shall neglect to attend that service on notice Given them either by any of the Majestrates or any two or three of the comission officers or towne councell those townes shall [forfeite] five shills. p' man for every day wanting therin to be levied as aforsaid; for the publick use or the other Townes as aforsaid, and if any p'ticular p'sons shall refuse to attend the order of theire p'ticular comaunder to march forth as aforsaid unlesse a satisfactory reason shalbe given to the officers and councell shall alsoe forfeite five shillings a day for every such neglect to be levied as aforsaid and Improved by the comission officers and towne councell of that place for the publicke service of those townes; and it is further ordered for the better Managemont of such expeditions that the souldery mett together may chose one to take the conduct of the whole being one of the comission officers of one of the said Townes; whome they shall reddily obey as theire comaunder in cheiffe; whoe is heerby Impowered to acte with the advice of his councell; The comaunders of the severall squadrons; and such other descreet men of his companie as hee shall see cause to advise with in surprisall, repelling, p'suing or distruction of the enimie as occation and oppertunitie may present for the mutuall defence of those townes or any other in destresse as may be, and these to be his or theire sufficient discharge.

1677.

It is enacted by the Court, That all such p'sons in this Gov'ment whoe have served under Comission in the late warr against the Natives shall not be compellable to serve in the Milletary Companie in any lower capacitie then Comission officers; and those officers whoe served in lower degree shall returne to theire former station.

It is enacted by the Court, That the order made by the Generall Court, October the fourth, 1675, respecting carrying of armes to the Meeting, be put in execution by all such p'sons as are by the Lawes of this Collonie required to beare armes viz.: the one halfe of the Companie one day and the other the other day and soe continewed untill futher order to Contrary from the Gov' and Councell.

It is enacted by the Court, That the order of Court made Anno 1644 allowing Matchcockes be repealed, and that all p'sons required by the lawes of this Collonie to keep and maintaine armes be att all times provided with sufficient fix feir lockes or snaphance musketts or other servicable peeces not exceeding four foot and an halfe longe; nor under Colliver bore, on penaltie of six shillings to be levied on the estate of all and every such p'son or p'sons as by order are appointed to keep and maintaine the same; and that every such p'son required to keep and maintaine armes shall for every fier locke or snaphance be alwaies provided with thirty flints on penaltie of twelve pence fine.

It is enacted by the Court, that the Comission officers in each Towne of this Gov'-ment doe speedily put in execution the order of Court made the fourth of July (73) for serching for defects of armes and amunition.

It is enacted by the Court, that the Order of Court bearing date 1640 shall by the Milletary Comission officers of this Jurisdiction be put in execution againe, viz.: The order concerning Training; with this limitation and addition that wheras formerly the Milletary Companies were required to traine six times in a yeer they are to traine or be exercised but four times in a yeer; and that they not onely traine theire souldiers in theire postures and motions but alsoe at shooting att Markes, &c.

1681.

It is ordered by the Court, that every Towne in this Jurisdiction choose three men to be Joyned together with those of the Comission officers and theire towne Councell.

It is enacted by the Court in reference unto Milletary discipline, That all the Milletary Companies in this Gov'ment be made compleat in theire officers of as able and fit men as they may be.

It is enacted by this Court, That every souldier in this Jurisdiction that beares armes be furnished with all convenient speed with a compleat sword or cutlas.

It is ordered by this Court, that the Comission officers of the Milletary Companies of each Towne in this Gov'nnent doe take care that one fourth p'te of the said Milletary Companies doe bringe theire armes fixed to the Meetings every Lords daye; with every souldier bearing armes six charges of powder same shott, viz., beginning from the beginning of April to the end of October yeerly, and every yeer as well in times of peace as warr; onely in times of danger they shalbe increased as the Milletary Comaunders and Towne Councell shall see cause, and that such as palpably neglect or refuse to p'forme theire duty therin shall forfeite two shillings for every such neglect and ten shillings in case it appeers to be in contempt; To be gathered by order from the Comission officers to the Constable, and where it appeers that any doe ordinarily and p'posely keep from meeting because they would not bringe theire armes as aforsaid to be summoned to the Court to have such reasonable fines as to the Court shall seem meet, saveing such townes wherby agreement amongst themselves they have such a number of men proportionable to aforsaid order constantly to carry theire armes on every Lords day to the meetings.

**1683.**

This Court doth order that Swansey and Middlebery shall chose some for Officers To lead theire Milletary Companies and Instruct them in Marshall disiplyne, and that orders to each of those Townes to send such to the Court as they shall see Cause to choose.

This Court taking Notice of the neglect of some Townes and Milletary Companies in not choosing of Milletary comaunders according to order of Court; when they have bin required therunto; by warrant from the p'sedent of the councell of warr, This Court therefore orders that if any Towne and Milletary Companie in the collonie shall neglect to choose Milletary comaunder or comaunders which they shalbe required according to former order of the Court to choose by warrant from the presedent of the councell of Warr that the councell of Warr shall appoint such comissioners officer & officers in such Townes and Companies as they shall Judge Meet and nessesary.

**1686.**

Agreed on by the Generall Court, that there be no Generall Training or regimental muster this year 1686.

Ordered &c., that in each Millitary Company a Comittee be Chosen by the Company consisting of so many men as added to the Commision Officers of such Company will make the number five, who shall have power with the Comission Officers to judge delinquents, determine & dispose of fines for the good of the Company and to inflict millitary punishment upon offenders according to law as occasion may require.

**1689.**

Ordered by this Court and the authority therof, that the Chief Comanders of each regiment, as was in the year 1686 before the late alteration of Government, be Continued in theire several places and have the same power they had by theire severall Comissions at that time and are soe to continue untill this Court doth otherwise order. As also that the Captains, Leiu'ts and Ensignes or so many of them as are living that were in Comission in the year 1686, before the alteration of the Government, be also continued in their severall places and have the same power they had by theire severall Comissions at that time and are so to continue untill this Court shall further Order, and in the meantime such Towns as had not then Officers Comissionated at that time or where any Officers are since dead, for a supply of all such Towns they are in the severall Towns to make Choice according to law of such Officers as are or shall be wanting, and to present them to the Generall Court for approbatior by the first opportunity.

And for as much as the Towns of Marshfield & Swansey have manifested some dislike to theire Captains, The Court therefore orders that the Companies of those Towns be comanded by the Lieut's and Ensignes of theire severall Towns untill the next Generall Court.

GENERAL ORDERS AND SPECIAL ORDERS ISSUED CONCERNING THE
EXPEDITIONS OF WAR IN WHICH PLYMOUTH COLONY ENGAGED.

## PEQUOT WAR.

**1637, June 7th.**

It is concluded and enacted by the Court, that the Colony of New Plymouth shall
send forth ayd to assist them of Massachusetts Bay and Conectacutt in their warrs
against the Pequin Indians in reveng of the innocent blood of the English wᶜʰ the ᵈᵈ
Pequins have barbarously shed and refuse to give satisfaccon for.

It is also enacted by the Court that there shalbe thirty p'sons sent for land service
and as many others as shalbe sufficient to mannage the barque. Leiftennant William
Holmes is elected to goe leader of the said company. Mr. Thomas Prence is also
elected by lott to be for the councell of warr and to goe forth wᵗʰ them.

The Names of the Souldiers that willingly offer themselves to goe vpon the ᵈᵈ Service wᵗʰ Mr. Prence & the Leiftenᵗ.

### VOLUNTARIES.

Thomas Clarke, Richard Church, Constance Southerne, John Barnes, Mr. Nathaniel
Thomas & his mann, Mr. Goarton, John Cooke if his family can be p'uided, Mr. Stee-
phen Hopkins, John Heyward, Thomas Williams, Nicholas Presland, Thomas Pope,
Philip Delanoy, Francis Billington, Henry Willis, Perregrine White, Caleb Hopkins,
Samuel Nash, Robte Mendall, Henry Sampson, George Soule, Samuell Jenney, Tho-
mas Redding, Louve Brewster or Joseph Robinson his man, Edward Holman, Willm
Paddy, Richard Clough, Henry Ewell, Joseph Biddle, Willm Tubbs, George Kenne-
rick, Thomas Halloway, John Irish, John Jenkins, Jacob Cooke, Giles Hopkins, John
Phillips, Thomas Goarton.

### SUCH AS WILL GOE IF THEY BE PREST.

Mr. Thomas Hill, Thomas Boardman, James Coole.

It is also enacted by the Court, that Mʳ Hopkins and John Winslow for the towne
of Plymouth, Mr. Howland and Jonathan Brewster for the towne of Ducksborrow,
and Mr. Gilson and Edward Foster for the towne of Scituate, shalbe added to the
Gou'nor and Assistants to assesse men toward the charges of the souldiers that are
to be sent forth for the ayde of the Massachusetts Bay and Connectacutt.

Wheras according to the order of the Court the Gou'nor and Assistants, wᵗʰ the
help of Mr. Hopkins and John Winslow for the towne of Plymouth, Mr. Howland
and Jonathan Brewster for the towne of Ducksborrow, and Mr. Gilson & Edward
Foster for the towne of Scituate, haue mett together & considered of the charge in
setting forth the souldiers and fynd that it will amount vnto the sume of two hundred pounds, the wᶜʰ is appoynted & concluded to be payd in manner following, viz.:
one hundred pounds by the township of Plymouth & the liberties thereof, fifty
pounds by the township of Ducksborrow, and thother fifty pounds by the towneship of Scituate.

A warrant was made to Mr. Hatherly & the inhabitants of Scituate p'sently to
make an equall assessment whereby the said sume may be p'sently made up for the
p'sent expedition.

## ALARM OF 1642.

**1642, Sept. 27th.**

This Court was occationed by the Indians to p'uide forces against them for an offensiue & defensiue warr; and though all the inh'i'ts were warned yet they appeared by
their seuall deputies as they had liberty to doe.

The Court being mett together & haueing intelligence of a genall conspiracy intended by the natives to cutt of all the English in this land, tooke the same into serious consideracon and duly wayiug such informacons wᶜʰ they haue receiued together
wᵗʰ circumstanc concurring there wᵗʰ all do adjudge it absolutely neefull & requisite
to make speedy p'paracon throughout gouerment for a defensive and offensiue warr
against them as if they were p'sently to be sent forth.

It is agreed and concluded that Mr. Edward Winslow, Mr. Tymothy Hatherly, &
Captaine Miles Standish shalbe sent into the Bay to & haue power to agitate and

conclude w<sup>th</sup> them for a p'sent combinacon w<sup>th</sup> them in the p'sent warrs and to treate w<sup>th</sup> them about a further combinacon or league but not to conclud that w<sup>th</sup> out consent of the Court here.

Their comission is as followeth:—Mr. Edward Winslow, Mr. Tymothy Hatharley, and Captaine Miles Standish are deputed and authorized by the Gen'all Court, this day to treate and conclude w<sup>th</sup> such comissioners as the Gou'nor & Court of Massachusetts shall appoynt for that purpose, vpon such heads & p'posicons as the Lord shall direct them for our combineing together mutually in a defensiue and offensiue warr for our p'sent defence against the intended surprisall of the natives; and also to treate & conferr w<sup>th</sup> them about a further combinacon & league to be concluded betwixt vs for future tymes and to certyfy this Court of the head therof that vpon our approbacon of the same they may be confirmed by a Gen'all Court.

It is also agreed & concluded that Captaine Miles Standish shall goe Captaine to lead those forces that shalbe sent forth; and that Mr. Thomas Prence shall go w<sup>th</sup> him to be his counsell and advise in the warrs &c.; and that Willm Palmer shalbe lieftenant and Peregrine White the anncient bearrer.

It is agreed vpon & concluded that the charges for & about y<sup>e</sup> souldiers w<sup>ch</sup> are to be sent forth shalbe payd by euery towneship according to their rates to the publicke charges, viz.:

| | £b. | s. | d. | | £b. | s. | d. |
|---|---|---|---|---|---|---|---|
| Plym. | 05 | 05 | 00 | Barnestable | 02 | 10 | 00 |
| Duxbor. | 03 | 10 | 00 | Yarmo. | 02 | 10 | 00 |
| Scittuat | 04 | 00 | 00 | Taunton | 02 | 10 | 00 |
| Sandwood | 03 | 00 | 00 | Marshfield | 02 | 00 | 00 |

And so according to this p'porcon, for a greater or lesser sum.

THE COUNSELL OF WARR.

The Gouern<sup>r</sup>     Mr. Tymothy Hatherley     Mr. Wm. Vassell
Mr. Edward Winslow     Mr. John Browne     Capt. Standish
Mr. Thom. Prence     Mr. Wm. Thomas     Mr. Thom. Dimmock
Mr. Wm. Collyer     Mr. Edm. Freeman     Mr. Anthon. Thacher

If any of these be absent when they should come together, the townes where such dwell are to send other sufficient men in their stead.

Whereas the towneshipps w<sup>ch</sup> in the gou'ment are maruelously vnprouided of leade and powder to secure our p'sent dangers and that to supply the extreme wants therof and to p'cure po'der and lead no course can be found out but by sale of some moose skins and other skins out of the gouerment, w<sup>ch</sup> those that hold the trade are p'hibited to doe by a certaine clause in their graunt, the Court, takeing the same into serious consideracon, and fynding the danger to be so great and euery mans life in such hassard the Court doth vpon due caution order that no advantage shalbe taken against the said p'tners of the trade for the p'cureing of leade and po'der for p'sent supply by sale of moose skins or other skins out of the gou'ment. And the Court doth further order, that the p'tners shall furthw<sup>th</sup> do the same to p'cure there wants supplyd p'uided that the townes bring in corne for them to be delified vpon the receipt of the pod<sup>r</sup> & lead, and that when pod<sup>r</sup> & lead is p'cured those townes shalbe first p'uided that are in greatest want.

1643, March 7.
Mr. Edward Winslow & Mr. Willm Collyer are elected by the Court to go to treate w<sup>th</sup> Massachusetts Bay &c. about y<sup>e</sup> combynacon.

June 6.—The first Teusday in July the ma<sup>trates</sup> meete and eich towne are to send such men as they shall think fitt to joyne w<sup>th</sup> them to consult about a course to saueguard ourselves from surprisall by an enemie.

August 20th.—The Court hath allowed & established a millitary discipline to be erected and mayntained by the townes of Plymouth, Duxborrow & Marshfield and haue also heard their orders and established them, viz.:—*

---

* There is a close resemblance in several of these orders to the rules and regulations adopted and put in practice by the "Great Artillery Company" at Boston, founded in 1638, and which company still continues to exist under the name of the "ANCIENT AND HONORABLE ARTILLERY COMPANY."

That Miles Standish shalbe captaine for this yeare; Nathaniell Thomas, leiftennant for this yeare; Nathaniell Sowther, clark of the band or company; Mathew Fuller, Samuell Nash, serjeants.

## ORDERS.

1. That the exercises be alwayes begunn and ended with prayer.

2. That there be one procured to preach them a sermon once a yeare, viz., at the elec'con of their officers, and the first to begin in Septemb^r next.

3. That none shalbe receiued into this millitary company but such as are of honest and good report, & freemen, not servants, and shalbe well approued by the officers & the whole company, or the major part.

4. That euery p'son after they have recorded their names in the millitary list shall from tyme to tyme be subject to the comaunds and orders of the officers of this millitary company in their places respectively.

5. That euery delinquent shalbe punished at the discretion of the officers and the millitary company, or the major part therof, according to the order of millitary discipline & nature of the offence.

6. That all talking, and not keepeing sylence, during the tyme of the exercise, jereing, quarrelling, fighting, de'pting collars w^thout lycense or dismission, &c., or other misdemeanor, so adjudged to be by the officers and the company or the maj^r part thereof, to be accounted misdemeanors, to be punished as aforesaid.

7. That every man that shalbe absent except he be sick or some extraordinay occation or hand of God vpon him, shall pay for every such default II.s. And if he refuse to pay it vpon demaund, or w^thin one month after, then to appeare before the company & be distrayned for it & put out of the list.

8. That if any man shall vpon the dayes appoynted come w^thout his armes or w^th defective armes shall forfaite for euery trayneing day as followeth :

|                                                    |     | d. |
| For want of a muskett or a peece approued euery tyme | .  . | VI. |
| For want of a sword                                  | . . . . . . . . . | VI. |
| For want of a rest                                   | . . . . . . . . | VI. |
| For want of bandelires                               | . . . . . . . | VI. |

Six months tyme giuen to p'uide in.

9. That euery man that hath entered himsef vpon the millitary list, and hath not sufficient armes, & doth not or will not p'cure them w^thin six monthes next ensuing, his name to be put out the list.

10. That there be but XVI^teene pikes in the whole company, or at the most for the third p^t, viz.: VIII. for Plymouth, VI. for Duxborrow and two for Marshfield.

11. That all that are or shalbe elected cheefe officers in this millitary company shalbe so titled and foreuer afterwards be so reputed except he obtayne a heigher place.

12. That euery man entred into the millitary list shall pay VI.d. the quarter to the vse of the company.

13. That when any of this millitary company shall dye or depart this life, the company vpon warening shall come together w^th their armes and interr his corps as a souldier and according to his place and quallytye.

14. That all that shalbe admitted into this millitary company shall first take the oath of fidellyty, if they haue not taken it already, or els be not admited.

15. That all postures of pike and muskett motions, rankes & files &c., messengers, skirmishes, seiges, batteries, watches, sentinells, &c., bee alwayes p'formed according to true millitary discipline.

16. That all that will enter themselues vpon this company shalbe p'pounded one day, receiued the next day, if they be approued.

The like liberty is graunted to the townes of Sandwich, Barnestable and Yarmouth, for the erecting of a millitary discipline amongst them p'uided they be men of honest and good report and freemen.

## ALARM OF 1643-4.

1643, October 10.

This Court was called vpon occation of the insurrection of the Indians ag$^{st}$ the Dutch and English there and haue plotted to cutt of the English and to beginn w$^{th}$ the Dutch, many of whom they haue already cutt off.

It is concluded and agreed vpon by the Court, that thirty men according to our p'porcon w$^{th}$ the confederates, shalbe forthw$^{th}$ made ready for the warr and be sufficiently p'uided w$^{th}$ armes compleate & other p'uisions and to be in continuall readynes to go forth w$^{th}$ the confederates when they shalbe called. The rule w$^{ch}$ was thought most equall for number of p'sons in euery towneship was to take one of a score in euery towneship as they are to make ready as followeth in euery towne:

Plymouth, seauen.  
Duxborrow, five.  
Scituate, five.  
Sandwich, three.  

Taunton, three.  
Barnestable, three.  
Yarmouth, two.  
Marshfeild, two.  

} XXX$^{tie}$ p'sons in all.

The rates of euery towneship to this charge are as followeth:

| | £ | s. | d. | | £ | s. | d. | |
|---|---|---|---|---|---|---|---|---|
| Plymouth | 04 | 05 | 00 | Taunton | 02 | 10 | 00 | According to |
| Duxborrow | 03 | 00 | 00 | Barnestable | 02 | 10 | 00 | these p'porcons |
| Scituate | 04 | 10 | 00 | Yarmouth | 02 | 10 | 00 | to the hundred |
| Sandwich | 03 | 05 | 00 | Marshfeild | 02 | 10 | 00 | pound charge. |

It is ordered and agreed vpon by the Court that the comittees of euery towneship do speedyly make their number of men ready and furnished w$^{th}$ sufficient armes and p'uision and send their names to the Gou$^r$ & counsell of warr hereafter named w$^{th}$ all convenyent speed and a cattalogue of their armes.

The counsell of warr elected & authorized by the Court are:—

The Gouernor, who is also president thereof,  
Mr. Edward Winslow,  
Mr. Thomas Prence,  
Mr. Will'm Collyer,  
Capt. Miles Standish.

It is ordered and concluded vpon by the Court that the counsell of warr shall haue full power to order all things concerning the gen'all warrs for the gou'ment, especially in these p'ticulars following, viz.:—

That the counsell of warr shall haue full power to yssue out warrants to presse such a number of men in euery towne as by p'porcon the said towne is to set forth; and also to yssue forth warrants to the said townes for armes & p'uision for them, and so for a greater or lesser number or p'porcon as occation shall require according to the number of p'sons and rates now agreed vpon in this Court for eich towneship.

That when complaiut is made to the counsell of warr either by the officers or souldiers of any offences donn in tyme of seruice, the said counsell of warr shall haue full power to heare & determine & punish such offenders.

The armes w$^{ch}$ shalbe accounted sufficient for the furnishing of a souldier are these:

A muskett, either firelock or matchcock, so that they p'uide match w$^{th}$ all, a paire of bandeliers, or a pouch for po'der and bulletts, a sword and a belt, a worme & scowrer, a rest & a knapsack.

That the counsell of warr shall haue full power to choose a treasurer or treasurers for the p'sent service to make p'uision for them, and shall give an account to the countrey of their receipts and payments when they shalbe required.

That the losse of armes w$^{ch}$ shall happen in this expedition shalbe borne by the countrey according to their seuall p'porcons.

That all the armes w$^{ch}$ shalbe used in this expedition shalbe valued by the counsell of warr and a record of them taken and to whom they are deliu'ed by one therevnto appoynted.

That the comittees do send a list of their souldiers names w$^{th}$ their armes to the counsell of warr to Plymouth on Munday the XXIII of this instant Octob$^r$ or before.

That the counsell of warr shall haue full power to make choyce of a leader that shall leade this company, and one to goe w$^{th}$ him for counsell.

That euery souldier shall haue XVIII.s. p. month & dyett & pillage.

That euery souldier shall haue a months p'uision sent w$^{th}$ him, viz.: for euery souldier XXX$^{lb}$ of biskett, XII$^{lb}$ of pork or XX$^{lb}$ of beefe, and half a bushell of peas or meale; and that euery towne p'uide according to this p'porcon for so many men as they are to send forth.

That the leader of this company shall have fourty shillings p. month, and the serjeant XXX$^{s}$ p. month.

It is ordered by the Court that if the townesmen of Yarmouth cannot p'sently agree to appoynt a place for defence of themselves, their wiues and children, in case of a suddaine assault, that then the Court doth order and appoynt Leiftenant Willm Palmer, Anthony Thacher, Nicholas Symkins and Samuel Rider w$^{th}$ the constable, to appoynt a place and forthw$^{th}$ to cause the same to be fortyfyed w$^{th}$ all speede.

It is ordered by the Court that if the townesmen of Barnestable doe not p'sently agree to appoynt a place or places for the defence of themselues theire wiues and children against a suddaine assault, that then y$^{e}$ Court doth order that Mr. Thomas Dimmack, Anthony Annable, Henry Cobb, Henry Coggen & Barnard Lumberd, w$^{th}$ the constable, shall forthw$^{th}$ appoynt a place or places for their defence, and cause the same to be speedyly fortyfied for their defence.

### 1644, March 5.

Whereas Scituate is p'sented for not exerciseing of armes according to the order of the Court, it is ordered that they shall exercise eight tymes this yeare according to the act of the Court and that it shalbe in the liberty of the millitary officers of that towne to call forth such squadrons or files as hee shall think fitt to be exercised eight tymes ouer more.

The p'porcon and Names of the Souldiers in eich Towne sent forth in the late Expedition against the Narrohiggansets & their Confederats.

The first company viz., XVI$^{teene}$ went forth the XV$^{th}$ August 1645.

Plymouth VIII men: six w$^{th}$ those that went out first, and two w$^{th}$ those y$^{t}$ went out last:—
John Tompson, Richard Foster, John Bundy, Nicholas Hodges, John Shaw, Samuel Cutbert; These VI were forth XVII days.
John Jenkins, John Harman; These two were forth XIII dayes.

Duxborrow, six men w$^{ch}$ went w$^{th}$ those that went out first:—
Serjeant Sam Nash, Will'm Brewster, Will'm Clarke, John Washborne, Nathaniell Chaundler, Edward Hall; These six were forth XVII dayes.

Marshfeild, foure men w$^{ch}$ went forth w$^{th}$ those that went out first:—
Luke Lillye, Twyford West, Will'm Hayle, Roger Cooke; These foure were forth XVII dayes.
These following went forth the XVIII$^{th}$ of August, 1645.

Sandwich, flue men w$^{ch}$ went forth w$^{th}$ those that went last:—
Thomas Burges, Thom$^{s}$ Greenfeild, Laurence Willis, Thomas Johnson, Rob'te Allen; These fiue men were forth XIII dayes.

Scittuate, eight men w$^{ch}$ went forth w$^{th}$ those that went last:—
John Turner, Georg Russell, Jeremiah Burrows, Hercules Hill, Edward Saunders, Nathaniell Moate, John Robinson, Richard Toute; These eight men were forth XIII dayes.

Barnestable, foure men w$^{ch}$ went forth w$^{th}$ those that went last:—
John Foxwell, John Russell, Jonathan Hatch, Francis Crocker; These foure men were forth XIIII dayes.

Yarmouth, flue men w$^{ch}$ went forth w$^{th}$ those that went last:—
Will'm Northcoate, Will'm Twyneing, Teague Joanes, Henry Wheildon, Will'm Chase, drummer; These fiue men were forth XIIII dayes.

Those all returned the 2d of September, being Tewsday, and were disbanded the day following being Wensday.

There was deliued to eich souldier 1$^{lb}$ of poder, and 3$^{lb}$ of bullets apeece and 1$^{lb}$ of tobaccoe, at their going forth.

The townes of Taunton and Rehoboth als Seacunck, were freed from sending forth any men in regard they are frontire townes, and billited the souldiers during the tyme they were forth.

COST OF THE EXPEDITION AGAINST THE NARRAGANSET INDIANS IN 1645.

The charges of this Expedition.

| | £. | s. | d. |
|---|---|---|---|
| Inpris⁰ giuen to the captaine, but not to be a presedent for after tymes, for himself & his man | 10 | 00 | 00 |
| To Serjeant, now Leiftennant, Nash | 02 | 10 | 00 |
| To Plymouth for VI men, 17 dayes | 05 | 02 | 00 |
| To Duxborrow for V men, 17 dayes | 04 | 05 | 00 |
| To Marshfield for IIII men, 17 dayes | 03 | 08 | 00 |
| To Plym. for two men more, 13 dayes | 01 | 06 | 00 |
| To Scittuate for eight men, 13 dayes | 05 | 04 | 00 |
| To Sandwich for fiue men, 13 dayes | 03 | 05 | 00 |
| To Barnestable foure men, 14 dayes | 02 | 16 | 00 |
| To Yarmouth five men, 14 dayes | 03 | 10 | 00 |
| And to the drummer wᶜʰ was one of Yarmouth ou' & aboue 5s. | 00 | 05 | 00 |
| | 41 | 11 | 00 |

| | £. | s. | d. |
|---|---|---|---|
| It. for a line to Mr. Hanbury | 00 | 02 | 00 |
| It. ½ dussen of kniues giuen to messengers | 00 | 02 | 06 |
| It. for casting of shott | 00 | 05 | 00 |
| It. for drumheads | 00 | 07 | 00 |
| It. spent of the money & beads the capt. had | 02 | 05 | 05 |
| It. worke done by Gorame | 00 | 04 | 00 |
| It. James Coles bill | 14 | 02 | 00 |
| It. A horse hire XI dayes | 00 | 11 | 00 |
| It. 25ˡᵇ of po'der taken at the barke by the captaine to bring the men hoame againe | 02 | 10 | 00 |
| It. 75ˡᵇ of biskett the capt. had at the bark to vittaile his men homewards for wᶜʰ is allowed 1 C waight | | 16 | 00 |
| It. allowed toward the carriage of p'uisions to Secunck wᶜʰ came by sea out of the Bay | 02 | 00 | 00 |
| Tobaccoe afterwards allowed 27s. 4d. | 01 | 07 | 04 |
| Sum total | 66 | 03 | 03 |

The barrell of po'der the souldiers spent & deliued to diuers of the townes, was not accounted, nor 300ˡᵇ of leade wᶜʰ Mr. Prence bought, nor the bullets the soldiers had forth wᶜʰ was not returned, nor what losse would be required to take the p'uisions againe beside the charge of euery p'ticuler towne wᵗʰ their souldiers in setting them forth, nor 5s. Mr. Prenc pay'd for casting shott and canvas bags for to put bread & p'uision in.

The sale of euery towne to this charg followeth.       Verte.

The Rates of the seuall Townes to the Charges of the Warrs.

| | £. | s. | d. |
|---|---|---|---|
| Plymouth | 12 | 02 | 03 |
| Duxborrow | 08 | 11 | 00 |
| Scittuate | 12 | 17 | 06 |
| Sandwich | 09 | 07 | 09 |
| Taunton | 05 | 02 | 06 |
| Barnestable | 06 | 02 | 06 |
| Yarmouth | 07 | 02 | 06 |
| Marshfeild | 07 | 02 | 06 |
| | 70 | 08 | 06 |

The Court for speciall consideracon did abate XXˢ. to Barnestable and 40ˢ. to Taunton, wᶜʰ is the reason they are not equall wᵗʰ Yarmouth and Marshfeild, but shall not be a presedent for after tymes; and Rehoboth was not rated at all, both because it was a new plantacon, and billited all the souldiers freely during all the tyme they stayed there.

12

The Sumes the Townes are to pay their Souldiers, and what wilbe comeing to y[e] Treasurer:

| | Souldiers. | | | Treasurer. | | |
|---|---|---|---|---|---|---|
| | £. | s. | d. | £. | s. | d. |
| Plymouth payes | 06 | 08 | 00 | 05 | 14 | 03 |
| Duxborrow " | 06 | 15 | 00 | 01 | 16 | 00 |
| Scituate " | 05 | 04 | 00 | 07 | 13 | 06 |
| Sandwich " | 03 | 05 | 00 | 06 | 02 | 06 |
| Barnestable " | 02 | 16 | 00 | 03 | 06 | 06 |
| Yarmouth " | 03 | 10 | 00 | 03 | 12 | 06 |
| Marshfeild " | 03 | 08 | 00 | 03 | 14 | 06 |
| Taunton " | 00 | 00 | 00 | 05 | 02 | 06 |
| Sum tot. | 31 | 06 | 00 | 37 | 02 | 03 |

& added to it w[ch] was remayning of the peaye & 20s. £1, 16s., 00d.

| | £. | s. | d. |
|---|---|---|---|
| The captaine rec. in peaye . . . . . . | 03 | 01 | 05 |
| More in money . . . . . . . | 01 | 00 | 00 |
| Spent thereof & lay'd out . . . . . . | 02 | 05 | 05 |
| Remayneth in his hands . . . . . . | 01 | 16 | 00 |
| In the Treasurers hands . . . . . | 38 | 18 | 03 |
| Due to himself . . . . . . . | 10 | 00 | 00 |
| The remainder to the country is . . . | 28 | 18 | 03 |

The Court doth order that euery towne shall pay their owne souldiers what is due vnto them for their wages and returne the rest to Plymouth to the Treasurer, at Mr. Paddys house towards the payment of other charges about the expedition prouided that euery souldier allow by deduction of his wages what hee hath taken vp of any man to furnish him for his seruice and like to returne theire armes and bullets againe or els allow for them.

1646, March 5.

The company for the Kennebeck trade brought in an account into the Court for the yeare 1644, w[ch] came that yeare but to thirty pounds, and also an account how it was disbursed for the countreyes use, w[ch] the Court accepted and allowed, and they are thereof discharged; and likewise towards the rent for the yeare 1645, there was an account exhibited whereby there appeared to be in the store for the countreys use six barrells of pouder, three hundred waight of leade and pounds of bulletts, and foure pounds nineteene shillings and six pence remayneing due to the country from them besides thirty shillings for a case of bottels w[ch] was not cleared, that they were spent for the countreys use; but the 300 waight of leade is not yet pay'd for.

And XVI[lb] of pouder to Marshfeild.

It. XX[lb] of pouder to Taunton.

It. XVI[lb] of pouder to Barnestable.

And baggs to put po'der in.

These p'cells of po'der were remayneing of the seauenth barrell of po'der, the rest being spent by the souldiers in the last expedition.

P'POSICONS.

That the towns p'uide sufficient armes for so many men as their p'portion wilbe to set forth that they may be in p'sent readynesse if any suddaine occation fall forth.

1646, June 2.

The Counsell of Warr chosen & nominated by Court for this ensuing yeare: Mr. Edward Winslow, p'sident, Mr. Thomas Prence, Captaine Miles Standish, Mr. Tymothy Hatherley, Mr. John Browne, Mr. John Alden, Capt. Will'm Poole.

It is enacted by the Court, that these or any three of them meeting together, shall haue power and authoryty to make orders for matters of warr and to yssue forth warrants &c.; but if but two of them do meete, then to haue the consent and approbacon of the Gou. in what they doe; and that when these do so meete together, they shall haue power to choose such p'sons to their counsell and assistance as they shall think good (if they please) so they exceed not the number of foure p'sons, and if any man shall refuse to doe the service when they are so warned or called therevnto, that then such p'son or p'sons shalbe fyned as the counsell of warr shall think meete so it exceede not fourty shillings to the colonies use; and that these shall haue power to determine in any offence concerneing warr either donn before this day or after, before thend of this ensuing yeare, and for all p'sons as well strangers as our selues for any thing donn w^th in this gou'ment and shall haue power to choose a p'sident amongst themsewles and to make orders about such thinges as shalbe needfull.

## TROUBLE WITH THE INDIANS IN CONNECTICUT IN 1649.

**1649, June 8.**

Wheras diuers sad iniurius practises to the murthering of sum of the English haue been com'ited by the natives to the westward against the said English at Stanford & other places, with diuers insolent & threatening speaches by them allso spoken, wherby the com'issioners for the Vnited Colinyes are ocationed to vse theire best endeavors for the rectifying of the said abuses; and being vncertaine whether there may bee need of a warr with the said natives for y^t end & haue therfore signifyed vnto the seuerall Vnited Colinyes y^t they may bee in a redines if ocation should bee.

It is therfor ordered by the Court y^t forthwith due p'uision bee made both of men and amunition, with poulder & shot & victailes and other nessesaryes for fourty men for the space of three monthes, sutable for such an ocation, & y^t euery towne respectiuely prouid for theire owne men.

The Court haue generally nominated and voted Captaine Standish to bee vnder the concideration of a generall officer or comissary generall, to haue the ouersight of the seuerall millitary companies within this gouerment, both for the viewall of theire armes & to comaund the said companies vpon spetiall ocations; & Captaine Standish aforsaid doth condecend therunto.

**1651, August 4.**

Warrants were signed and directed to the cunstables of seuerall townes for to leuy the fines for the defects in armes.

**1652, June 3.**

The Court haue ordered Mr. Hatherly that hee take course that the miletary company of Scittuate doe traine according to order this yeare and that hee see that some fitt p'sons bee joyned with the cunstables of Scittuate to take view of theire amunicion and to see that they haue poweder and shott according to order.

Likewise the cunstable of Sandwidge by a warrant is required to call vpon the leiftenant and Willm Newland to traine the milletary companie of Sandwidge, and if hee refuse, to appoint theire sergeant Peeter Wright to do it.

**1653, April 6.**

The milletary orders agreed on and concluded are as followeth. First that the summe of fifty pounds bee raised of the seuerall townes within the gouerment according to theire proportions in other rates, in such pay as will answare for our p'tes of the powder and shott, armes and lockes sent out of England to bee reddy against such time as we shalbee required to answare for y^t, and that the said powder and shott &c. be receiued and kept for the p'sent att Capt. Willets and Mr. Paddyes warchouse att Boston.

That the milletary officers of euery companie shall p'sent the defects of the armes of theire companies at the next Court of Asistants.

That a milletary watch in euery towne be continued vntell further order to the contrary.

That all men though aboue the age of sixty bee required either by finding a sufficient man or in theire owne p'sons to watch according to order as shalbee agreed vpon in each towne excepting such as through both age and pouerty are disabled, and that such widdowes as haue estates beare theire p'te by finding one to watch according to theire proportions.

The Court recomend to euery towne to prouide som place or places to retreat vnto, that thether they may bring theire wiues and children in time of eminent danger for theire better securitie.

That euery towne that shalbee defectiue in the want of a drumm att any time for the space of two monthes shall forfeite the summe of forty shillings to the collonies vse. That shalbee defective in coullers the space of six months foure pounds.

That a considerable companie of half pikes bee prouided in euery towne att the charge of the townshipp, videlecet, wher 80 men are able to beare armes theire twenty to bee prouided and soe proportionable to theire number bee they greater or lesser.

That euery towne prouide halberts for the sergiunts of theire milletary companie,

That euery towne that hath aboue fifty men bearing armes shall haue powder answarable to a barrell for euery fifty men and soe bullets proportionable therunto.

That noe man make an allarum without apparent danger.

That in case one gun bee shott of in the night whiles the milletary watch is kept within any townshipp yᵗ shalbee taken as an allarum to the said towne and answered by any man that shall heare the same.

That three guns or continued shooting or the beat of a drumm in the night shalbee an allarum to bee taken from towne to towne.

That in case any towne shalbee destressed by reall assault vpon them, such towne as haue certaine intelligence therof shall affoard releife.

### PREPARATIONS FOR WAR WITH THE DUTCH AT NEW YORK IN 1653.

Haueing receiued intelligence from the comissioners mett att Boston of theire agitations about and conserning a warr with the Duch in these p'tes of America and serivaly weyinge and delibberating vpon such ground and reasons with theire cercomstances as by the said comissioners haue been propounded enduceing therunto they came to these conclusions following: Videlecett, that whatsoeuer shalbee vndertaken or donn in, aboute or conserning the said warr or any thinge conduceing therunto shalbe acted and goe forth in the name and by the authoritie of the state of England.

2ᶜᵒⁿᵈˡʸ That in case theire shalbee a concurrance of the other jurisdictions with vs heerin viz., all things acted in and aboute the p'mises shalbee acted vnder God in the name of the state of England as aforsaid, and that vpon returne of the messengers sent by the comissioners to the Munhatoes or other certaine intelligence further grounds and reasons shall appeer to bee of weight nessesitateing a warr with said Duch, they will bee in a reddines through the healp of God to assist and engage therinn according to theire proportions and vtmost abillities.

And for that end and purpose preparacon was made as followeth.

Warrants were issued out in the name of the state of England for the pressing of the number of sixty men, able and fitt for warr if need shall require, which number was to bee taken out of the seuerall townes within this jurisdiction according to theire proportions viz.:

| | | | |
|---|---|---|---|
| Out of Plymouth | 7. | Yarmouth | 6. |
| Duxburrow | 6. | Barnstable | 6. |
| Scittuate | 9. | Marshfeild | 6. |
| Sandwidge | 6. | Rehoboth | 6. |
| Taunton | 5. | Eastham | 3. |

The constables of the seuerall townes were ordered by the warrants directed vnto them to haue these proportions of men in a reddines and to giue notice vnto theire seuerall townes to provide sufficient armes for euery man that shalbee pressed out of theire seuerall townes as aforsaid.

The comaunders chosen and appointed to goe forth on the said expedition, in case there shalbee occation, are Capt. Myles Standish for captaine, Leiftenant Thomas Southworth for leiftenant, and Hezekiah Hoare of Taunton for ensigne.

Moreouer two barkqes were alsoe pressed to attend the expedition aforsaid, videlecett, the barkqe in which George Watson sayleth together with him the mʳ therof, and John Smith Junior of Plym' and Joseph Green, with all things belonging to the said barkqe nessesarie for the said expedition.

In like mannor the barkqe in which Richard Knowles sayleth, with him the master therof, was pressed for the same purpose with John Younge and William Walker and all things nessesarie for theire vse belonging to the said barkqe.

June 9.

Ordered that all such as were pressed by warrants issued out by the late counsell of warr be forthwith released.

1654, June 20.

The counsell of warr mett att Plymouth the 20ᵗʰ of June, 1654, att which meeting warrants were issued out in the name of his highness the Lord Protector of England, Ireland and Scotland, for the pressing of the number of fifty men to bee taken out of the seuerall townes of this jurisdiction to goe forth with Major Robert Sedgwicke and Capt. John Leueritt on an intended expedition against the Duch att the Monhatoes. The proportions of each townes are as followeth:

| Plymouth, 6 men. | Sandwich, 4 men. | Marshfeild, 5 men. |
| Duxburrow, 6. | Taunton, 5. | Rehoboth, 4. |
| Scittuate, 8. | Yarmouth, 4. | Eastham, 3. |
| | Barnstable. 5. | |

These being well prouided for were to goe forth vnder the comaund of Captaine Myles Standish whoe was ordered to be theire comander in cheife; Leiftenant Mathew Fuller was ordered to goe forth with him as leiftenant on this expedition; and Hezekiah Hoare was appointed to bee ensigne bearer.

### PREPARATIONS FOR WAR WITH NINIGRET.

**1654, October 3d.**

The comissioners being returned from theire last meeting informed the Court that they had determined with the rest of the comissioners of the other collonies to send a certaine number of horse and footmen on a special message to Ninnegrett the Niunticke Sachem; and in case nessesitie should further require, that they had joyntly agreed to send a 2ᶜᵒⁿᵈ supply of men out of the 4 Vnited Collonies to warr against Ninnegrett; whervpon warrants were forthwith directed to the cunstables of each towne to presse the number of men out of each towne as followeth according to their seuerall proportions.

| Plymouth, | 6. | Yarmouth, | 4. |
| Duxburrow, | 6. | Barnstable, | 5. |
| Scittuate, | 8. | Marshfeild, | 5. |
| Sandwich, | 4. | Rehoboth, | 4. |
| Taunton, | 5. | Eastham, | 4. |

### COST OF THE EXPEDITION AGAINST NINIGRET.

**1655, Oct. 4.**

The proportions of each towne of what they are to pay towards the charge of the expedition the last yeare in sending out souldiers against Ninnegrett the Nyanticke Sachem.

| | £. | s. | d. |
|---|---|---|---|
| Plymouth | 04 | 01 | 06 |
| Duxburrow | 03 | 13 | 08 |
| Scittuate | 06 | 14 | 02 |
| Sandwig | 04 | 16 | 01 |
| Taunton | 03 | 14 | 01 |
| Yarmouth | 03 | 14 | 01 |
| Barnstable | 04 | 01 | 06 |
| Marshfeild | 03 | 14 | 01 |
| Rehoboth | 06 | 14 | 02 |
| Eastham | 02 | 19 | 08 |
| | 44 | 03 | 00 |

### PREPARATIONS MADE FOR WAR WITH AWASHOUKS, THE SQAW-SACHEM OF SACONETT.

**1671, June 5th.**

This Court haue agreed and voated that some force be raised and sent to the Indians att Saconett, to fech in theire armes and in defect therof theire p'sons as occation may require. And for the management of this enterprise it is refered to the councell of warr or soe many of them as shall meet soe as they be nine in number, viz., the major p'te of them concurring.

The names of such as are aded to the Majestrates to be off the Councill of Warr.

| Mr. Josias Winslow, Seni', | Leift. Morton. |
| James Walker, | Cornett Studson. |
| Thomas Huckens, | Ensigne Eames, |
| Nathaniel Morton, | Isacke Chettenden. |

Three shillings a day is allowed for a man and his horse, to all such as were imployed in the late expedition for the fetching in of armes from the Indians, and this allowance to be p'manent for the future vntill it shalbe otherwise ordered.

And likewise for any teame of foure oxen and an horse and a man to goe with them that have bine and are to be imployed in the countryes seruice to haue fiue shillings a day.

July 8, 1671.

It was agreed that a hundred men should be pressed out of the seuerall townes of this jurisdiction in an equall proportion to be in a reddines att Plymouth on Monday the seauenth of August next to goe forth on the said expedition vnder the comand of Major Josias Winslow as comaunder in cheife. It was further ordered by the councell of warr, that Leiftenant John Freeman shallbe a second to the major in the said expedition. And Mr. Constant Southworth comissary.; Captaine Fuller to supply the place of a leiftenant and a sarjean; and Mr. Willam Witherell and Elisha Hedge for sarjeants.

PRESENT APPEARANCE OF ASSONET FOUR CORNERS IN FREETOWN.
[The place of assembling, July, 1671.]

It was also agreed that forty of our trustiest Indians should also be procured to be in a reddines for to goe forth to be healpfull in the said enterprise. The eight day of August next to be the time of theire setting forth; on which day the townes of Taunton, Rehoboth, Bridgwater and Swansey are to cause theire souldiers that are to be sent forth to giue meeting to the major and the rest of the company att or neare Assonett about John Tisdall's farme. It was agreed that the comaunder in cheif shall haue allowed vnto him 10s a day. A leiftenant 06s a day. A sarjeant 04s a day. An ordinary souldier, horse and man 03s a day. The Proportions of the Men pressed out of the seuerall Townes of this Jurisdiction to goe forth on the aboue mencioned Expedition

| Plymouth | 9 | Marshfeild | 8 |
|---|---|---|---|
| Duxburrow | 5 | Rehoboth | 9 |
| Scittuate | 14 | Eastham | 5 |
| Sandwich | 10 | Bridgwater | 5 |
| Taunton | 12 | Swansey | 4 |
| Yarmouth | 9 | Middleberry | 2 |
| Barnstable | 10 | | — |
| | — | | 33 |
| | 69 | | |

In all one hundred and two.

## PREPARATIONS MADE IN 1673 FOR A WAR WITH THE DUTCH AT NEW YORK.

1673, Dec.

This Court vpon serious consideration of the injurious actings of the Duch our naighbours att New Yorke, in the surprissall of seuerall vessells and goods of our confeaderats, and refusing to make just satisfaction for the same vpon demaund; being alsoe informed of theire threats to invade his ma⁻ subjects on Longe Iland, and other p'tes of this countrey, and that they still continew theire men of war abroad to the great predjudice of this country in respect of theire trade and to the disturbance of our peace otherwise; minding alsoe that they have declared these theire actings to be grounded on the nationall quarrell between them and vs in Europe, and accordingly declare theire comission and orders to be to doe all possible spoile and damage to the states enimies by land and water; and soe haueing reason to expect that as theire numbers and strength may increase, theire insolences towards vs will alsoe grow higher,        for our more nessesarie defence wee judge it requisite to indeauor theire . remouall, and haue resolued that theire is just ground of a warr against them and although the season of the yeare is in some respects discurraging, yett haueing reason to thinke that our enimies will have recrute of men &c., early in the springe, wee judge it best with all possible speed to procecute the said expedition and shall indeauor to goe our p'tes therin altho not according to what wee are propoftioned by our confeaderates, wherein wee are apparently ouer rated, yett to the vtermost of our abillities, viz. to raise and maintaine one hundred men in the expedition, if wee can att p'sent be supplyed with what is nessesarie for theire march or voyage.

And that instructions be giuen to the comaunders in cheife, first to sumons them to yeild with theire promise of injoying theire estates and liberties.

The names of the comaunders chosen by the Court were:—

        Captaine James Cudworth for Captaine.
        Mr. John Gorum        for Leiftenant.
        Mr. Michaell Peirse     for Ensigne.

                    FOR SARJEANTS.

        Willam Witherell,        John Witherell,
        Thomas Harvey,         Phillip Leanard.

Captaine Mathew Fuller was chosen the surjean selected for this expedition, if on the motion of it to the Court of the Massachusetts &c., it be approued by them.

The souldiers wages agreed by the Court was

|  | s. | d. |
|---|---|---|
| To a private souldier . . . . . . . | 2 | 00 p. day. |
| To a drumer . . . . . . . . . | 2 | 06 p. day. |
| To a serjeant . . . . . . . . | 3 | 00 p. day. |
| To an ensigne . . . . . . . . | 4 | 00 p. day. |
| To a leiftenant . . . . . . . . | 5 | 00 p. day. |
| To a captaine . . . . . . . . | 6 | 00 p. day. |

The Gouʳ bestows a drum towards the expedition, and the other to be had att Taunton, one pair of cullers to be had att Swansey, the other from

        Four halberts ; Serjeant Tompson,        one.
                    From Scittuate,        one.
                    Captaine Willett,        one.
                    Leiftenant Hunt,        one.

## KING PHILIP'S WAR, 1675.

1675, October 4.

Major James Cudworth was vnanimously chosen and reestablished in the office of a generall or comaunder in cheiffe to take the charge off our forces that are or may be sent forth in the behalfe of the colonie against the enemie as occation may require.

And serjeant Robert Barker to be his leiftenant of his p'ticulare companie; Capt. John Gorum to be captaine of the other companie and Ensigne Jonathan Sparrow to be his leiftenant. Leift. John Browne is appointed and impowered by the Court to be capt. of the guard att Mount Hope.

It is ordered by the Court that twenty flue men, well prouided with armes and amunition be pressed to be and lye in garrison att Mount Hope and that the souldiers that are there att p'sent be forthwith released.

Mr. Thomas Huckens was chosen comissary generall of the forces of this jurisdiction.

The proportions of the salleries allowed by the Court to the comaunders and comon souldiers which haue bin forth in the late expeditions out of this collonie against the Indians, or may be for the future imployed on the countryes occasions :

|  | s. | d. |  |
|---|---|---|---|
| Imp'. to the generall . . . . . ., | 06 | 00 | a day. |
| To a captaine . . . . . . . . | 05 | 00 | a day. |
| To a leift. . . . . . . . . . | 04 | 00 | a day. |
| To Capt. Mathew Fuller, as surjean generall of the forces of this collonie, and for other good service p'formed in the countryes behalfe against the enemie, in the late expeditions or which may be done for the future as occation may require, the Court alloweth him . . | 04 | 00 | a day. |
| To the capt. of the guard at Mount Hope . | 04 | 00 | a day. |
| To an ensigne . . . . . . . . | 03 | 00 | a day. |
| To a comissary generall . . . . . . | 04 | 00 | a day. |
| To a serjeant . . . . . . . . | 02 | 06 | a day. |
| To a corporall . . . . . . . . | 02 | 00 | a day. |
| To a comon souldier . . . . . . | 01 | 06 | a day. |

The proportions of the souldiers to be pressed out of each towne of this jurisdiction to goe forth as occation may require.

| Plymouth, | 15 | 2 | Barnstable, | 16 | 3 | ⎧ To the garison att |
|---|---|---|---|---|---|---|
| Duxburrow, | 08 | 1 | Marshfeild, | 13 | 2 | ⎬ Mount Hope to be |
| Scittuate, | 2J | 4 | Rehoboth, | 15 | 2 | ⎩ subtracted out of them. |
| Sandwich, | 16 | 3 | Eastham, | 08 | 2 | 157 |
| Taunton, | 20 | 3 | Bridgwater, | 08 | 1 | 025 |
| Yarmouth, | 15 | 2 |  |  |  |  |
|  |  |  |  | 157 | 25 | 182 |

The rates alowed for the horses prest or imployed in the expedition against the enemie att Mount Hope and places adjacent, viz.: flue shillings for the vse of euery horse that hath bin returned to the owner within one month after the advance on the said expedition, and 10ˢ p. horse for all that are returned to the owner since the said month or shalbe returned within 28 dayes after the date heerof, and twenty shillings for euery such horse or mare that shall not be returned within the said 28 dayes vnlesse there shalbe another horse in steed therof deliuered within the said time.

Joseph Burge, for his abusing of the watch att Sandwich by entering into the gaurd and assaying to take away a gun and beating one of the gaurd which opposed him therin, is fined flue pound viz., six shillings to the constable for bringing him to the Court and ten shillings to John Dexter, the son of Ensigne Dexter, which was beaten as aforsaid, and flue shillings a peece to the said Ensign Dexter and his son for theire coming vp to and attending on the Court on the said busines, and the remainder of the said flue to the country.

Memorand.: that seuen shillings and sixpence is abated of what is due to the country from the said Burge.

At a Meeting of the Councell of Warr for the Jurisdiction of New Plymouth, held att Marshfeild the sixt Day of December, 1675.—

An order directed from the said Councell to the seuerall plantations within this jurisdiction as followeth

Gentlemen Souldiers :

The prouidence of God soe disposing that wee are still exercised vnder the callamitie of a warr and the councells and authoritie of the seuerall collonies resoluing that there is a nessesitie of sending forth a considerable force with all possible speed, it is desired and required that each collonie and euery p'ticular towne p'esent theire ablest and most suitable men to be improued in that seruice and the Gou' and Councell of this gou'ment request that our people in the seuerall plantations therof will expresse theire woonted chearfulnes and currage in ingageing therin; and for youer incurragement therunto you may please take notice that our Gou' is designed to haue the conduct of all the vnited forces of whose p'ticular fauor and kindnes you may be well assured and also that speciall and effectual care is and shalbe taken that those that goe forth shall in all respects be comfortably prouided for according to the season and seruice, and that the lands and other proffitts of the warr that haue bin obtained or by the blessing of God shalbe gained shalbe kept as cecurtie for the souldiers pay that haue bin and shalbe improued and shall not be sold or disposed of but to answare that end.

The worⁱᵖᵘˡˡ Capt. Bradford and Captaine John Gorum are your p'ticular comaunders. Such as cheerfully tender themselues to the expedition or to presse shalbe looked vpon with singular respect.

By order of the Councell

NATHANIEL MORTON, *Secretary.*

It is ordered by the councell that the milletary officers of each towne of this jurisdiction shall, the next day after the army marcheth forth, exercise the one halfe of his companie in armes; and the next day after the other halfe, and soe euery day after, the one half each day to be in armes where the officers shall appoint vntill further order.

The councell of warr haue ordered and appointed Major Cudworth, Cornett Robert Studson and Isacke Chettenden presse masters for the pressing of able and fitt men att Scittuate to goe forth on the p'sent expedition against the Indians.

An order directed to yᵉ milletary Comission Officers of this jurisdiction as followeth,

Genᵗˡᵉ: You are heerby required to procure youer men pressed to be in a reddines to march soe as they attaine to meet at Prouidence on the tenth of December next; and in order thervnto, that they randezvous on the seauenth of the said month att Plymouth, on the eight att Taunton, att Rehoboth on the 9ᵗʰ and Prouidence on the tenth as aforesaid; and that you see that they be nôt onely able and fitt men, but alsoe well fitted with clothing nessesary for the season, and prouided with knapsackes and amunition according to order viz., halfe a pound of powder and 4 pound of bulletts to each man. Fayle not.

It is ordered by the councell of warr for this jurisdiction that if any p'son henceforward being pressed into the countryes seruice in the expedition against the Indians, and shall neglect or refuse to goe forth on the seruice being thervnto ordered and required by authoritie euery such p'son shall forfete ten pounds in money or the full vallue therof to the vse of the towne to which hee appertaineth; but in case noe estate can be found of the said p'ty to satisfy the same that then hee shalbe forthwith comitted and suffer imprisonment soe that it exceed not six monthes.

It is ordered by the councell of warr for this jurisdiction that if any man that is ordered by the councell where hee liues to be pressed shall leaue his owne towne and goe to another within this collonie, that the constable where hee is vpon notice giuen him of his absenting himselfe from the presse, that constable is required and shall by vertue heerof presse the said p'son into the seruice and forthwith convey him vnto the constable of the towne to which hee appertaines.

The Proportions of the Souldiers to be raised out of each Towne of this Jurisdiction by Order of the Councell of Warr as followeth:

| | | | | | |
|---|---|---|---|---|---|
| Plymouth, | 11. | Taunton, | 13. | Rehoboth, | 15. |
| Duxburrow, | 06. | Yarmouth, | 10. | Eastham, | 09. |
| Scittuate, | 17. | Barnstable, | 13. | Bridg-water, | 07. |
| Sandwich, | 11. | Marshfeild, | 10. | | |

At a Meeting of the Councell of Warr for this Jurisdiction held att Marshfeild the 29ᵗʰ Day of February, 1675 [this was old style, it would be 1676 as we now reckon time], Actes and Orders were made and concluded as followeth: . .

Wheras great damage and prejudice may acrew vnto this juriadiction by the withdrawing of the inhabitants therof in this time of publicke calamitie and trouble, it is therfore ordered by the councell of warr for this jurisdiction that all the inhabitants scated in this gou'ment shall and doe abide in each towne of this collonie to which hee belongs and not depart the same on p'ill of forfeiting the whole p'sonall estate of each one that shall soe doe to the collonies vse except it be by the speciall order or allowance of the Gou' or any two of the other majestrates; and that it shalbe lawful for any majestrate of this gou'ment takeing notice of the intensions of any inhabitant of this collonie to withdraw as aforsaid, to make seizure of the p'sons of such theire estates, and to seize all such barques, boates or carts as shalbe found to be imployed in transporting of the goods of such inhabitants intended to withdraw as aforsuid.

13

The Men appointed to be of the Towne Councell in each Towne of this Jurisdiction:
Plymouth: Nathaniel Morton, Joseph Warren, Joseph Howland.
Duxburrow: Mr. John Alden, Mr. Constant Southworth, Mr. Josias Standish.
Scittuate: Cornett Robert Studson, Isacke Chettenden, Edward Jenkens.
Sandwich: Mr. Richard Bourne, Mr. Edmond Freeman Junr, Thomas Tobey Senir.
Taunton: James Walker, William Harvey, John Richmond.
Yarmouth: Mr. Edmond Hawes, John Miller, Jeremiah Howes.
Barnstable: Mr. Thomas Hinckley, Mr. Thomas Huckens, Mr. Barnabas Laythrop.
Marshfield: Anthony Snow, Nathaniel Thomas, Nathaniel Winslow.
Rehoboth: Mr. Nathaniel Paine, Mr. Nathaniel Cooper, Mr. Daniel Smith.
Bridg'water: Mr. William Brett, Mr. Samuell Edson, John Wilkis Senir.
Eastham: Mr. John Freeman, Jonathan Sparrow, Marke Snow.

The said towne councells together with the comission officers, or the major p'te of the whole concurring, shall haue power to order all watches and wardings and garrisons in theire respectiue townes, and the setting forth of scoutes for the safty of townes, and to take care that the townes stocke of amunition to which they belong may be supplyed, and haue power to call the towne together to make a rate to defray the charge therof as occation may require, and to dispose the said stocke into such places as they shall judge most convenient; and whosoeuer shall neglect, or refuse, to watch or ward being required and ordered so to doe, shall forfeite fiue shillings for euery default, to be leuied by distresse on his estate if he haue any to answare it; and if noe estate, then to be sett necke and heeles, by order of the comission officers, not exceeding halfe an houre; and for euery neglect of p'formance of theire duty in watching or warding one houre after the time appointed to sett it to be, fined one shilling; and after the first houre expired the captaine of the watch shall hier another to watch or ward, and the whole fine of fiue shillings to be payed by delinquent; and such fines soe gathered shalbe comitted to the comission officers or towne councell to be improued for the supply in the defects in watching and warding abouesaid and for other nessesary occations.

It is further ordered by the councell that the watches shall continew from sun seting vntill the sun rise, and the warding to be from sun riseing to sunseting successiuely, and that none shalbe accepted to watch or ward but with fixed armes and suitable amunition, and in case any doe come without the same they shalbe returned againe and the fine of fiue shillings shalbe speedily exacted.

The councell doe agree that the souldiers now vnder presse from the southern townes be att Plymouth on Weddensday the eighth of this instant in order vnto a further march and with them 20 or 30 of the southern Indians, whoe together with the other whoe are vnder presse to goe forth vnder the comaund of Captaine Michael Peirse and Leiftenand Samuell Fuller.

The councell of warr now assembled doe comend it to the seuerall townshipps in this jurisdiction to make some payment to the souldiers first sent out against the Indians in p'te of what is due to them for that seruice especially to the poorer sort who need some supply for theire familyes and the councell doth heerby declare that such payments made as aforsaid shalbe allowed to the respective townes in the generall publicke accoumpt when it shalbe orderly settled and proportioned.

The councell of warr now assembled doe order that the Namassachesett Indians be speedily remoued to Clarkes Iland and ther to remaine and not to depart from thense without lycense from authoritie vpon paine of death.

Wheras it is judged very nessesary and likely to be beneficiall that a garrison should be kept att the house of Joseph Barstow both in respect to the towne of Scittuate and the country,—The councill doe therfore order that speedily a garrison be erected and kept att the said house with about 10 or 12 men; and for the further ordering therof it is refered vnto the comission officers and towne councell of Scittuate.

Att a Meeting of the Councell of Warr for this Jurisdiction att Plymouth the 10th Day of March anno Dom. 1675, Orders and Conclusions were made and ordered as followeth:

In reference to the forces abroad the councell haue ordered and doe impower the president and such of the councell as are neare vnto him that in case they shall see reason by any inconvenience that may appeer to them by theire p'mitting the said forces to continew out they are impowered heerby to require them home againe.

And further that in case notice may be giuen from the other Vnited Colonies to require that our p'te of the thousand men should be sent forth the Gou' is heerby requested to send into the Bay and to respect the case vntill the generallitie of the councell can meet againe.

Memorand.: that the order formerly voated prohibiting shooting bee putt in reall and vigorouse execution.

In order to the keeping of a garrison att Barstowes the councell doe order and allow two men on the countryes charge vntill the army now forth returne hom againe.

In reference vnto the offenciue fact that Robert Barker in breaking away from the army when they were on theire march in a mutinous way, and by his example aluring others to come away with him, to the great scandoll, prejudice and disparragement of the collonie and p'ticularly vnto the comaunder in Cheiff, viz., the generall.

Forasmuch as vpon his late examination hee doth in some measure take to his great offence the councell do centance him heerby to be degraded from the honor and office of a leiftenant and to pay a fine of fifteen pounds to the vse of the collonie in currant siluer money of New England, and to defray the charge of his late imprisonment. The councell doe alsoe order that all such as came away from the army with the said Robert Barker'or followed him in a disorderly way shall likewise forfeite theire wages as to that expedition.

The Fines of the seuerall delinquent souldiers:

|  | £ | s. | d. |
|---|---|---|---|
| Simon Rouse fined | 01 | 00 | 00 |
| Jonathan Winslow | 01 | 00 | 00 |
| John Hewitt | 01 | 00 | 00 |
| Daniel Butler | 08 | 00 | 00 |
| Zacheriah Jenkins | 08 | 00 | 00 |
| Ephram Allin | 08 | 00 | 00 |
| William Alline | 04 | 00 | 00 |
| Zacheriah Coleman | 08 | 00 | 00 |
| John Nolman | 08 | 00 | 00 |
| Joseph Coleman | 08 | 00 | 00 |
| Thomas Coleman | 08 | 00 | 00 |
| John Rance | 08 | 00 | 00 |
| John Northy | 01 | 00 | 00 |
| The constables of Taunton for pressing Joseph Deane, a man vnfitt to goe forth on seruice | 04 | 00 | 00 |
| John Crossman | 08 | 00 | 00 |
| Thomas Lincon | 08 | 00 | 00 |
| Jonathan Harvey | 02 | 00 | 00 |
| Ezra Bourne | 02 | 00 | 00 |
| The constables of Bridgwater for pressing Samuell Laythrop illegally and hee a man vnfitt to goe forth on the seruice, fined | 02 | 00 | 00 |
| And likewise for not pressing John Willis legally | 02 | 00 | 00 |
| John Smith, the son of Mr. John Smith of Sandwich, for neglecting to goe forth a souldier, notwithstanding his plea of nessesitie of keeping att home, yett fined | 02 | 00 | 00 |
| John Fuller, the son of Samuell Fuller of Barnstable, for the same, notwithstanding his plea, fined | 02 | 00 | 00 |

Off Sandwich, fiue defective and wanting of theire number the last presse.

Off Bridgwater, fiue wanting in one presse and foure in another.

In reference to the clearing vp of the case respecting John Smith Junir of Sandwich aforsaid, which case was left on inquiry, the constable of Sandwich appeered before the councell and affeirmed that hee made publicke'proclamation att Sandwich in reference to the souldiers, that they should be supplyed with clothes and nessesaaries for the expedition, and tendered him the said Smith in p'ticular seuerall thinges with which hee might haue bin supplyed if hee had seen cause.

Euery of those fornamed were fined as aforsaid for not going forth being pressed, and some of them for neglecting, being constables, to executing theire office concerning such, and the townes responsible to pay for not makeing vp theire number of men.

A son of Ralph Jones excused himselfe by reason of his father falling sicke about the time of the souldiers goeing forth.

Wheras the Court for the incurragement of the souldiers sent forth on the first expedition against the Indians, did order and engage according to thexe desire that they should haue their pay in money or lands; and noe way at p'sent appeering to raise monyes, doe theirfore for theire satisfaction order that certaine tracts of land be assigned to the vallue of about one thousand pounds to be deuided amongst them for the payment of theire respectiue p'tes, due vnto them; the said tracts assigned being att Showamett supposed to be neare the vallue of 500$^d$; att Assonet Necke 200$^£$; att Assowamsett 200$^£$; and about Agawam and Sepecan, one hundred pound; soe as the said tractes shalbe more p'ticularly viewed and vallued as att mony price according to such indifferent rates as they might haue bine esteemed worth when the said order was made; and for the better effecting therof, the Treasurer, Major Cudworth, Cornett Studson and James Walker are desired and appointed to take view therof and make reporte therof to the Court or councell for the settleing of the same att such reasonable rates as to them shall seeme meet to be deuided to the said souldiers or sold for theire pay or discharge of other nessessarie dues occationed by this warr.

It is aloe further ordered that the sume of one thousand pound be assessed on the seuerall townes of this gou'ment to be payed in clothing, prouisions or cattle att mony prise; an indifferent good ordinary cow being to be vallued att forty fiue shillings and other cattle according to that proportion for the payment of such of the souldiers whose needy condition may call for other supplyes more suitable for theire families than lands, and such other smale dues to others of them as may be by them desired and judged convenient by those betrusted in the scuerall townes for the management of that affaire, together with the defraying such other charges as hath bin occationed by these warrs according to order. The proportions to the seuerall townes of the said sume of one thousand pounds are as followeth :

| | £ | s. | d. | | £ | s. | d. |
|---|---|---|---|---|---|---|---|
| Plymouth, | 99 | 03 | 06 | Yarmouth, | 74 | 15 | 06 |
| Duxburrow, | 46 | 11 | 00 | Barnstable, | 99 | 03 | 06 |
| Bridgwater, | 46 | 11 | 00 | Marshfield, | 75 | 08 | 00 |
| Scittuate, | 165 | 09 | 00 | Rehoboth, | 136 | 19 | 00 |
| Taunton | 92 | 13 | 06 | Eastham, | .66 | 16 | 06 |
| Sandwich, | 92 | 13 | 06 | | | | |

FORM OF WARRANT DIRECTED TO THE PEOPLE OF THE DIFFERENT TOWNS FOR THE
COLLECTION OF THIS TAX.

Wheras youer townes p'te of the sum of 1000 £. to be leuied for the defraying the charge of this warr according to order in that case prouided amounts to the sum of       these are therfore in his ma$^{ties}$ name to will and require you p'sently on receipt heerof to call youer towne together to make a rate for the defraying the said sume, to be payed in clothing, prouision or cattle att the prises in the said order prouided about the middle of May next according to the Treasurers order to be disposed to those appointed by the towne councell or such other order as the Treasurer shall appoint for the ends aforsaid. Fayle not.

The 29th of March, 1676.

The councell of warr for this jurisdiction ordereth as followeth : in reference vnto a p'sent exegencye and straite that is on vs by reason of the neare approach of our enimies whoe haue fiered the greatest p'te of one of our fronteer townes and that wee haue reason to expect that they may p'sist on in theire hostilitie, and assault other townes before wee are aware, the councell doe agree and order that the number of three hundred English souldiers be raised and pressed out of our collonie, and one hundred Indians, well fitted to goe forth and to be reddy for a march the eleuenth of Aprill next. The Proportions of Men pressed out of the seuerall Townes of this Gou'ment :

| Plymouth, | 30 | Taunton, | 30 | Rehoboth, | 30 |
|---|---|---|---|---|---|
| Duxburrow, | 16 | Yarmouth, | 26 | Eastham, | 18 |
| Scittuate, | 50 | Barnstable, | 30 | Bridgwater, | 16 |
| Sandwich, | 28 | Marshfield, | 26 | | |

It is ordered by the councell that such youthes as are vnder the age of sixteen yeers and notwithstanding are able to p'forme seruice in watching and warding shalbe required soe to doe, and p'forme theire duty therin as others, being soe judged by the comaunders or towne councell.

The Treasurer is desired and ordered to procure the bread for the souldiers in a reddines to attend the expedition, And to procure a competency of bulletts for the souldiers in their said intended expedition as hee shall judge meet.

**1670, June 7.**

Vpon consideration of the nessesitie of sending forth some forces to be by the healp of God a meanes of our safty and preservation, the Court came to a conclusion and doe heerby voate that one hundred and fifty English and fifty Indians be with the best speed that may be raised and prouided and sent forth towards the frontiere p'tes of this collonie to be vpon motion to scout to and frow for the safty of the collonie, the time appointed of sending forth is on Weddensday the 21 of this instant

**June. 1676.**

The proportions of the men and money to be raised for the seting forth in the expedition aforsaid is as following:

| THE PROPORTIONS OF MEN. | | MONEY. | | | |
|---|---|---|---|---|---|
| Plymouth, | 15 | Plymouth, | 16£ | 00s. | 00d. |
| Duxburrow, | 9 | Duxburrow, | 9 | 10 | 00 |
| Scittuate, | 25 | Scittuate, | 26 | 10 | 00 |
| Sandwich, | 15 | Sandwich, | 16 | 00 | 00 |
| Taunton, | 15 | Taunton, | 16 | 00 | 00 |
| Yarmouth, | 13 | Yarmouth, | 14 | 00 | 00 |
| Barnstable, | 15 | Barnstable, | 16 | 00 | 00 |
| Marshfeild, | 13 | Marshfeild, | 14 | 00 | 00 |
| Rehoboth, | 15 | Rehoboth, | 16 | 00 | 00 |
| Eastham, | 10 | Eastham, | 10 | 15 | 00 |
| Bridgwater, | 9 | Bridgwater, | 09 | 10 | 00 |
| | 154 | | | | |

**1676, June 7.**

It is ordered by the Court and the authoritie therof that each towne make a rate to pay all theire souldiers and officers which haue bin out on the countryes seruice from first to last theire full due in such specue as by the last rate for their payment in p'te was ordered, vnlesse any of them desire rather to stay to haue it in land; and that the seuerall townes bring or send in an accoumpt of theire p'ticular distinct disbursements to July Court next that soe there may be a right proportioning of the whole charge of this warr vpon the seuerall townes.

It was agreed and ordered by the Court, that ten hogsheds of bread be procured for and towards the expedition intend and a thousand waight of bulletts. And that the sume of twenty or thirty pounds be improued in the paying of the collonis debts att Rhode Iland.

A p'sell of amunition deliuered to som souldiers lately gon forth was to Marshfeild men 37lb of bulletts and 14 pound of powder.

To Duxburrow men 23 pound of bulletts.

To Daniel Turner of Scittuate 4 pound of bulletts.

The names of such souldiers of Scittuat whoe desired to be satisfyed in lands for such seruice as they p'formed for the conntry, with the sumes due to them on that accoumpt is as followeth:

| | £ | s. | d. |
|---|---|---|---|
| Imp'. Leifte Isake Bucke . . . . . | 10 | 00 | 00 |
| Zacheriah Daman . . . . . . . | 06 | 06 | 01 |
| John Daman . . . . . . . | 06 | 05 | 07 |
| Richard Prowtey . . . . . . . | 06 | 12 | 03 |
| Cor. John Bucke . . . . . . . | 08 | 09 | 05 |
| Jonathan Jackson . . . . . . . | 06 | 05 | 04 |
| Thomas Clarke . . . . . . . | 05 | 05 | 02 |
| Will'am Hatch . . . . . . . | 02 | 01 | 00 |
| Walther Bridges . . . . . . . | 05 | 18 | 07 |
| Joseph Garrett . . . . . . . | 05 | 09 | 07 |
| Richard Dwelley . . . . . . . | 11 | 13 | 07 |
| Charles Stockbridge for Benjamin Woodworth | 07 | 09 | 00 |

July the 7<sup>th</sup>, 1676.

It was ordered by the Court, that the seuerall townes of this jurisdiction should send in some one of each towne of this jurisdiction to giue meeting to the majestrates on the 19 of this instant July, att Plymouth to settle theire accompts respecting the charges of this p'sent warr, on paine of forfeiting euery towne that shall neglect ten pounds to the vse of the collonie.

The 22<sup>cond</sup> of July, 1676.

The councell haue ordered that all such voulenteers as shall or haue sett forth to oppose the enimie in case they shall take any prisoners, they bearing the charge of the expedition, shall haue the one halfe of them for theire paines and venture from the day of the date heerof, includeing those prisoners alsoe last brought in by Benjamine Church and his companie.

It is ordered by the councell, that euery towne of this gou'ment shall pay theire souldiers and officers what is due to them for theire seruice against our comon enimie since last June Court, wherin that noe towne may be oppressed, that they bringe in theire disbursments vnto the next Generall Court, that soe there may be an equall ballence of charges.

Nov. 1.

This Court engaged, that Charles Stockbridge and others of such of Scittuate as listed theire names to take theire pay in land shalbe payed for theire seruice for the countrey in mony out of the prise of those lands which shalbe first sold which is appointed for the payment of souldiers, &c.

1677, March 6.

In reference vnto a kettle appertaineing to James Walker Juni<sup>r</sup>, taken away by Jerrud Talbutts soldiers, but not returned, the Court haue ordered that the said souldiers shall forthwith make payment of 31s. currant siluer mony of New England, vnto the said James Walker or his order in full satisfaction for the said kettle.

July 3<sup>d</sup>.

The sume of tweenty pounds is allowed by the Generall Court vnto Thomas Baxter a maimed souldier, whoe hath lost the vse of one of his hands in the time hee was in the countreyes service.

New Plymouth Colony Debter.

| | | | |
|---|---:|---:|---:|
| 84 <sup>lbs</sup> of biskett to Generall Cudworth . . . | 00 | 18 | 00 |
| gallons of wine to ditto . . . . . . . | 00 | 08 | 00 |
| bagg & runlett not returned . . . . | 00 | 00 | 00 |
| sheep deliuered by John Sanford, by of Comis- | | | |
| ~~sesary vnder ye souldiers come ouer from Mount~~ | | | |
| Hope . . . . . . . . . . | 04 | 11 | 00 |
| 1 <sup>lb</sup> 3<sup>d</sup> 16 pound of biskett delified to John Abbitt by | | | |
| Generall Cudworth's order . . . . . | 02 | 10 | 00 |
| | 08 | 07 | 00 |

Sign<sup>d</sup> by PELEG SANFORD.

The above written accompt is allowed by the Court held in June, 1682, Peleg Sanford Esq. his Accompt appointed to be rded at June Court, 1682.

---

# KING WILLIAM'S WAR.

1689, August 14.

Mr. Nath<sup>el</sup> Byfield, Capt. Jonathan Sparrow, & Leiut. Isaac Little chosen to be of the councill of war.

In refference to the motion made by the honourable Councill & Generall Convention of our friends & neighbours at Boston, for our advice & assistance in repelling & suppressing the barbarous heathen, that have comitted many barbarous murders and outrages on the easteren parts on the subjects of the crown of England, this Generall Court declare their concurrence therein according to our weak capacity, and do committ the management thereof to Thomas Hinkley, and John Walley, Esq<sup>rs</sup> their comission<sup>rs</sup> chosen for that end, both for the inquiry into the grounds of s<sup>d</sup> war, for farther satisfaction, & to order all other suitable means & actions as they shall se cause, with the advice and concurrance of such as may be comissionated thereunto by our friends and ancient confederates of the Massachusetts and Conecticut, or by any other of their ma<sup>ties</sup> colonies that may be concerned therein, as may through God's blessing conduce to the comon good & safty of the whole against the comon enimie, according to such instructions as are by the Court given to them. That such due encouragement may be given to souldiers that if it may be there may be enough raysed to go volluntarly, without pressing, such encouragement to be six shillings per weeke, money or monies value for each private souldier, and eight or ten pound pr head to our company of souldiers, for every fighting man of the enimy whose scalp shall be brought in, to such person or officer as shall be appointed to take notice or knowledge thereof, and also to have all the persons as they shall take & captivate, and all portable plunder divided amongst them.

And if any souldier of ours shall be maimed in s<sup>d</sup> war and thereby disabled to maintaine themselves, he or they to be provided for, relieved and maintained in such capacity as he or they lived in before concerned in s<sup>d</sup> war, and also to have victuals & amunition allowed while upon the expedition.

That in regard the other colonies are better stored with provision and amunition then our selves, they may disburse on the publique faith to be repaid in time convenient.

That care be forthwith taken to engage the Mowhawke Indians with us against our said enimins by sending some meet person to them with a present, and to treat with them in order there to.

Ordered by this Court and the authority therof, that if any person English or Indian, apprehend and bring before authority any man that is an Indian enimie, he shall have ten pounds for a reward if he bring him alive & five pounds if killed, provided it be evident it be an enimie Indian. Alsoe ordered, that the military officers of each town forthwith use their endeavour to encourage English & Indians to a volluntary going out in this present expedition under comand of Capt. Church, and such persons to list and give an account therof to said capt. or other officer. And if for the Indians souldiers they or the selectmen or any inhabitant supply them with any thing for their present necessity & encouragement, it shall be allowed or paid to them by the Treasurer out of the next rate.

It is ordered by this Court that the proportion for men and armes for each towne for the present expedition shall be as followeth : each man to be provided with a well fixt gun, sword or hatchet, a horne or cartouch box, suitable amunition, & a snapsack.

| | Men. | Armes. | | Men. | Armes. | | Men. | Armes. |
|---|---|---|---|---|---|---|---|---|
| Plymouth, | 4 | 3 | Barnstable, | 4 | 3 | Bristol, | 3 | 2 |
| Scituate, | 6 | 5 | Eastham, | 4 | 3 | Taunton, | 4 | 4 |
| Marshfield, | 3 | 3 | Sandwich, | 3 | 3 | Rehoboth, | 4 | 3 |
| Duxburough, | 2 | 2 | Yarmouth, | 3 | 3 | Dartmouth, | 3 | 2 |
| Bridgwater, | 3 | 2 | Rochester, | 1 | 1 | Swansey, | 3 | 2 |
| Middleborough, | 1 | 1 | Monamoy, | 1 | 1 | Freetown, | 1 | 1 |
| | | | Succonessett, | 1 | 1 | Little Compton, | 2 | 2 |

It is ordered by this Court and the authority thereof, that if there do not appear a competent number of English souldiers in each town of this colony to go vollunteers under the conduct of Capt. Church or some other officer, as shall be by the councill of war appointed to go out upon the present expedition to suppress the heathen that are enimies within any part of this countrey, that then such a number shall be pressed as shall be by the councill of war agreed upon in the severall towns where vollunteers enough do not appear.

It is ordered by this Court that the majors of the severall regiments forthwith take care to procure a perfect list of all the males in their respective regiments of what rank or quality soever from the age of sixteene to sixty yeares, and to deliver the same to one of the comissioners of this colony at ór before the fourteenth day of this instant October, by them to be caryed to Boston in order to proportion the charge of the present warr.

Ordered that towards the bearing of the charge of the present warr there be forthwith levyed and raysed by the select men or raters of each town and village in this colony the sums hereafter set downe and agreed on by this Court, viz.:

| | £ | s. | d. | | £ | s. | d. | | £ | s. | d. |
|---|---|---|---|---|---|---|---|---|---|---|---|
| Plymouth, | 60 | 00 | 00 | Barnstable, | 60 | 00 | 00 | Dartmouth, | 40 | 00 | 00 |
| Duxbury, | 25 | 00 | 00 | Sandwich, | 60 | 00 | 00 | Bristol, | 35 | 00 | 00 |
| Scituate, | 88 | 00 | 00 | Yarmouth, | 41 | 00 | 00 | Taunton, | 60 | 00 | 00 |
| Marshfield, | 45 | 00 | 00 | Eastham, | 46 | 00 | 00 | Rehoboth, | 48 | 00 | 00 |
| Bridgwater, | 28 | 00 | 00 | Rochester, | 08 | 00 | 00 | Swansey, | 40 | 00 | 00 |
| Middlebury, | 14 | 00 | 00 | Monamoy, | 07 | 00 | 00 | Little Compton, | 35 | 00 | 00 |
| Foords Farmes, | 02 | 00 | 00 | | | | | Freetown, | 08 | 00 | 00 |

The severall sums to be paid to the constables of each towne and village at or before the 25th day of November next, the same to be paid by the constables in each town & village to such as the Generall Court shall appoint, the severall sums to be paid one third in money, one third in grain, Indian corne at two shillings pr bushell, rye two shillings and six pence pr bushell, barly two shillings pr bushell, wheat four shillings pr bushell, the other third in biefe at ten shillings pr C., and porke at two pence pr pound, the charge of transportation after it is delivered pr order aboard any vessel to be allowed by the publique. It is alsoe agreed that this proportion be onely for this rate and that there be a way found with all convenient speed for a valluation of the estates of the colony in order to the making of a just proportion which when found out and determined each town be allowed or advanced accordingly; or, if any, for the corne or provision part, pay that which for price and specie sattisfie any souldiers that went in the service it shall be accepted and there shall be care taken that the souldiers English and Indians be paid by the counties where they lived or were raysed, and care taken as much as may be in the whole to prevent transportation. Farther agreed that any person that for the corne part or provision part of this rate will pay money shall have one sixth part abated.

October ye 2d 1689.

Ordered by the Court the select men of each town take care forthwith to take a valluation of the estates of each town and village according to the prises hereafter mentioned, viz.:

| | £ | s. | d. |
|---|---|---|---|
| Every ox at . . . . . . . . . . | 02 | 10 | 0 |
| Every cowe . . . . . . . . . . | 01 | 10 | 0 |
| Every steere & heiffer of 3 year old . . . . | 01 | 10 | 0 |
| Every two year old at . . . . . . . . | 01 | 00 | 0 |
| Every yearling at . . . . . . . . | 00 | 15 | 0 |
| Every horse & mare at . . . . . . . . | 02 | 00 | 0 |
| Every two year old colte at . . . . . . | 01 | 00 | 0 |
| Every yearling colte . . . . . . . . | 00 | 10 | 0 |
| Every swine of a year old & upwards at . . . . | 00 | 06 | 0 |
| Sheep of a year old and upward, by ye score . . . | 05 | 00 | 0 |
| Land in tillage, every acre . . . . . . | 00 | 05 | 0 |
| Meadow and English pasture, every acre at . . . | 00 | 05 | 0 |

Vessels and trading estate not more than half price.
Faculties and personall abilities at will and doome; the
like where any neglect or refuse to give in a just account
of their ratable estate.

Dec. 25.

John Thacher, } Esqrs
John Walley, }
Mr. John Saffin,
Capt. Jonathan Sparrow,
Mr. Stephen Skeff &
Leiut. Isaac Little.

{ Chosen and appointed by this Court as a Committee to take and adjust the accounts and charges of the war relating to the late expedition against the Indians, and to make report thereof to this Court to the end that souldiers & others concerned may have their wages and dues paid with all convenient speed.

It is ordered by this Court, &c. that there be a comittee chosen in each county to settle the charges of the war and disbursments in their respective counties, and to adjust the accounts of all officers and souldiers that have been in the service, & to order payment to all officers, souldiers & other persons that have disbursed for the war in such ways as may be most suitable & convenient for them, and most advantageous to the colony.

Ordered that Major Church shall have ten pounds allowed him (besides what he hath received from the Bay) more than his wages by the weeke and that his weekly wages as a major in yᵉ late expedition be 40 shillings, and that Major Church shall have 5£ cash and Capt. Bassitt 3£ cash part of what is due to them from the colony, paid to them by the constables of Plymouth out of the last rate.

That Leiut. William Southworth have 25 shillings pʳ weeke for his service in the warr.

That Capt. Edmonds have 20ˢ pʳ weeke for his service.

That Leiut. Smith have 20ˢ pʳ weeke for his service.

That John Stetson have 15ˢ pʳ weeke for his service & being helpfull to yᵉ comissary.

That each English serjeant have 12ˢ pʳ weeke; each corporall, 9ˢ pʳ weeke; and that Benjamin Bantum yᵉ clerk have 9ˢ pʳ weeke.

That each Indian capt. have 12ˢ & each leiut. 9ˢ pʳ weeke.

And that Capt. John Hunter have nine shillings pʳ weeke for his service in the expedition aforesaid.

That Capt. Bassitt have 30ˢ pʳ weeke as capt., and 5ˢʰⁱˡˡ pʳ weeke for his assistance of the comissary.

1690, May 20.

Ordered by this Court and the authority thereof, that there be sixty men forthwith raysed in the colony to be sent by water to Albany or elswhere to joyne with the forces of New Yorke, Massachusetts or Conecticot, &c., for the defence of sᵈ places or other service of their maᵗⁱᵉˢ against the comon enemy; the men to be raysed in each town according to the proportions hereafter set down, viz.:

| | | | | | |
|---|---|---|---|---|---|
| Plimouth, | 5 | Barnstable, | 5 | Bristol, | 3 |
| Duxburough, | 3 | Sandwich, | 4 | Taunton, | 5 |
| Scituate, | 6 | Yarmouth, | 4 | Rehoboth, | 4 |
| Marshfield, | 3 | Eastham, | 4 | Dartmouth, | 3 |
| Bridgwater, | 3 | Rochester, | 1 | Swansey, | 3 |
| Middleborough, | 1 | Monamoy, | 1 | Little Compton, | 2 |
| | | Succoneasset, | 1 | Freetowne, | 1 |

Ordered by this Court and the authority thereof, that the proportions of men now agreed on to be raysed for their maᵗⁱᵉˢ service be impressed in the severall towns by warrant under the hands of the town council or the major part of them, and where there is no town council by warrant from the selectmen of such town or townes or the major part of them, and where there is no town council nor select men, to be impressed by warrant from the major of the regiment; sᵈ town councils, select men or majors are hereby ordered and required to impress or cause to be impressed the severall proportions of men upon Wednesday next and not before, and that the whole be ready on or before the second day of June next to attend such service as then shall be required of them.

Ordered, that all constables, serjeants, corporals or other persons that the warrants from the town council, select men & majors are or shall be directed too in matters they are impowered relating to this present expedition, are hereby required to execute the same and to be aiding and assisting as there may be occasion.

Ordered, that the town council, all or either of them, endeavour forthwith to p'cure from the inhabitants of the severall townes so much money as to make up 20 shillings for every man orderd to be sent forth from each town, and whatsoever any inhabitant shall disburse or lend on that account or that shall be impressed for fitting out the souldiers shall be repaid by the countrey or discounted out of the next rate; said money to be brought to next June Court to be disposed as sᵈ Court shall order.

Ordered, by this Court, that all such as are or shall be impressed for the countreys service against the comon enemy, and shall refuse or neglect the service, they are to pay as a fine the sum of four pounds in money or not paying the same by warrant from the town council, select men, or major, which gave the warrants forth, such person or persons to be imprisoned untill the fine be paid, and others to be impressed in their roome, which fines shall by the town council be improved for buying armes & amunition for a stock for the town, unles they se cause to dispose any part thereof for the fitting or encouragement of such as shall be impressed in their stead, unles such person or persons shall appeal to the council of warr and give security to answer the same.

14

*New Plimouth, Aprill ye 2d, 1690.*

By the President & Council of War.

Ordered, that a watch be forthwith kept and maintained in every town & village of this colony of so many persons as the town councill in each town or village shall appoint.

And that in such towns where the said town councill shall judge it needfull, principlely and especially in all sea port towns & places, that some persons be appointed to ward in the day time as s<sup>d</sup> councill shall direct.

Ordered, that the comission officers of every millitary company in this colony cause a speedy search to be made in their severall respective towns, to see and know how persons are provided w<sup>th</sup> armes and amunition, & to proceed in that matter as y<sup>e</sup> law directs.

Ordered, that the town councill and select men of the town of Plimouth, with all convenient speed cause cariages to be made for the great guns in s<sup>d</sup> town, and that all s<sup>d</sup> guns be speedily mounted or put on said cariages and brought into the towne, & planted where they may be most serviceable advantageous & convenient for the anoyance of an enemy & defence of the towne.

1690, June 5.

Ordered, that for the present expedition for Canady or places adjacent, that the souldiers already impressed be made up, the proportions for each town as is hereafter set down:

| Armes. | | Men. | Armes. | | Men. |
|---|---|---|---|---|---|
| 4 | viz. Plimouth, | 13 | 4 | Barnstable, | 12 |
| 2 | Duxborough, | 7 | 3 | Sandwich, | 10 |
| 2 | Marshfield, | 7 | 3 | Yarmouth, | 10 |
| 5 | Scituate, | 16 | 2 | Eastham, | 10 |
| 2 | Bridgwater, | 8 | 1 | Succonessett, | 2 |
| 1 | Middleborough, | 3 | 1 | Manamoy, | 2 |
| | | | 1 | Rochester, | 2 |
| 16 | | 54 | 15 | | 48 |

| Armes. | | Men. |
|---|---|---|
| 2 | Bristoll, | 6 |
| 3 | Swansey, | 7 |
| 2 | Little Compton, | 4 |
| 3 | Dartmouth, | 8 |
| 4 | Taunton, | 14 |
| 3 | Rehoboth, | 10 |
| 1 | Freetown, | 2 |
| 18 | | 51 |

Ordered, by this Court, that in this present expedition there be raysed fifty Indians, 22 in the county of Barnstable, 22 in the county of Bristoll and six in the county of Plimouth. If such do not present as are to the sattisfaction of one or more of the magistrates of the coûnty, or the comander of the company, that then by warrant from a magistrate such be impressed as are most fitt. And that Plimouth county take care to provide armes and other necessaries for eighteene men, Barnstable county for fifteene men and Bristoll county for seventeene men.

The officers and souldiers now to be raysed to march at such time and rendevouse at such places as they shall receive orders from one or both of the comissioners of the colony, one or both of which are hereby impowered to grant warrants to impress vessels, men, armes, amunition or any other thing needed, and can be procured within the colony for this present expedition.

Ordered, that if the officers now appointed for this expedition either do not accept or are prevented by the hand of God, or any should otherwise be wanting, that the Govern<sup>r</sup> with the consent of two magistrates appoint and comissionate others, as there may be need.

Ordered, &c., that the persons which shall be appointed press masters to impress souldiers for their ma<sup>ties</sup> service, shall have full power to impress any men appointed, to be impressed for the town which he or they shall be press masters for in any town in this colony.

Capt. Joseph Silvester, Mr. John Goram, chosen for captains for the present expedition.

Jabiz Snow, Sam¹ Gallop, leiftenants; Preserved Abel or John Butterworth, Sam¹ Lucos, ensignes.

1690, June 3.

Barnabas Lothrop, Esqʳ, John Walley, Esqʳ and Capt. Nathˡ Thomas:

Appointed a comittee to receive and take account of the late comittees of yᵉ counties of Barnstable and Bristoll, and of yᵉ town councills or constables in each towne of yᵉ county of Plimouth, respecting yᵉ money & prouision raysed for payment of souldiers & charge of yᵉ war in yᵉ last rate.

Nov. 4.

Capt. Nathaniel Thomas, Leiut. Isaac Little, are appointed a comittee to take & adjust the accounts of what the colony is indebted to particular (persons) for money lent or other debts of the colony ———— to yᵉ making a rate for the speedy———— the same.

Resolved and agreed on by the Generall Court, that 1350 pounds be forthwith raised pʳ rate upon all the rateable inhabitants of the colony for the payment of all known debts of the colony relating to the present war, and otherwayes excepting the charges about armes for yᵉ expedition to Caᴀda.

. The one half of sᵈ sum to be paid in money, the other half in wheat at 4s. pʳ bushel, barley at 2s., rye at 2s. 9d., Indian corne at 2s. 6d. pʳ bushell, porke at 45 shillings pʳ barrell, biefe at 28 shillings pʳ barrell, butter in firkin or pott at 6d. pʳ

---

NOTE.—Capt. Joseph Sylvester was a son of Richard Sylvester and wife Naomi Torrey. For his military services and those of his company they received a grant of wild land from the general court of Massachusetts, which grant was thought to have been in Maine, but upon the establishment of the line was found to be in New Hampshire, and in 1765 their heirs received a new grant in Maine to compensate for that lost in N. Hampshire, and this 2d grant was what, July 7, 1786, was incorporated as the township of TURNER, in Maine. In this expedition of 1690, Capt. Sylvester commanded one of the companies, and 16 of his soldiers were Scituate men, several of whom together with himself are thought to have lost their lives in that service. Benjamin Stetson, John Perry and William Perry, three of his soldiers who lived to return home, were witnesses to Capt. Joseph Sylvester's will. In the local militia of Scituate, Joseph Sylvester was commissioned captain, October 2, 1689.

Mr. John Gorham was of Barnstable. He was born Feb. 20, 1651. He was a son of the Capt. John Gorham who died in the service of his country while commanding a company stationed in Swansea (Feb. 5, 1676). John the son probably did not accept this appointment as captain in the expedition of 1690, but is probably identical with the John Gorham who served as a captain in an expedition against the French and Indians in Maine in 1696, and in the same service as a Lieut. Colonel in 1704.

Preserved Abel and John Butterworth, one of whom was to have been commissioned as an Ensign, were both Rehoboth men.

Samuel Gallop, appointed to be a lieutenant, was promoted to and served as a captain in the expedition of 1690.

The following is a roll of Capt. Samuel Gallop's company in that expedition:

Commissioned Officers.—Samuel Gallop, Captain; Preserved Abel, Lieutenant; Solomon Smith, Ensign.

Non Commissioned Officers.—Samuel Sabin and William Hack, Sergeants; John Querk and Nicholas Peck, Corporals.

Private Soldiers.—Ichabod Peck, William Robinson, Daniel Carpenter, Jacob Carpenter, Daniel Sheperson, Noah Sabin, John Ormsby, John Wall, Samuel Butterworth, Henry Thomas, John Daviss, Samuel Luther, Morris Ronam, Ungass Callee, Zachariah Curtis, Richard Tuells, Thomas Tuells, Thomas Crossman, John Bright, Nicholas Hall, John Smith, John Bagley, Joseph Jones, Daniel Fisher, John Eddy, Samuel Holloway, Daniel Phillips, Miles Garden, John Haskins, William Ripley, Thomas Traintor, Carlo Caree, Philip Braseel, John Price, William Hillyerd, Jonah Meredith, Thomas Hart, William Newland, Philip Allen, William Ellis, John Cupowo, John Thomas, Sam. Tutusk, Dickens ———, Simon Tom, Joshua Thomas, James Trask, James Pumshot, Obed Wickum, Obediah ———, Benjamin Jacob, Abel Wasunks, Sam Hunter, Joseph Jeckewot, Sam Umpatune, Job ———, Jeremiah Jones.

Commissioned, 3; Non Commissioned, 4; Private Soldiers, 57; Total, 64.

Doubtless quite a number of the private soldiers above enumerated were Indians.

Daniel Carpenter, a soldier in this company, in a letter directed to his father William Carpenter, of Rehoboth, said that the company remained at Plymouth eight days waiting for the vessels that were to convey the soldiers, and upon the 27th (probably of June), 1690, sailed out of Plymouth in five shallops about noon, and arrived at Nantasket before night, where they expected to remain until the 30th instant.

The soldiers Traintor and Caree were from Freetown.

pound, in less quantity by pound, 5d.; all s<sup>d</sup> grain & provisions to be good & merchantable.

The Court allow to Leiv<sup>t</sup> Little for his trouble & charge in receiving and delivering the loan money for Canada expedition, &c., the sum of 40 shillings to be paid out of this rate.

This Court order that the Goven<sup>r</sup>, Assistants, Secretary, and Chief Marshall shall have one third part of what is allowed and due to each of them paid in money.

Barnabas Lothrop Esq<sup>r</sup>, Mr. Stephen Skeff and Capt. William Bassett:
Are appointed a comittee for the county of Barnstable.
John Cushing Esq<sup>r</sup>, Leivt. Isaac Little and Sam<sup>l</sup> Sprague:
Are appointed a comittee for the county of Plimouth.
Daniel Smith Esq<sup>r</sup>, Capt. Thomas Leonard and Sam<sup>l</sup> Gardiner:
Are appointed a comittee for the county of Bristol.

The s<sup>d</sup> comittees of each county are appointed to meet at their severall county towns upon the third Tuesday of this instant November, then and there to receive and prepare the accounts of the severall persons to whome the colony is indebted; which being performed the whole comittees, viz., all the persons above named, are to meet at Plimouth on the first Tuesday of December next, who are hereby impowered to adjust and allow all such accounts of souldiers and others as to them shall seeme just and reasonable, and to order bills to the severall county Treasurers for payment of y<sup>e</sup> same to such as y<sup>e</sup> colony is indebted unto.

And the said county Treasurers are hereby impowered to require & receive the said severall sums that shall be levyed & raysed upon the towns in their respective counties, of the severall constables who shall colect and gather the same, and upon receipt thereof to give acquittances & other discharges to s<sup>d</sup> constables.

The Court allow to each of s<sup>d</sup> comittee 3s. p<sup>r</sup> day, for what time they shall necessarily be imployed in the colonies concerns as aboves<sup>d</sup>.

The Court allow 4d. p<sup>r</sup> meal to those that billetted souldiers.

The proportion of each town & village in the colony towards the afores<sup>d</sup> sum of 1350 pounds is as followeth:

| | £ | s. | d. | | £ | s. | d. |
|---|---|---|---|---|---|---|---|
| Plimouth, | 84 | 15 | 00 | Barnstable, | 112 | 10 | 00 |
| Scituate, | 163 | 10 | 00 | Yarmouth, | 104 | 02 | 09 |
| Marshfield, | 67 | 13 | 00 | Sandwich, | 93 | 15 | 00 |
| Duxbury, | 55 | 05 | 00 | Eastham, | 93 | 19 | 06 |
| Bridgwater, | 57 | 07 | 06 | Rochester, | 13 | 15 | 00 |
| Middleborough, | 21 | 16 | 06 | Monamoy, | 18 | 18 | 09 |
| | | | | Succonessett, | 15 | 03 | 09 |
| | 451 | 07 | 00 | | 452 | 04 | 09 |

| | £ | s. | d. |
|---|---|---|---|
| Bristoll, | 39 | 06 | 09 |
| Taunton, | 100 | 16 | 09 |
| Rehoboth, | 79 | 07 | 09 |
| Dartmouth, | 82 | 10 | 00 |
| Swansey, | 56 | 05 | 00 |
| Little Compton, | 75 | 00 | 00 |
| Freetowne, | 13 | 01 | 00 |
| | 446 | 08 | 00 |

By the councill of war at Plimouth Octob<sup>r</sup> y<sup>e</sup> 9<sup>th</sup>, 1690, Thomas Tomson of Middleborough, being p<sup>r</sup> order of the major part of the town councill of s<sup>d</sup> Middleborough impressed for the service of their mat<sup>ies</sup> at Canada, and refusing to attend that service is sentenced to pay a fine of four pounds in money to the said town councill for the use of s<sup>d</sup> town or be imprisoned till the same be paid with fees, &c.

James Soul of Middleborough, for the same, is sentenced as abovesaid.

By the councill of war at Plimouth, Novemb<sup>r</sup> y<sup>e</sup> 6<sup>th</sup>, 1690, Joseph Halley, Jun<sup>r</sup> of Sandwich, being p<sup>r</sup> order of the town councill of s<sup>d</sup> Sandwich, impressed for the service of their mat<sup>ies</sup> against y<sup>e</sup> Indian enemy eastward, & in regard of his ill deportment after pressed, & not appearing at the time & place appointed, is sentenced to pay a fine of 4 pound money. But in regard it appears to this councill that he was not well when the souldiers were to march, the councill remit half s<sup>d</sup> fine, ordering that he pay to the town councill for y<sup>e</sup> use of said town y<sup>e</sup> sum of 40s. in money, & fees, &c.

---

# PROFESSIONAL LISTS.

---

# CLERGYMEN.

## BARNSTABLE COUNTY.

| Name of Town. | Name of Clergyman. | When Settled. | When Dismissed. | Cause of Dismissal. |
|---|---|---|---|---|
| Barnstable— | John Lothrop | Sept. 3, 1639 | Nov. 8, 1653 | Death. |
| | Thomas Walley | ......1663 | Mar. 24, 1678 | Death. |
| | Jonathan Russell | ......1683 | | |
| Eastham— | John Mayo | ......1646 | ......1655 | |
| | Thomas Crosby | | | |
| | Samuel Treat | ......1672 | Mar. 18, 1717 | Death. |
| Rochester— | Seth Arnold | ......1684 | About 1716 | Death. |
| Sandwich— | William Leverick | | | |
| | John Smith | ......1676 | ......1688 | |
| Yarmouth— | Marmaduke Andrews | | | |
| | John Miller | ......1646 | | |
| | Thomas Thornton | ......1662 | ......1692 | |
| | John Cotton | ......1691 | April 26, 1705 | Death. |

Richard Bourne was settled as the pastor of an Indian Church at Marshpee, in 1670, and died in 1685, when he was succeeded in the ministry by an Indian named Simon Popmonet, whose ministry continued about 40 years; from 1729 to 1742, the preacher to the Indians was Joseph Bourne, a grandson of the aforenamed Richard Bourne. For a few years immediately after 1742, Solomon Briant, an Indian, was the minister.

## BRISTOL COUNTY.

| Name of Town. | Name of Clergyman. | When Settled. | When Dismissed. | Cause of Dismissal, or Place of Removal. |
|---|---|---|---|---|
| Bristol— | Benjamin Woodbridge | ......168 . | | |
| | Samuel Lee | | | |
| Dartmouth— | John Cooke* | ......16 | Nov. 23, 1695 | Death. |
| Rehoboth— | Samuel Newman | June 4, 1645 | July 5, 1663 | Death. |
| | Noah Newman | March, 1668 | April 18, 1678 | Death. |
| | John Angier | ......1679 | ......1693 | Ill health. |
| Swansea— | John Myles* | Oct. 30, 1667 | Feb. 3, 1683 | Death. |
| Taunton— | William Hooke | Sept. 3, 1639 | ......1644 | New Haven. |
| | Nicholas Street | Sept. 3, 1639 | Nov. 29, 1659 | New Haven. |
| | George Shove | Nov. 17, 1665 | April 21, 1687 | Death. |
| | Samuel Danforth | Sept. 21, 1687 | Nov. 14, 1727 | Death. |

* John Cooke and John Myles were Baptist Ministers.

## PLYMOUTH COUNTY.

| Name of Town. | Name of Clergyman. | When Settled. | When Dismissed. | Cause of Dismissal, or Place of Removal. |
|---|---|---|---|---|
| Bridgewater— | James Keith | Feb. 18, 1664 | July 23, 1719 | Death. |
| Duxbury— | Ralph Partridge | June 7, 1637 | . . . . . . 1658 | Death. |
| | John Holmes | . . . . . . 165 . | Dec. 24, 1675 | Death. |
| | Ichabod Wiswall | . . . . . . 1676 | July 23, 1700 | Death. |
| Marshfield— | Richard Blinman | | | |
| | Edward Bulkley | . . . . . . 1642 | . . . . . . 1658 | Concord. |
| | Samuel Arnold | . . . . . . 1658 | Sept. 1, 1693 | Death. |
| Plymouth— | Ralph Smith | . . . . . . 1629 | | |
| | John Reynor | . . . . . . 1636 | | |
| | John Cotton | . . . . . . 1669 | | |
| Scituate— | Giles Saxton | . . . . . . 1631 | . . . . . . 1634 | Boston. |
| | John Lothrop | Jan. 18, 1635 | Sept. 3, 1639 | Barnstable. |
| | Charles Chauncey | . . . . . . 1641 | . . . . . . 1654 | Cambridge. |
| | William Wetherell | Sept. 2, 1645 | April 9, 1684 | |
| | Henry Dunster | . . . . . . 1654 | Feb. 27, 1659 | |
| | Nicholas Baker | . . . . . . 1660 | Aug. 22, 1678 | Death. |
| | Thomas Mighill | Oct. 15, 1684 | Aug. 26, 1689 | |
| | Jeremiah Cushing | May 27, 1691 | Mar. 22, 1705 | |

# PHYSICIANS.

## BARNSTABLE COUNTY.

| Where Located. | Name. | Term of Practice. | Remarks. |
|---|---|---|---|
| Barnstable— | Matthew Fuller. | | |

## BRISTOL COUNTY.

| Where Located. | Name. | Term of Practice. | Remarks. |
|---|---|---|---|
| Bristol— | Isaac Waldron | | |
| Taunton— | Samuel Danforth | Sept. 21, 1687, to Nov. 14, 1727 | d. Nov. 14, 1727. |

## PLYMOUTH COUNTY.

| Where Located. | Name. | Term of Practice. | Remarks. . |
|---|---|---|---|
| Duxbury— | Comfort Starr<br>Samuel Seabury<br>Samuel Seabury, Jr. | about 1638 to<br>about 1659 to Aug. 5, 1681 | rem. to Boston.<br>d. Aug. 5, 1681. |
| Plymouth— | Samuel Fuller | | |
| Scituate— | Charles Chauncey | about 1641 to 1654. | rem. to Cambridge. |

# LAWYERS.

## BARNSTABLE COUNTY.

| Where Located. | Name. | Term of Service. | Remarks. |
|---|---|---|---|
| Barnstable— | Thomas Hinkley | from about 1645. | |

## BRISTOL COUNTY.

| Where Located. | Name. | Term of Service. | Remarks. |
|---|---|---|---|
| Bristol— | John Saffin<br>Nathaniel Byfield | from about 1689. | |
| Taunton— | Samuel Danforth* | Sept. 21, 1687, to Nov. 14, 1727 | d. Nov. 14, 1727. |

## PLYMOUTH COUNTY.

| Where Located. | Name. | Term of Service. | Remarks. |
|---|---|---|---|
| Scituate— | Edward Foster<br>John Saffin<br>John Hoar<br>John Barker<br>John Cushing<br>Thomas Turner | 1633 to about 1644<br>1649 "    "    1670<br>——— "    "    1669<br>1676<br>1680<br>1690 | d. in or near 1644.  [Bristol.<br>rem. to Boston, thence to<br>rem. to Concord, Mass. |

* Was Clergyman, Lawyer and Physician while at Taunton.

## LAWS CONCERNING PROFESSIONAL MEN, WITH DATES OF THE SEVERAL ENACTMENTS.

### CLERGYMEN OR MINISTERS.

**1655, June 5.**

Wheras there hath been many complaints of want of due maintainance of the minnesters as some have reported : It is therefore enacted, That noe Pastore or Teacher of any Congregation shall remove before his complaint hath been tendered to the Majestrates, and they have heard both sides.

That upon such complaints if there appears to bee a reall defect in the hearers of the minnesters soe complaining, the Majestrates shall use all gentle means to p'suade them to doe theire duty heerin. But if any of them shall not heerby bee reclaimed, but shall persist through plaine obstinacy against an ordinance of God that then it shalbee in the power of the Majestrate to use such other meanes as may put them upon theire duty.

**1657, June 3.**

Wheras this Generall Court taking into theire seriouse consideration the great defect that either is or like to be in y$^e$ severall Townshipes in this jurisdiction for want of an able Godly Teaching Minnestry, and the great prejedice to the soules of many like to ensue ; and being desirouse according to our duties that such defects should not bee for want of due Incurragement to such as either are or shalbee imployed in soe good a worke of the Lord, for his houner and the good of soules. And in consideration that in as much as the severall Townshipes graunted by the Government; was that such a Companie might bee received as should maintaine the publicke worshipe and service of God, there doe therefore judge that the whole body Church and towne are mutually ingaged to support the same ; And therefore order and agree, That in whatsoever Towneship there is or shalbee an able Godly Teaching Minister which is approved by this Government, that then four men be chosen by the Inhabitants or in case of theire neglect, chosen by any three or more of the Majestrates to make an equall and just proportion upon the estates of the Inhabitants according to their abillities to make up such a convenient maintainance for his comfortable attendance on his worke as shalbe agreed upon by the Church in each township where any is with the concurrence of the rest of the Inhabitants if it may be had, or by the Majistrates aforesaid in case of their apparent neglect, and that destresse according as in other just cases provided bee made upon such as refuse to pay theire proportions which is in justice due. But in case there bee any other way wherby any township doe or shall agree that may effect the end aforesaid, this law not to be binding on them.

It is enacted by the Court, that wheras minesters maintainance is to be raised by rate according to order of Court bearing date 1657, which upon neglect is to be taken by distresse, as by the said order doth appear ; yet for preventing off offence and it may be of destresse, This Court doth order : That the Majestrate of each towne where there is any ; and the Celectmen or any of them where there is noe Majestrate ; be heerby impowered upon notice of default heerin to summon every such p'son or p'sons to the next Court, to answare the said neglect, and in case such p'son or p'sons doe not make out just cause for such neglect, they shalbe amerced double the sume proportioned to him or them to the Collonies use, to be disposed of by the Court.

[For further enactments concerning the collection of Minister's Rates, see at the bottom of page 66 of this book.]

## ·PHYSICIANS.

1642, Sept. 6th.

If any children or elder persons shalbe sent or come from one Towne to another to be nursed, schooled or otherwise educated, or to a Phisician or Chirurgeon to be cured of any disease or wound, &c., yet they come to stand in need of releafe, they shalbe releeved and mayntained by the Townships whence they came or were sent from, and not by that Towneship where they are so nursed, educated or at cure, and in case they come or be sent from any Towne or place out of this Colony, then if the nurse, educator, physicon or Chirurgeon, take not sufficient securyty of the person to be nursed, educated or cured, to discharge the Towneship of and from all cost and charge which shall or may come and befall the said Towneship in which hee or they is so to be nursed, educated or cured; Then they, the said nurse, educator, phisicon or Chiurgeon as neglects the same, shall discharge the said Towneship of them themselves.

## ATTORNEYS OR LAWYERS.

1681, July 7.

It is ordered by this Court, that there shall not be allowed above five shillings cost for any attorney or attorneyes to any one action, and where there shall happen to be but one attorney entertained but one day in any one action, then to have two shillings and sixpence only allowed him for costs therin.

Liberty is granted by this Court to any person to improve one or two Attornies to help him in his Pleas provided they be persons of good repute, and such as the Court shall approve, and the said Attornies are required as to be faithful to their Clyent so also to avoid fraudulent pleas, that may have a tendency to mislead the Court or darken the case.

# RHODE ISLAND COLONY.

## CIVIL LISTS.

**1647—1700.**

16

# COLONIAL OFFICERS.

## GOVERNORS.

| Name. | Residence. | Term of Service. |
|---|---|---|
| John Coggshall | Newport | May 19, 1647, to May 16, 1648. |
| Jeremiah Clarke | Newport | May, 1648, to May 22, 1649. |
| John Smith | Warwick | May 22, 1649, to May 23, 1650. |
| Nicholas Easton | Newport | May 23, 1650, to May 18, 1652. |
| John Smith | Warwick | May 18, 1652, to May 16, 1653. |
| Gregory Dexter | Providence | May 16, 1653, to May 16, 1654. |
| Nicholas Easton | Newport | May 16, 1654, to May 22, 1655. |
| Roger Williams | Providence | May 22, 1655, to May 19, 1657. |
| Benedict Arnold | Newport | May 19, 1657, to May 22, 1660. |
| William Brenton | Portsmouth | May 22, 1660, to May 22, 1662. |
| Benedict Arnold | Newport | May 22, 1662, to May 2, 1666. |
| William Brenton | Portsmouth | May 2, 1666, to May 5, 1669. |
| Benedict Arnold | Newport | May 5, 1669, to May 1, 1672. |
| Nicholas Easton | Newport | May 1, 1672, to May 6, 1674. |
| William Coddington | Newport | May 6, 1674, to May 3, 1676. |
| Walter Clarke | Newport | May 3, 1676, to May 2, 1677. |
| Benedict Arnold | Newport | May 2, 1677, to Nov. 8, 1678. |
| John Cranston | Newport | Nov. 8, 1678, to May 5, 1680. |
| Peleg Sanford | Portsmouth | May 5, 1680, to May 2, 1683. |
| William Coddington | Newport | May 2, 1683, to May 6, 1685. |
| Henry Bull | Newport | May 6, 1685, to May 5, 1686. |
| Walter Clarke | Newport | May 5, 1686, to the time that the Government was interrupted by Sir Edmund Andros. |
| Henry Bull | Newport | Feb. 26, 1690, to May 7, 1690. |
| John Easton | Newport | May 7, 1690, to |
| Caleb Carr | Newport | |
| Walter Clarke | Newport | to May 4, 1698. |
| Samuel Cranston | Portsmouth | May 4, 1698, to 1727. |

## DEPUTY GOVERNORS *(Beginning under Charter 1663).*

| Name. | Residence. | Term of Service. |
|---|---|---|
| William Brenton | Newport | Nov. 25, 1663, to May 2, 1666. |
| Nicholas Easton | Newport | May 2, 1666, to May 5, 1669. |
| John Clarke | Newport | May 5, 1669, to May 4, 1670. |
| Nicholas Easton | Newport | May 4, 1670, to May 3, 1671. |
| John Clarke | Newport | May 3, 1671, to May 1, 1672. |
| John Cranston | Newport | May 1, 1672, to May 7, 1673. |
| William Coddington | Newport | May 7, 1673, to May 6, 1674. |
| John Easton | Newport | May 6, 1674, to May 3, 1676. |
| John Cranston | Newport | May 3, 1676, to Nov. 8, 1678. |
| James Barker | Newport | Nov. 8, 1678, to May 7, 1679. |
| Walter Clarke | Newport | May 7, 1679, to May 5, 1686. |
| John Coggeshall | Newport | May 5, 1686, to the time that the Government was interrupted by Sir Edmund Andros. |
| John Greene | Warwick | May 7, 1690, to May 1, 1700. |
| Walter Clarke | Newport | May 1, 1700, to |

From 1647 to 1663 the chief magistrates of this colony were denominated or styled PRESIDENTS instead of Governors. In 1651, William Coddington went to England, and procured from the Council of State a commission dated April 3, 1651, constituting him Governor for life of Rhode Island, Canonicut, &c. With this commission he returned to Rhode Island about the first of August, 1651: but all the English inhabitants upon the main land in Rhode Island government refused to submit to the authority thus obtained by William Coddington, and appointed Roger Williams and John Clarke to proceed to England to procure the repeal of Coddington's commission, which after much opposition they effected in 1652. Mr. Williams soon after returned to Rhode Island, but Mr. Clarke remained as the colony's agent in England, till he obtained the charter granted by Charles II., and dated at Westminster July 8, 1663.

## SECRETARIES *(or General Recorders).*

| Name. | Residence. | Term of Service. |
|---|---|---|
| William Dyre | Newport | May 19, 1647, to May 16, 1648. |
| Philip Sherman | Portsmouth | May 16, 1648, to 1651. |
| John Greene, Jr. | Warwick | 1651, to May 17, 1653. |
| William Lytherland | Newport | May 17, 1653, to May 20, 1656. |
| John Sanford | Portsmouth | May 20, 1656, to May 21, 1661. |
| Joseph Torrey | Newport | May 21, 1661, to May 2, 1666. |
| John Sanford | Portsmouth | May 2, 1666, to May 5, 1669. |
| Joseph Torrey | Newport | May 5, 1669, to May 3, 1671. |
| John Sanford | Portsmouth | May 3, 1671, to May 3, 1676. |
| John Coggeshall | Newport | May 3, 1676, to May 1, 1677. |
| John Sanford | Portsmouth | May 1, 1677, to [Andros, 1686]. |
| Weston Clarke | Newport | Feb. 26, 1689, to May 6, 1691. |
| John Coggeshall | Newport | May 6, 1691, to 1692. |
| John Easton | Newport | 1692, to |
| Weston Clarke | Newport | 1695, to |

## TREASURERS.

| Name. | Residence. | Term of Service. |
|---|---|---|
| Jeremiah Clarke | Newport | May 19, 1647, to May 22, 1649. |
| John Clarke | Newport | May 22, 1649, to |
| Randall Holden | Warwick | May 18, 1652, to May 16, 1653. |
| John Coggshall | Newport | May 16, 1653, to Sept. 12, 1654. |
| Richard Borden | Portsmouth | Sept. 12, 1654, to May 22, 1655. |
| John Sanford | Portsmouth | May 22, 1655, to May 21, 1661. |
| Caleb Carr | Newport | May 21, 1661, to May 22, 1662. |
| John Sanford | Portsmouth | May 22, 1662, to May 4, 1664. |
| John Coggeshall | Newport | May 4, 1664, to May 1, 1672. |
| Peter Easton | Newport | May 1, 1672, to May 2, 1677. |
| Thomas Ward | Newport | May 2, 1677, to May 1, 1678. |
| Peleg Sanford | Newport | May 1, 1678, to May 4, 1681. |
| Weston Clarke | Newport | May 4, 1681, to May 6, 1685. |
| John Woodman | Newport | May 6, 1685, to [Andros, 1686]. |
| John Holmes | | Feb. 26, 1689, to May 4, 1703. |

## SERGEANTS.

| Name. | Residence. | Term of Service. |
|---|---|---|
| Alexander Partridge | Newport | May 16, 1648, to May 22, 1649. |
| Richard Knight | Newport | May 22, 1649, to |
| Hugh Bewitt | Providence | May 18, 1652, to |
| Richard Knight | Newport | May 17, 1653, to May 22, 1655. |
| George Parker | Portsmouth | May 22, 1655; died in 1656. |
| Richard Knight | Newport | Oct. 11, 1656, to May 17, 1659. |
| James Rogers | Newport | May 17, 1659, to May 1, 1677. |
| Thomas Fry | E. Greenwich | May 1, 1677, to May 7, 1679. |
| Edmund Calverly | Warwick | May 7, 1679, to |
| Thomas Fry | E. Greenwich | May 4, 1681, to May 3, 1682. |
| Edmund Calverly | Warwick | May 3, 1682, to [Andros, 1686]. |
| Thomas Fry | E. Greenwich | Feb. 26, 1689, to |

The title of Sergeant seems to have been dropped and that of Sheriff adopted, though the duties of the officer remained the same as before.

## SHERIFFS.

| Name. | Residence. | Term of Service. |
|---|---|---|
| Thomas Townsend | Portsmouth | May 6, 1696, to |
| Jirch Bull | Kingstown | May 4, 1698, to May 3, 1699. |
| Thomas Mallett | Newport | May 3, 1699, to May 4, 1703. |

## ATTORNEYS.

| Name. | Residence. | Term of Service. |
|---|---|---|
| John Easton | Newport | May 17, 1653, tọ May 16, 1654. |
| John Cranston | Newport | May 16, 1654, to May 26, 1656. |
| John Easton | Newport | May 20, 1656, to May 19, 1657. |
| John Greene, Jr. | Warwick | May 19, 1657, to May 22, 1660. |
| John Easton | Newport | May 22, 1660, to May 22, 1663. |
| John Sanford | Portsmouth | May 22, 1663, to May 4, 1664. |
| John Easton | Newport | May 4, 1664, to May 4, 1670. |
| John Sanford | Portsmouth | May 4, 1670, to May 3, 1671. |
| Joseph Torrey | Newport | May 3, 1671, to May 1, 1672. |
| John Easton | Newport | May 1, 1672, to May 6, 1674. |
| Peter Easton |  | May 6, 1674, to May 3, 1676. |
| Weston Clarke | Newport | May 3, 1676, to May 2, 1677. |
| Edward Richmond | Newport | May 2, 1677, to May 5, 1680. |
| Weston Clarke | Newport | May 5, 1680, to May 4, 1681. |
| Edmund Calverly | Warwick | May 4, 1681, to May 3, 1682. |
| John Pococke | Newport | May 3, 1682, to May 3, 1683. |
| Weston Clarke | Newport | May 2, 1683, to May 7, 1684. |
| John Pococke | Newport | May 7, 1684, to May 6, 1685. |
| Weston Clarke | Newport | May 6, 1685, to May 5, 1686. |
| John Williams |  | May 5, 1686, to [Andros, 1686]. |
| John Pococke | Newport | May 7, 1690, to |
| John Smith |  | May 6, 1696, to |

## SOLICITORS.

| Name. | Residence. | Term of Service. |
|---|---|---|
| John Greene, Jr. | Warwick | May 22, 1655, to May 20, 1656. |
| Richard Bulgar |  | May 20, 1656, to May 19, 1657. |
| James Rogers | Newport | May 19, 1657, to May 22, 1660. |
| Richard Bulgar |  | May 22, 1660, to May 21, 1661. |
| Peter Tallman | Portsmouth | May 21, 1661, to May 22, 1662. |
| Richard Bulgar |  | May 22, 1662, to May 4, 1664. |
| Lawrence Turner | Newport | May 4, 1664, to May 3, 1665. |
| William Dyre | Newport | May 3, 1665, to May 1, 1667. |
| Edward Richmond | Newport | May 1, 1667, to May 1, 1668. |
| William Dyre | Newport | May 6, 1668, to May 5, 1669. |
| Edward Richmond | Newport | May 5, 1669, to May 3, 1671. |
| William Harris | Providence | May 3, 1671, to May 1, 1672. |
| Edward Richmond | Newport | May 1, 1672, to May 7, 1673. |
| Robert Williams | Providence | May 7, 1673, to May 1, 1678. |
| Edmund Calverlye | Warwick | May 1, 1678, to May 5, 1680. |
| Robert Williams | Providence | May 5, 1680, to May 4, 1681. |
| Edmund Calverly | Warwick | May 4, 1681, to May 3, 1682. |
| Richard Barnes | Newport | May 3, 1682, to May 7, 1684. |
| John Pococke | Newport | May 7, 1684, to. |

# OFFICERS APPORTIONED TO EACH TOWN.

## EAST GREENWICH. INCORPORATED OCT. 31, 1677.

| Date. | GOVERNOR'S ASSISTANTS. | REPRESENTATIVES. |
|---|---|---|
| 1678 | | Sergt. Clement Weaver, Sergt. Thomas Dungin. |
| 1679 | | John Heath, Sergt. Thomas Nicholls. |
| 1680 | | John Heath, John Spencer. |
| 1681 | | Thomas Dungin, John Sanford. |
| 1682 | | John Heath, John Sanford. |
| 1683 | | Clement Weaver, John Sanford. |
| 1684 | | George Vaughan, Thomas Frye. |
| 1685 | | Thomas Nicholls, Henry Mathewson. |
| 1686 | | Thomas Nichols, John Sanford. |
| 1687 | | [Government interrupted by Sir Edmund Andros.] |
| 1688 | | |
| 1689 | | Capt. Clement Weaver, Thomas Nicholls. |
| 1690 | | Giles Pearce, Lieut. Samuel Bennett, Thomas Fry, Thomas Nicholls. |
| 1691 | | |
| 1692 | | |
| 1693 | | |
| 1694 | | |
| 1695 | | John Spencer, Thomas Fry. |
| 1696 | | |
| 1697 | | |
| 1698 | | Thomas Nichols, George Vaughan. |
| 1699 | | |
| 1700 | | John Spencer. |

June 12th, 1678, John Spencer was chosen a CONSERVATOR OF THE PEACE.

## EAST GREENWICH.—ACT OF INCORPORATION.

Voted, wheras at the General Assembly held for the Collony, at Newport, in May last, it was ordered that a certaine tract of land in some Convenient place in the Narragansett country shall be laid forth into hundred acre shares with the house lots, for the accommodatinge of soe many of the inhabitants of this Collony as stand in need of land, and the Generall Assembly shall judge fit to be supplyed. In pursuance of said act of the Generall Assembly this present court doe enact and declare that the said tract of land be forthwith layd forth to containe five thousand acres, which shall be divided as followeth : five hundred acres to be laid in some place neare the sea, and as commodious as may be for a towne, which said five hundred acres shall be divided into fifty house lots, and the remainder of said five thousand acres, beinge four thousand five hundred acres, shall be divided into fifty esqual shares or great divisions; and that each person hereafter named and admitted by this Assembly to have land in the said tract, shall have and enjoy to him and his heires and assigns forever, in manner and forme, and under the conditions and limitations hereinafter expressed, one of the said house lots and one great division, containing in the whole one hundred acres.

And further this Assembly do enact, order and declare, that the persons before named, that is to say, John Spencer, Thomas Nicolls, Sr., Clement Weaver, Henry Brightman, George Vaughan, John Weaver, Charles Macarty, Thomas Wood, Thomas Frye, Benjamin Griffin, Daniel Vaughan, Thomas Dungin, John Pearce Mason, Stephen Peckham, John Crandall, Henry Lilly, John Albro, Jr., Samuel Albro, Philip Long, Richard Knight, John Peckham, Thomas Peckham, William Clarke, Edward Lay, Edward Richmond, Edmund Calverly, John Heath, Robert Havens, John Strainge, Jr., John Parker, George Browne, Richard Barnes, Samson Balloo, Jonathan Devell, Benjamin Mowry, Joseph Mowry, William Wilbore, Jr., Gyles Pearce, James Batty, John Remington, Benjamin Gorton, Henry Dyse, John Knowles, Stephen Arnold, Jr., William Hawkins, John Sanford, John Gorton and John Houlden are the persons unto whom the said tract of land is granted, and who shall possess and enjoy the same, their heires and assigns, accordinge to the true intent and meaning of this present grant. And to the end that the said persons and their successors, and proprietors of the said land from time to time, may be in a better capacity to manage their publick affaires, this Assembly doe enact and declare that the said plantation shall be a towne, by the name and title of East Greenwich, in his Majesty's Collony of Rhode Island and Providence Plantations, with all rights, libertys, and priviledges whatsoever unto a towne appertaininge; and that the said persons above mentioned, unto whom the said grant is made, are by the present Assembly and the authority made and admitted the freemen of the said towne, and they, or soe many of them as shall be then present, not being fewer than twelve on the said land are required and empowered to meet together upon the second Wednesday in April next, and constitute a towne meetinge, by electinge a Moderator, a Town Clerke, with such constables as to them shall seem requisite; and alsoe to choose two persons their Deputys to sitt in General Assembly, and two persons, one to serve on the Grand Jury and one on the Jury of tryals, in the General Court of Tryalls, and soe the like number and for the said services of the said Court from time to time.

And to the end that the said plantation may be speedily settled and improved accordinge to the end of this present court in the granting thereof : be it enacted and ordained that each person mentioned in this present grant shall, within one year after the publication thereof, make a settlement on his house lott by building a house fit and suitable for a habitation ; and in case any person who hath any of the said house lotts shall neglect or refuse by himself, or his assignee to build accordingly, he shall forfeit both the house lott and greater division, to be disposed by any succeedinge General Assembly as they shall see cause.

And further, this Assembly doe enact and declare that if any person unto whom the said land is granted, by this present act, shall at any time within one and twenty years after the date thereof, sell, grant, make over or otherwise dispose of any of the land or lands hereby granted unto him, unto any other person interested in the said plantation, that then the said person or persons soe selling, or any other person or persons whatsoever without liberty had and obtained from the Generall Assembly, that then the said person or persons so selling or disposing of the land, shall lose all other lands whatever that he is possessed of in the said plantation, and alsoe the lands soe disposed of to be and remaine to this Collony, anything to the contrary thereof in this present act declared notwithstandinge. (See pages 587, 588, 589 and 590 of Volume II. Rhode Island Colonial Records.)

## JAMESTOWN.

## KINGSTOWN. INCORPORATED OCT. 28, 1674.

17

| Date. | REPRESENTATIVES. | Date. | REPRESENTATIVES. |
|---|---|---|---|
| 1679 | Ebenezer Slocum, Capt. John Foanes. | 1679 | [No Representatives received at the Court.] |
| 1680 | Capt. John Foanes, Ensign Nicholas Carr. | 1680 | |
| 1681 | Ebenezer Slocum, Capt. John Foanes. | 1681 | |
| 1682 | Ebenezer Slocum, Oliver Arnold. | 1682 | |
| 1683 | Ebenezer Slocum, Ephraim Morse. | 1683 | |
| 1684 | Ebenezer Slocum, Caleb Carr, Jr. | 1684 | |
| 1685 | Ebenezer Slocum, Nicholas Carr. | 1685 | |
| 1686 | Josiah Arnold, Joseph Morey. | 1686 | [Government interrupted by Sir Edmund Andros.] |
| 1687 | [Government interrupted by Sir Edmund Andros.] | 1687 | |
| 1688 | | 1688 | |
| 1689 | | 1689 | |
| 1690 | | 1690 | Thomas Gould, John Watson. |
| 1691 | | 1691 | |
| 1692 | | 1692 | |
| 1693 | | 1693 | |
| 1694 | | 1694 | |
| 1695 | | 1695 | |
| 1696 | Ebenezer Slocum, Nicholas Carr. | 1696 | Andrew Willett, Lodowick Updike. |
| 1697 | | 1697 | |
| 1698 | Joseph Morey, John Hull. | 1698 | Capt. John Foanes, Capt. Andrew Willett. |
| 1699 | Nicholas Carr, Joseph Morey. | 1699 | George Vaughan, Henry Straight. |
| 1700 | | 1700 | Capt. Edward Greenman. |

ACT OF INCORPORATION.—Voted, by the King's authority in this Assembly, it is approved the Generall Councills acts in obstructing Connecticutt Collony from useinge jurisdiction in the Narragansett country, and the Councills establishing a towne shipp there, and the callinge it Kingstown, with liberty as hath been granted to New Shoreham. (See page 525, Volume II., Rhode Island Colonial Records.)

In 1678 Thomas Gould and John Greene were made Conservators of the Peace for Kings Towne, and Jireh Bull and Capt. John Foanes were appointed to the same office in 1683, with Daniel Vernon, as Town Clerk, Samuel Albro, Treasurer, Thomas Mumford, Henry Gardner, John Andrew and James Hazleton, Constables, and Job Jenine, Town Sergeant.

# RHODE ISLAND COLONY.

## NEWPORT. Settled by the English in 1629.

| Date. | Governor's Assistants. | Representatives. |
|---|---|---|
| 1640 | Nicholas Easton, John Coggshall | |
| 1641 | John Coggshall | |
| 1642 | Nicholas Easton, John Coggshall | |
| 1643 | Nicholas Easton, John Coggshall | |
| 1644 | Nicholas Easton, John Coggshall | |
| 1645 | | |
| 1646 | | |
| 1647 | | |
| 1648 | William Coddington | William Dyer, Easton, John Clarke, James Weedan, James Barker, Joseph Clarke. |
| 1649 | John Clarke | |
| 1650 | John Clarke | |
| 1651 | | |
| 1652 | | |
| 1653 | Nicholas Easton | Benedict Arnold, Richard Tew, John Coggshall, John Easton, William Lytherland, Thomas Gould. |
| 1654 | Edward Smith | Capt. Joan Cranston, Benedict Arnold, John Easton, Edward Smith, John Gould, Joseph Clarke, John Greene, Obadiah Holmes, Richard Knight, Henry Bull. |
| 1655 | Benedict Arnold | William Haviland, Obadiah Holmes, John Easton, Joseph Torrey, Peter Easton, Robert Griffin, Benedict Arnold, Richard Tew, John Richmond, Daniel Gould. |
| 1656 | John Coggshall | Benedict Arnold, John Easton, John Cranston, Richard Tew, Joseph Clarke, John Gould, John Greene. |
| 1657 | Richard Tew | Caleb Carr, Obadiah Holmes, Joseph Torrey, John Easton, John Crandall, Robert Griffin. |
| 1658 | Joseph Clarke | John Easton, Caleb Carr, John Crandall, Joseph Torrey, Edward Smith, William Weeden, Benedict Arnold. |
| 1659 | Joseph Clarke | Nicholas Easton, Richard Tew, Capt. John Cranston, John Easton, William Harris, John Greene, Peter Easton, Caleb Carr, John Sweet, Thomas Gould. |
| 1660 | Benedict Arnold | William Brenton, Benedict Arnold, Caleb Carr, John Easton, Joseph Torrey, William Jeffrey. |
| 1661 | Benedict Arnold | Benedict Arnold, William Dyer, John Gould, John Crandall, William Weeden, Joseph Torrey, George Gardiner, Caleb Carr. |
| 1662 | Richard Tew | Benedict Arnold, Richard Tew, Henry Timberlake, John Crandall, Edward Larken, Joseph Torrey, John Coggshall, William Brenton, John Easton, John Cranston. |
| 1663 | Richard Tew | |

| | | |
|---|---|---|
| 1664 | John Coggshall, James Barker | Richard Tew, John Gould, John Easton, Joseph Torrey, Caleb Carr, William Dyer, John Clarke. |
| 1665 | John Card, James Barker | John Clarke, John Card, Capt. John Cranston, Edward Smith, John Gould. |
| 1666 | Richard Tew, William Coddington | John Clarke, Nicholas Easton, Henry Bull, John Cranston, Joseph Torrey, William Dyer, Edward Smith, Thomas Harte. |
| 1667 | Peleg Sanford, John Easton | John Clarke, James Barker, William Reape, Capt. John Cranston, Peter Easton, Walter Clarke, John Coggshall, John Clarke, William Case, John Cowdall, Edward Thurston. |
| 1668 | Capt. Peleg Sanford, Capt. John Cranston, John Easton | John Clarke, Capt. John Cranston, Caleb Carr, Lt. Joseph Torrey, Joseph Clarke, Edward Greenman. |
| 1669 | Peleg Sanford, John Cranston | John Coggshall, Joseph Torrey, Caleb Carr, Edward Greenman, Joseph Clarke, James Barker. |
| 1670 | John Cranston, John Coggshall | John Coggshall, Caleb Carr, Joseph Torrey, Edward Greenman, Walter Clarke, Peleg Sanford, James Barker, Richard Bayley. |
| 1671 | John Cranston, John Coggshall | John Clarke, Caleb Carr, Peter Easton, Joseph Torrey, Richard Bayley, James Barker, Wm. Weeden. |
| 1672 | Francis Brindley, John Easton | Walter Clarke, Henry Bull, John Gould, Peter Easton, Edward Thurston, Weston Clarke, Daniel Gould. |
| 1673 | Daniel Gould, Walter Clarke, John Easton | Walter Clarke, Peter Easton, John Wood, Daniel Gould, John Gould, Henry Bull, Edward Thurston, Thomas Clifton, William Case, John Greene. |
| 1674 | Daniel Gould, Walter Clarke | Edward Thurston, John Wood, William Case, Peter Easton, Thomas Clifton, Henry Bull, Joseph Torrey, Caleb Carr, James Parker, William Weeden. |
| 1675 1676 1677 1678 | Edward Thurston, Henry Bull John Coggshall, James Barker James Barker, Peleg Sanford James Barker, Capt. Peleg Sanford | John Coggshall, William Case, Peter Easton, John Wood, Thomas Clifton, John Read. |
| 1679 | Caleb Carr, Thomas Ward | Caleb Carr, Thomas Ward, Edward Richmond, John Greene, James Barker, Jr., John Rogers, Caleb Carr, Thomas Ward, Lt. Edward Richmond, Lt. John Greene, William Coddington, Ensign John Bliss. |
| 1680 | Caleb Carr, Thomas Ward | William Coddington, Peter Easton, Benedict Arnold, Henry Bull, Capt. John Greene, Benjamin Smith, John Potter. |
| 1681 | Caleb Carr, William Coddington | James Barker, Sr., Edward Thurston, Peter Easton, Henry Bull, Richard Dunn, Philip Smith. |
| 1682 | Caleb Carr, William Coddington | Lieut. John Bliss, Edward Greenman, John Woodman, Capt. Roger Goulding, Edward Thurston, Sr., John Holme. |
| 1683 | Caleb Carr, John Coggshall | James Barker, Sr., John Coggshall, Thomas Ward, Edward Thurston, Sr., Philip Smith, Nathaniel Coddington. |
| 1684 | Caleb Carr, John Coggshall | James Barker, Sr., Edw'd Thurston, Sr., Thos. Ward, Walter Rubary, Philip Smith, John Woodman. |
| 1685 | Caleb Carr, Major John Coggshall, John Easton | James Barker, Sr., Edward Thurston, Sr., Thomas Ward, John Rodman, Nathaniel Coddington, Capt. Roger Goulding, |
| 1686 | John Coggshall, Edward Thurston, John Easton | James Barker, Sr., Thomas Ward, Benedict Arnold, Edward Thurston, John Woodman, Nathaniel Coddington. |
| 1687 | John Easton | [Government interrupted by Sir Edmund Andros.] |

## NEWPORT (CONTINUED).

| Date. | GOVERNOR'S ASSISTANTS. | REPRESENTATIVES. |
|---|---|---|
| 1688 | Edward Thurston, John Easton | James Barker, Benedict Arnold, Henry Bull, Jonathan Holmes, Edward Thurston, Jr., John Wood. |
| 1689 | Edward Thurston, Benedict Arnold | James Barker, Jonathan Holmes, Philip Smith, Caleb Carr, John Tillinghast, John Wood. |
| 1690 | Caleb Carr, Benedict Arnold, Edward Thurston | Jonathan Holmes, Philip Smith, James Barker, Jr., John Easton, Jr., Nowell New, Lawrence Turner. |
| 1691 | | |
| 1692 | | |
| 1693 | | |
| 1694 | | |
| 1695 | | |
| 1696 | James Barker | Capt. Jonathan Holmes, Capt. John Stanton, Jeremiah Clarke, William Peckham, Lieut. Thomas Weaver, Thomas Gould. |
| 1697 | | |
| 1698 | Capt. James Barker, Capt. Nathaniel Coddington | Capt. Henry Tew, Capt. Jonathan Holmes, Jeremiah Clarke, William Peckham, William Weeden, John Easton, Jr. |
| 1699 | Capt. James Barker, Walter Clarke | Benedict Arnold, Nathaniel Sheffield, Isaac Martindale, Capt. Jonathan Holmes, Jeremiah Clarke, John Easton, Jr. |
| 1700 | Isaac Martindale | Jonathan Holmes, John Easton, Jr. |

## NEW SHOREHAM. INCORPORATED Nov. 6, 1672.

### Indian name—MANISSIS.

| Da | REPRESENTATIVES. |
|---|---|
| 1665 | James Sands and Thomas Terry were admitted to represent the interests |
| 1674 | of the people of Block Island, which in 1672 |
| 1675 | became the township of New Shoreham. |
| 1676 | |
| 1677 | |
| 1678 | Capt. John Sands. |
| 1679 | John Williams. |
| 1680 | John Sands. |
| 1681 | John Rathbone. |
| 1682 | James Rathbone. |
| 1683 | John Rathbone. |
| 1684 | John Rathbone. |
| 1685 | |
| 1686 | [Government interrupted by Sir Edmund Andros.] |
| 1687 | |
| 1688 | |
| 1689 | |
| 1690 | Capt. John Sands. |
| 1691 | |
| 1692 | |
| 1693 | |
| 1694 | |
| 1695 | |
| 1696 | Joshua Raymond. |
| 1697 | |
| 1698 | |
| 1699 | |
| 1700 | |

## ACTION OF THE COLONIAL COURT CONCERNING BLOCK ISLAND (SUBSEQUENTLY SHOREHAM).

**March, 1664.**

Resolved by this Assembly, That the Governor and deputy Governor be desired to send to Block Island to declare vnto our friends the inhabitants therof, that they, are vnder our care, and that they admitt not of any other to beare rule over them but the power of this Collony; and that James Sands, who is a freeman of this Collony, come in to the Governor or deputy Governor to take his ingagement as Constable, or Conservator of the peace theare; and that the most able and deserving men are warned in to the next Court in May, to be informed of their priviledge, and such to be free made of the Collony. (See Vol. II. page 32, Rhode Island Colonial Records.)

## ACT OF INCORPORATION.

**November 6th, 1672.**

Voted, that the petition of the inhabitants of Block Island to this Court for their beinge granted the liberty and priviledge of a towneship, shall be adjitated.

Voted, fforasmuch as the inhabitants of Block Island, viz.: Mr. James Sands, Mr. Thomas Terry and others expressed in their paper, have presented their request to have granted and enacted by this Assembly, that they may have liberty of a towne, and like libertyes (according to the charter), with other townes in this Collony, and their reasons showed of their said request of a towneship, &c., and the said called Shoreham.

18

This Assembly have considered the said petition and weighed their reasons, and senceably see a great necessity of the preservation of his Majesties peace more fully than as yett is provided for on the said Block Island, with more conveniency and ease to the said inhabitants, they liveinge remote and beinge soe farr in the' sea, cannot without great danger and charge accomplish their peace and safety but as aforesaid; and alsoe consideringe their numbers and quality as thought fitt by this Assembly, for such betrust and fitt to enjoy such liberty.

Therefore, bee it enacted and by this Assembly is enacted, that the said Mr. James Sands, Mr. Thomas Terry and the rest of the freemen on record expressed in their said paper read in this Assembly, shall have and hereby have towneship authority and liberties as followeth for the preservation of his Majesties peace. The said ffreemen of this his Majesties Collony (inhabitants of the said Block Island), shall upon the reception of this act (with all convenient speed) assemble themselves together in some convenient place on said Island, and then and there shall choose two of the said free men, able and well qualified for the preservation of his Majesties peace; the said two persons to be elected by the major part of such freemen as shall assemble at the said time and place. And beinge elected (as afore said), the two persons names shall be returned to the Governor and Deputy Governor, or either of them (in the absence of the other), who shall engage the said two persons elected upon their or either of their appearance, at Newport, or to be required by writt there to appeare, if they appeare not without writt, whose engadgement shall be accordinge to the tenure of the engadgement of other officers, consideringe their offices.

And that the said elected and engadged persons'shall be called Wardens; the first that shall be elected shall be called head Warden, and the second elected Deputy Warden. Butt for all future Wardens soe elected shall have power as followeth, viz., when a new choyce is made of another head Warden immediately he shall be engadged by the Deputy Warden, and a new Deputy Warden beinge chosen shall be engadged by the head Warden last chosen, by the then election. Soe beinge elected and engadged shall be impowered as followeth, viz: shall have authority or either of them shall have authority to send forth writts in his Majesties name under their hands, to require the said freemen to meet upon all just occasions, and elect two for Deputys to sitt in the law makeinge Assembly of this his Majesties Collony when by writt required thereto, and Deputys to sitt in such Assefnblys as are mentioned in the pattent and send them thereto; though by reason of winde, weather and distance by sea, writts should fayle to be sent to them to require them.

And by writt to require the said freemen to meete four times in the yeare for their said towne affaires, for the makinge of such order or bye lawes as may be needfull for theire better management of their affaires amonge them selves, accordinge to their constitution not opugninge the lawes of his Majesties realme of England, his patent, nor the laws of this Colloney, agreeable thereto; and that the said Wardens or one of them require the said freemen to meete for the first of the said four mecteings as soone as convenient after they are engaged to thelre said office, from which said meetinge shall begin the said yeare.

And at the said first meetinge of the said freemen of the said Island, the major part of them being met shall elect a Clerke, and shall provide a book or books as need shall require; and that the said Wardens or either of them in the absence of the other, shall engage the said Clerke to the faithfull performance of his office accordinge to the tenure thereof; and that the said Clerke record in the book or books of the acts of the freemen in their towne affaires as to lands and bounds thereof, all publications of marriages to bee returned to him by the publishers; all marriages, all births, all burials, all actions, to bee there commenced and the progress thereof.

And to make such returns to the Assembly or Court of Tryalls of this Collony as need shall require and the law injoyne such Clerks to performe, all and every other thinge pertaininge to the office of the Towne Clerke of this Collony, though not herein exprest.

And that the said freemen (the major part of them met) àt the said first Court quarter meetinge, shall elect a Sergeant for the said freemen to meetings by the aforesaid writts, and to searve other writts; who shall bee engaged to the faithfull performance of his office according to the tenure thereof, by the said Wardens or one of them.

And that the aforesaid freemen (the major part of them met) at the said first quarter meetinge shall elect a Constable or Constables if need require, two or more for the apprehension of the breakers of the peace, wanderinge persons, fellows, and to doe any other thinge appertaininge to the office of a Constable.

And that the said freemen at the said meetinge shall choose three wise honest men who shall be added to the two Wardens, for the Town Councill, to have like authority as other Towne Councills have.

PORTSMOUTH. Settled by the English in 1638.

| Date. | Governor's Assistants. | Representatives. |
|---|---|---|
| 1647 | John Sanford | Capt. ——— Morris, John Tripp, George Lawton, William Almy, John Briggs, Samuel Wilbur, Jr. |
| 1648 | William Baulston | |
| 1649 | John Sanford | |
| 1650 | John Porter | |
| 1651 | | |
| 1652 | | |
| 1653 | Richard Borden | |
| 1654 | Richard Borden | William Baulston, Rich'd Borden, John Roome, Thos. Cornell, John Briggs, Wm. Hall, John Tripp. |
| 1655 | John Roome, William Baulston | William Baulston, John Roome, John Tripp, John Briggs, Thomas Lawton, Thomas Brownell. |
| 1656 | William Baulston | William Baulston, John Roome, Richard Borden, Philip Sherman, William Wodell, John Sanford, William Hall, John Babcock. |
| 1657 | William Baulston | William Almy, Richard Borden, William Baulston, John Freeborn, John Sanford, John Greene, Edward Greenman. |
| 1658 | William Baulston | Benedict Arnold, William Baulston, John Tripp, Henry Pearcy, John Almy, John Sanford. |
| 1659 | William Baulston | Benedict Arnold, William Baulston, Roger Williams, Joseph Clarke, Samuel Wilbur, John Sanford, John Briggs, John Roome, John Porter, James Babcock. |
| 1660 | William Baulston | John Porter, William Hall, Samuel Wilbur, Lieut. John Albro, Edward Fisher, John Sanford, Wm. Brenton, Benedict Arnold, Philip Taber, Richard Morris, William Baulston. |
| 1661 | William Baulston | William Baulston, John Roome, John Briggs, Thomas Brownell, Lieut. John Albro, John Tripp, Thomas Lawton, Peter Tollman. |
| 1662 | William Baulston | Peter Tollman, William Baulston, John Sanford, Robert Hazard, Francis Broyton, Thomas Green, John Tripp, Samuel Wilbur, Thomas Brownell, John Briggs. |
| 1663 | William Baulston | William Baulston, John Briggs, John Tripp, Samuel Wilbur, Thomas Brownell, John Sanford, William Almy, Lot Strange, William Woodall, Francis Broyton, William Hall, Philip Taber. |
| 1664 | William Baulston, John Sanford | John Briggs, Thomas Brownell, Thomas Cornell, Samuel Wilbur, Wm. Wodell, Joshua Coggshall, Lot Strange. |
| 1665 | William Baulston, Samuel Wilbur | Samuel Wilbur, John Briggs, Philip Sherman, John Sanford, George Lawton. |
| 1666 | William Baulston, Samuel Wilbur | John Sanford, Thomas Lawton, John Albro, John Anthoney, John Card, Joshua Coggshall, Wodell, John Tripp. |
| 1667 | William Baulston, Samuel Wilbur | John Card, William Wodell, Wm. Hall, Robert Hazard, Philip Sherman, John Tripp, Joshua Coggshall, William |
| 1668 | William Baulston, Samuel Wilbur | William Hall, Lieut. John Albro, Joshua Coggshall, John Sanford, John Briggs, John Tripp, Edward Lay. |
| 1669 | William Baulston, Joshua Coggshall | John Sanford, John Briggs, John Tripp, Lot Strange, Capt. Samuel Wilbur, William Wodell. |

## PORTSMOUTH (CONTINUED).

| Date. | GOVERNOR'S ASSISTANTS. | REPRESENTATIVES. |
|---|---|---|
| 1670 | William Baulston, John Tripp | John Tripp, John Sanford, Lieut. John Albro, Thomas Cornell, Joshua Coggshall, Capt. Samuel Wilbur, Ensign Lot Strange, Robert Hazard. |
| 1671 | William Baulston, Lieut. John Albro | Thomas Cornell, William Sayton, Joshua Coggshall, John Sanford, John Tripp, George Lawton. |
| 1672 | William Baulston, Joshua Coggshall | William Wodell, William Hall, Edward Fisher, Anthony Emory, John Sanford, John Tripp, John Arthony, Lieut. William Codman. |
| 1673 | Joshua Coggshall, John Tripp | William Hall, William Wodell, William Codman, Robert Dennie, John Sanford, Edward Fisher, Adam Mott, John Borden. |
| 1674 | Joshua Coggshall, John Tripp | John Sanford, Lieut. William Codman, Ensign Lot Strange, William Wodell. |
| 1675 | Joshua Coggshall, John Tripp | |
| 1676 | Joshua Coggshall, William Codman | Capt. John Albro, George Lawton, Gideon Freeborn, William Wodell. |
| 1677 | Samuel Wilbur, Capt. John Albro | |
| 1678 | Samuel Wilbur, Capt. John Albro | John Sanford, Hugh Parsons, Lieut. William Corey, William Wilbur. |
| 1679 | Capt. John Albro, John Sanford | George Lawton, Lieut. William Corey, Lieut. Francis Brayton, Lieut. William Codman. |
| 1680 | Capt. John Albro, George Lawton | George Lawton, William Wodell, Capt. William Corey, John Borden. |
| 1681 | Maj. John Albro, George Lawton | Latham Clarke, William Wodell, Peleg Tripp, Arthur Cooke. |
| 1682 | William Codman, George Lawton | William Codman, Latham Clarke, Henry Brightman, William Wodell. |
| 1683 | Maj. John Albro, George Lawton | William Wodell, Major John Albro, Latham Clarke, Thomas Cornell, Thomas Greene, Sr. |
| 1684 | Maj. John Albro, George Lawton | William Wodell, Francis Brayton, Caleb Arnold, Robert Dennis. |
| 1685 | Maj. John Albro, George Lawton | Latham Clarke, Henry Brightman, John Coggshall, Joseph Nicholson. |
| 1686 | George Lawton, John Coggshall | William Wodell, John Coggshall, Peleg Tripp, Robert Hodgson. |
| 1687 | | |
| 1688 | | Government interrupted by Sir Edmund Andros. |
| 1689 | George Lawton | Latham Clarke. |
| 1690 | John Coggshall, George Lawton, Isaac Lawton | George Sisson, Gideon Freeborn, Henry Brightman, Robert Lawton. |
| 1691 | Robert Lawton, Henry Brightman | Henry Brightman, Latham Clarke, William Coggshall, John Keese. |
| 1692 | Henry Brightman | |
| 1693 | | |
| 1694 | | |
| 1695 | Henry Brightman | |
| 1696 | Joseph Sheffield | John Coggshall, Joseph Sheffield, William Corey, Isaac Lawton. |

| | | |
|---|---|---|
| 1697 | Capt. Joseph Sheffield | Joseph Whipple, Latham Clarke, Isaac Lawton, Robert Fish, Robert Lawton. |
| 1698 | Capt. Joseph Sheffield | George Brownell, Benjamin Hall, Isaac Lawton, John Borden. |
| 1699 | Capt. Joseph Sheffield | John Ward. |
| 1700 | | |

## PROVIDENCE. SETTLED BY THE ENGLISH IN 1636.

| Date. | GOVERNOR'S ASSISTANTS. | REPRESENTATIVES. |
|---|---|---|
| 1647 | Roger Williams | |
| 1648 | Roger Williams | |
| 1649 | Thomas Olney | |
| 1650 | William Field | |
| 1651 | | Thomas Olney, Thomas Harris, Wm. Withenden, Hugh Bennett, Robert Williams, Gregory Dexter. |
| 1652 | Thomas Olney | Robert Williams, Thomas Harris, Hugh Bewit, William Wickenden, Thomas Olney, Gregory Dexter. |
| 1653 | Thomas Olney | Robert Williams, Gregory Dexter, Richard Waterman, Thomas Harris, William Wickenden, Hugh Bewitt, Thomas Hopkins, James Ashton, Thomas Angell, Henry Brown. |
| 1654 | Thomas Olney, Thomas Harris | Gregory Dexter, John Sayles, Arthur Fenner, William Wickenden, Thomas Angell, James Ashton. Thomas Harris, Gregory Dexter, John Taylor, William Wickenden, John Browne, Henry Browne, Henry Reddick. |
| 1655 | Thomas Olney | Robert Williams, William Wickenden, Thomas Harris, Arthur Fenner, Richard Waterman, John Sayles, Roger Williams, Thomas Olney, William Field, Wm. Dyer, James Barker, Mathew West. |
| 1656 | Thomas Olney, William Field | Roger Williams, Thomas Olney, William Field, Harris, Waterman, Roberts, Hugh Benett, John Tripp. |
| 1657 | Arthur Fenner, Thomas. Olney | Thomas Harris, John Sayles, Henry Bull, Thomas Walwin, Samuel Bennet, Hugh Bewitt, John Smith, Thomas Olney, William Field, William Carpenter, James Sweet, Edward Enman. |
| 1658 | William Field, Roger Williams | Roger Williams, William Field, Thomas Olney, Richard Waterman, Roger Morey, James Ashton. |
| 1659 | William Field, Roger Williams | William Field, Thomas Olney, John Sayles, Arthur Fenner, Thomas Hopkins, James Ashton, Roger Williams, William Carpenter, Zachem Rhodes, John Smith. |
| 1660 | William Field, William Harris | William Brenton, William Field, Benedict Arnold, Arthur Fenner, William Carpenter, Thomas Hopkins, William Harris, John Fenner, Joseph Torrey. |
| 1661 | William Field, Arthur Fenner | William Field, William Arnold, Thomas Harris, Sr., Thomas Roberts, Zachery Rhodes, James Barker, Roger Williams, Thomas Olney, Joseph Torrey, Philip Taber, John Anthoney. |

## PROVIDENCE (CONTINUED).

| Date. | GOVERNOR'S ASSISTANTS. | REPRESENTATIVES. |
|---|---|---|
| 1662 | William Field, Thomas Olney | William Field, Arthur Fenner, Thomas Olney, Thomas Hains, Sr., William Harris, William Carpenter, Zachery Rhodes. |
| 1663 | William Field, Roger Williams | William Field, Thomas Olney, William Carpenter, Thomas Harris, Arthur Fenner, James Ashton, Zachery Rhodes, William Harris, Edward Thurston, Joseph Torrey, Richard Tew. |
| 1664 | William Field, Roger Williams | Gregory Dexter, Zachery Rhodes, John Throgmorton, William Carpenter, Arthur Fenner, William Wickenden. |
| 1665 | Arther Fenner, William Carpenter | John Throgmorton, Thomas Olney. |
| 1666 | Thomas Olney, Sr., William Carpenter | John Throgmorton, Wm. Harfis, Thos. Harris, Edw'd Enman, Lt. John Whipple, Wm. Wickenden. |
| 1667 | Wm. Carpenter, Wm. Harris, Arthur Fenner | Roger Williams, Thomas Olney, Sr. Stephen Arnold, John Throckmorton, Anthony Evernden, Thomas Hopkins, Shadrach Manton. |
| 1668 | William Carpenter, William Harris | John Throckmorton, Samuel Bennett, Edward Enman, Nathaniel Waterman, Anthony Everenden, Shadrach Manton. |
| 1669 | Wm. Carpenter, Wm. Harris, Thomas Olney, Jr. | John Sayles, Shadrach Manton, James Barker, John Whipple. |
| 1670 | Roger Williams, Thomas Olney, Wm. Carpenter | John Throgmorton, Thomas Harris, Capt. Arthur Fenner, Thomas Olney, Sr., Thomas Roberts. |
| 1671 | Roger Williams, William Carpenter, Thomas Harris | Thomas Olney, Sr., John Sayles, Shadrach Manton, Ephraim Carpenter, John Throckmorton, Anthony Everden, Stephen Arnold, Thomas Clemance, Thomas Roberts. |
| 1672 | Arthur Fenner, Thomas Harris | Arthur Fenner, Thomas Arnold, Edward Enman, Thomas Hopkins, William Harris, Samuel Reape, Pardon Tillinghast, Thomas Borden. |
| 1673 | William Harris, Thomas Harris | John Throckmorton, William Harris, Laura Wilkinson, Anthony Evernden, John Lapham, William Austin, Thomas Harris, Tollera Harris. |
| 1674 | William Harris, Thomas Harris, Sr. | John Whipple, Sr., Stephen Arnold, John Sayles, James Barker. |
| 1675 | Thomas Harris | |
| 1676 | William Harris, Capt. Arthur Fenner | Tolleration Harris, Edward Smith, William Austin, Valentine Whitman. |
| 1677 | John Whipple, Jr., Stephen Arnold | |
| 1678 | John Whipple, Jr., Stephen Arnold | Edward Enman, Samuel Bennit, Thomas Arnold, William Hankins, Jr. |
| 1679 | John Whipple, Jr., Capt. Arthur Fenner, Stephen Arnold | Capt. Arthur Fenner, William Carpenter, Richard Arnold. |
| 1680 | Capt. Arthur Fenner, Stephen Arnold | John Thornton, Pardon Tillinghast, James Mathewson, Edward Smith. |
| 1681 | Capt. Arthur Fenner, Joseph Jencks | John Whipple, Jr., Richard Arnold, Nathaniel Waterman, Thomas Harris, Jr. |

| Date. | | |
|---|---|---|
| 1682 | Capt. Arthur Fenner, Richard Arnold | Thomas Harris, Jr., Edward Smith, Thomas Arnold, John Whipple, Jr. |
| 1683 | Capt. Arthur Fenner, Richard Arnold | Thomas Field, Thomas Arnold, Thomas Fenner, Alexander Boleun. |
| 1684 | Capt. Arthur Fenner, Richard Arnold | Stephen Arnold, John Whipple, Jr., Henry Brown, Epenetus Olney. |
| 1685 | Capt. Arthur Fenner, Richard Arnold | Stephen Arnold, Sr., Thomas Field, Valentine Whitman, Thomas Harris, Jr. |
| 1686 | Capt. Arthur Fenner, Richard Arnold | Valentine Whitman, John Whipple, Epenetus Olney, John Angell. |
| 1687 | | Government interrupted by Sir Edmund Andros. |
| 1688 | | |
| 1689 | Joseph Jencks | James Barker. |
| 1690 | Joseph Jencks, Stephen Arnold | Stephen Arnold, Pardon Tillinghast, Lieut. John Dexter, Gideon Crawford. |
| 1691 | Joseph Jencks | Thomas Harris, Samuel Whipple, Thomas Fenner, Joseph Jencks, Jr. |
| 1692 | | |
| 1693 | | |
| 1694 | | |
| 1695 | | |
| 1696 | Joseph Jencks, Stephen Arnold | Thomas Olney, Richard Arnold, John Sprague, Lieut. John Dexter. |
| 1697 | | Joseph Williams, Richard Arnold, James Angell. |
| 1698 | Capt.Richard Arnold, Joseph Williams | Jonathan Sprague, Eliaba Arnold, John Wilkinson, Peleg Rhodes. |
| 1699 | Capt.Richard Arnold, Joseph Williams | Jonathan Sprague, Joseph Jencks, Jr. |
| 1700 | Joseph Williams | |

## WARWICK.

| Date. | GOVERNOR'S ASSISTANTS. | REPRESENTATIVES. |
|---|---|---|
| 1647 | Randall Holden | John Smith, Ezekiel Holman, John Warner, Robert Potter, Christopher Holmes, Peter Green. |
| 1648 | John Smith | |
| 1649 | Samuel Gorton | |
| 1650 | James Weeks | |
| 1651 | | Samuel Gorton, John Weeks, John Greene, Jr., John Smith, Robert Potter, Stukely Westcott, Ezekiel Holman, John Townsend, Richard Townsend, Walter Todd. |
| 1652 | Samuel Gorton | Ezekiel Holman, Stukely Westcott, John Townsend, Richard Townsend, Walter Todd, John Greene, Jr., Samuel Gorton, John Weeks, John Smith, John Greene, Sr., Randall Holden, Robert Potter. |

## WARWICK (Continued).

| Date. | Governor's Assistants. | Representatives. |
|---|---|---|
| 1653 | Stukely Westcott | Ezekiel Holman, Stukely Westcott, John Townsend, Walter Todd, Richard Townsend, John Greene, Jr., Henry Townsend, James Sweet, John Cooke. |
| 1654 | Randall Holden | John Greene, Sr., Randall Holden, Ezekiel Holman, John Greene, Jr., John Townsend, Richard Townsend. |
| 1655 | Randall Holden | John Greene, Sr., Stukely Westcott, Ezekiel Holman, John Greene, Jr., Richard Harcutt, Christopher Hanxhurst, Robert Potter, Randall Holden. |
| 1656 | John Weeks | John Greene, Sr., Ezekiel Holman, Walter Todd, John Weeks, John Greene, Jr., Samuel Gorton, Richard Bulger, John Sanford. |
| 1657 | Randall Holden | John Greene, Sr., Randall Holden, Samuel Gorton, John Weeks, John Greene, Jr., Walter Todd, Peter Greene. |
| 1658 | Randall Holden | Randall Holden, Samuel Gorton, John Weeks, John Greene, Jr., Ezekiel Holman, John Smith. |
| 1659 | Randall Holden | Randall Holden, John Smith, Samuel Gorton, John Greene, Richard Carder, Richard Townsend, Ezekiel Holman, James Sweet, Robert Westcott. |
| 1660 | John Greene | Randall Holman, Samuel Gorton, John Smith, John Greene, John Weeks, Richard Carder, Stukely Westcott. |
| 1661 | John Greene | John Smith, John Weeks, John Greene, James Greene, William Dyer, Sr., Peter Tallman, John Potter, Thomas Brownell. |
| 1662 | John Greene | John Smith, John Greene, John Weeks, Samuel Gorton, Randall Holden, James Greene. |
| 1663 | John Greene | John Greene, Samuel Gorton, Randall Holden, John Weeks, James Greene, Richard Carder, Walter Todd, Edmund Calverly. |
| 1664 | Randall Holden, Walter Todd | John Weeks, Sr., Walter Todd, Edmund Calverly, Richard Carder. |
| 1665 | John Greene, Randall Holden | Samuel Gorton, John Weeks, Richard Carder, Edmund Calverly, James Greene. |
| 1666 | Benjamin Smith, Capt. John Greene | Samuel Gorton, Capt. Randall Holden, John Weeks, Edmund Calverly. |
| 1667 | Capt. John Greene, Benjamin Smith | John Weeks, Richard Carder, James Greene, Edmund Caverly, Capt. Randall Holden, Thomas Greene, John Potter. |
| 1668 | Capt. John Greene, Benjamin Smith | John Weeks, Richard Carder, James Greene, Edmund Caverly. |
| 1669 | Capt. John Greene, Benjamin Smith | Capt. Randall Holden, Richard Carder, Thomas Greene, Edmund Caverly, Tobias Saunders, James Weeks. |
| 1670 | Capt. John Greene, James Greene | Capt. Randall Holden, James Greene, Richard Carder, Edmund Caverly, Stephen Wilcox, Job Almy, Amos Westcott, Samuel Stafford, Thomas Greene. |

| Year | | |
|---|---|---|
| 1671 | Capt. John Greene, Benjamin Smith | Benjamin Smith, Stukely Westcott, Walter Todd, Richard Carder, Amos Westcott, John Weeks, Edmund Caverly, Job Almy, Randall Holden. |
| 1672 | Capt. John Greene, Benjamin Smith | Capt. Randall Holden, Richard Carder, Thomas Greene, John Potter, John Weeks, James Greene, Eleazer Collins. |
| 19 1673 | Walter Todd, Job Almy | Capt. Randall Holden, Richard Carder, James Greene, Edmund Caverly, John Weeks, Benjamin Smith, Eliza Collins, Thomas Stafford. |
| 1674 | Job Almy, Samuel Stafford | Capt. John Greene, James Greene, Thomas Greene, Richard Carder, Samuel Stafford, Benjamin Smith, John Warner. |
| 1675 | Benjamin Smith, Benjamin Barton | Capt. Randall Holden, Capt. John Greene, John Weeks, James Greene. |
| 1676 | Capt. Rand'l Holden, Sam'l Gorton, Jr. | Capt. John Greene. |
| 1677 | Capt. John Greene, Samuel Gorton, Jr. | Walter Todd, Thomas Greene, Eliza Collins, John Cardor. |
| 1678 | Samuel Gorton, Thomas Greene | Edmund Caverly, Lieut. Benjamin Barton, Samuel Stafford, John Warner. |
| 1679 | Capt. Samuel Gorton, Thomas Greene | Randall Holden, Robert Burdick. |
| 1680 | Capt. Sam'l Gorton, Capt. John Greene | Thomas Greene, Benjamin Barton, Moses Lippitt, Knowles. |
| 1681 | Capt. Sam'l Gorton, Capt. John Greene | Benjamin Smith, Abiah Carpenter, Samuel Stafford, John Low. |
| 1682 | Capt. Sam'l Gorton, Capt. John Greene | Isreal Arnold, John Potter, John Warner. |
| 1683 | Capt. John Greene, Benjamin Barton | Benjamin Smith, Thomas Greene, Samuel Gorton, Moses Lippitt. |
| 1684 | Major John Greene, Thomas Greene | James, Greene, Sr., Benjamin Smith, Benjamin Barton, John Warner. |
| 1685 | Samuel Gorton, Benjamin Barton | Randall Holden, James Greene, Sr., Capt. Benjamin Gorton, Samuel Stafford. |
| 1686 | Major John Greene, Samuel Stafford | |
| 1687 | | Government interrupted by Sir Edmund Andros. |
| 1688 | Benjamin Smith, Major John Greene | James Greene, Peter Greene, John Warner, Israel Arnold. |
| 1689 | Benjamin Smith | Benjamin Barton, Samuel Stafford, Roger Burlingham, Moses Lippitt. |
| 1690 | Benjamin Smith | Randall Holden, Samuel Gorton, Isreal Arnold, Peter Greene, |
| 1691 | | |
| 1692 | | |
| 1693 | | |
| 1694 | | |
| 1695 | | |
| 1696 | Benjamin Smith | Benjamin Barton, John Carder, James Greene, Jr., Randall Holden. |
| 1697 | | |
| 1698 | Benjamin Smith | Peter Greene, James Carder, Moses Lippitt, Thomas Greene, Jr. |
| 1699 | Benjamin Barton | Randall Holden, Isreal Arnold, Job Greene, Moses Lippitt. |
| 1700 | Benjamin Smith, Benjamin Barton | Kendall Holden. |

## WESTERLY. Incorporated May, 1669.

| Date. | Governor's Assistants. | REPRESENTATIVES. |
|---|---|---|
| 1670 | | Stephen Wilcox, John Maxon, John Crandall. |
| 1671 | | John Crandall, Tobias Saunders. |
| 1672 | | Tobias Saunders, Stephen Wilcox. |
| 1673 | | |
| 1674 | | |
| 1675 | | |
| 1676 | | |
| 1677 | | |
| 1678 | | |
| 1679 | | Joseph Jencks. |
| 1680 | | Tobias Saunders, Henry Tew, Edward Thurston. |
| 1681 | | Tobias Saunders, Jeffrey Champlin. |
| 1682 | | Jeffrey Champlin, John Babcock. |
| 1683 | | Tobias Saunders, Robert Burdick. |
| 1684 | | Jeffrey Champlin, John Babcock. |
| 1685 | | Jeffrey Champlin, Robert Burdick. |
| 1686 | | Jeffrey Champlin, John Maxon. |
| 1687 | | |
| 1688 | | [Government interrupted by Sir Edmund Andros.] |
| 1689 | | John Maxon. |
| 1690 | | Tobias Saunders, William Champlin. |
| 1691 | | Capt. William Champlin, Henry Hall. |
| 1692 | | |
| 1693 | | |
| 1694 | | |
| 1695 | | |
| 1696 | | Capt. William Champlin, Nicholas Cotterell. |
| 1697 | Capt. Jeffrey Champlin | |
| 1698 | Capt. Jeffrey Champlin | Capt. William Champlin, Joseph Clarke. |
| 1699 | Capt. Jeffrey Champlin | Capt. William Champlin, Peter Crandall. |
| 1700 | Capt. Jeffrey Champlin | Capt. Wm. Champlin, Jos. Clarke, Lt. Peter Crandall. |

### ACT OF INCORPORATION.

This Court taking notice of the returne by the Committee to wit: Mr. John Easton, Mr. Benjamin Smith, James Greene, Edward Smith, Caleb Carr and William Weeden in reference to the petition or desire of the people inhabitting at Musquamacott and Pawcatucke, in the Kings Province, to be made a towneshipp, it being and lying within this jurisdiction, as by his Majestyes Letters Pattents it may appear, and considering the power by his Majestye given to this Assembly to order and settle townes, cityes and corporations, within this said jurisdiction, as shall seem meet; and seeing there doth alsoe appeare good evidence of the trust and good affection of the said people vnto his Majestyes Government established in this Collony, and being also sensibell that the said inhabitants have suffered in much vindicating the same, and are a competent number to carry on the affaires there as in condition of a towneship.   Bee it therefore enacted by this Assembly, and by the authority thereof, that the said inhabitants of Musquamcott being seated adjoyning to Pawcatucke, alias Narragansett or Norrogansitt river on the west part, and boundary of this Collony, and within that part thereof knowne by the name of the King's Province aforesaid, to wit: Mr. John Crandall, Mr. Tobias Sanders, and all such others as now are or hereafter shall be legally admitted as freemen and inhabitants in the said place called Musquamcott, &c., shall be knowne and called by the name of Westerly, and shall be reputed and deemed the fifth towne in this Collony; and shall have vse and enjoy all such priviledges, and exercise all such methods and formes for the well ordering their towne affaires as any other towne in this Collony may now vse and exercise; and they shall have liberty to elect and send two Deputyes, to sitt and act in the General Assemblys of this Collony from time to time, and are enjoyned to choose and send to the General Court of Trialls one grand juryman, and one for the Jury of triarls from time to time. (See pages 250 and 251, Vol. II. R. I. Colonial Records.)

# MILITARY LISTS.

## 1642—1700.

## MAJOR COMMANDANTS.

### WHILE THE MILITIA OF THE COLONY CONSTITUTED ONE REGIMENT.

| Name. | Residence. | Term of Service. |
|---|---|---|
| John Cranston | Newport | April 11, 1679, to May 7, 1679. |
| Peleg Sanford | Newport | May 7, 1679, to May 5, 1680. |
| John Albro | Portsmouth | May 5, 1680, to May 2, 1683. |

### WHILE THE MILITIA WERE DIVIDED INTO TWO REGIMENTS.

#### THE ISLAND REGIMENT.

| Name. | Residence. | Term of Service. |
|---|---|---|
| John Coggeshall | Newport | May 2, 1683, to May 6, 1685. |
| Roger Goulding | Newport | May 6, 1685, to |
| John Bliss | Newport | May 6, 1696, to May 3, 1698. |
| Samuel Cranston | Newport | May 3, 1698, to May 1, 1700. |
| Henry Tew | Newport | May 1, 1700, to May 5, 1702. |

#### THE MAIN LAND REGIMENT.

| Name. | Residence. | Term of Service. |
|---|---|---|
| John Greene | Warwick | May 2, 1683, to May 3, 1698. |
| William Hopkins | | May 3, 1698, to May 3, 1699. |
| John Dexter | Providence | May 3, 1699, to May 1, 1706. |

## MILITIA COMPANIES.

| Where Located. | Rank of Officers. | Names of Officers. | Date of Commission. | Date of Discharge. | Cause of Discharge. |
|---|---|---|---|---|---|
| East Greenwich— | Captains— | Clement Weaver | ......168 | | |
| Jamestown— | Captains— | Thomas Fry | | | |
| | | Samuel Bennett | | | |
| | Lieutenant— | John Foanes | | | |
| | Captains— | Thomas Paine | | | |
| | Lieutenant— | Nicholas Carr | August 2, 1692 | August 2, 1692 | Promotion. |
| | Ensigns— | Nicholas Carr | ......167 | | |
| Kingstown— | Captains— | George Cooke | August 2, 1692 | | |
| | | Andrew Willett | | | |
| | | Edward Greenman | | | |
| | | Jeffrey Champlain | ......169 | | |
| | Lieutenant— | Thomas Eldridge | ......169 | | |
| | Ensign— | John Eldridge | ......169 | | |
| Newport— | Captains— | Robert Jeffreys | March 17, 1642 | | |
| | | Jeremiah Clarke | March, 1644 | | |
| | | John Cranston | | | |
| | | John Greene | | April 11, 1676 | Promoted to Major. |
| | Lieutenants— | Roger Goulding | | | |
| | | Henry Tew | | | |
| | | Jeremiah Clarke | March 17, 1642 | May 6, 1685 | Promoted to Major. |
| | | Joseph Torrey | ......166 | May 3, 1699 | Promoted to Major. |
| | | Edward Richmond | ......167 | March, 1644 | Promoted to Captain. |
| | | John Greene | | | |
| | | John Bliss | ......168 | | |
| | | Thomas Weaver | | ......1680 | Promoted to Captain. |
| | Ensigns— | ...... Smith | | | |
| | | George Gardiner | March 17, 1642 | March, 1644 | Promoted to Lieut. |
| | | John Bliss | | | |
| | | James Berker | ......1644 | ......168 | Promoted to Lieut. |
| | | Weston Clarke | | | |
| New Shoreham— | Captain— | John Sands | | | |

| Town | Rank | Name | Date | Date | Remarks |
|---|---|---|---|---|---|
| Portsmouth— | Captains— | Richard Morris | March 17, 1642 | | |
| | | John Sanford | ....166 | | |
| | | Samuel Wilbur | Sept., 1669 | | |
| | | John Albro | | | |
| | | William Corey | | | |
| | | John Sheffield | ....1680 | May 5, 1680 | Promoted to Major. |
| | Lieutenants— | William Baulston | March 17, 1642 | | |
| | | John Sanford | March, 1644 | | |
| | | John Albro | ....165 | | |
| | | William Codman | ....167 | 166 | Promoted to Captain. |
| | | Francis Brayton | ....167 | 167 | Promoted to Captain. |
| | | Latham Clarke | | | |
| | | William Corey | | | |
| | Ensigns— | Thomas Cornell | ....167 | | |
| | | Lot Strange | March 17, 1642 | 1680 | Promoted to Captain. |
| | | | Sept. 1669 | | |
| Providence— | Captains— | Thomas Hains | ....166 | | |
| | | Arthur Fenner | ....166 | | |
| | | Roger Williams | ....167 | | |
| | | Andrew Edmunds | ....167 | May 3, 1699 | Promoted to Major. |
| | Lieutenants— | John Dexter | ....1698 | ....1698 | Promoted to Captain. |
| | | John Whipple | ....166 | | |
| | | John Dexter | ....169 | | |
| Warwick— | Captains— | Randall Holden | ....166 | | |
| | | John Greene | ....166 | | |
| | | Samuel Gorton | | | |
| | | Benjamin Gorton | | | |
| | | Edmund Calverly | | May 1, 1705 | Promoted to Major. |
| | | Peter Greene | | May 2, 1683 | Promoted to Major. |
| | Lieutenants— | Edmund Calverly | | | |
| | | Benjamin Barton | | | |
| | | James Carder | | | |
| Westerly— | Captains— | Jeffrey Champlin | | | |
| | | William Champlin | | | |
| | | James Babcock | | ....1676 | Promoted to Captain. |
| | Lieutenant— | Peter Crandall | | | |

## MILITARY LAWS AND ORDERS.

**1647, May.**

It is ordered that there is free Libertie granted for the free Inhabitants of yᵉ Province (if they will) to erect an Artillery Garden, and thôse that are desirious to advance the Art Military, shall have freedom to exercise themselves therein, and to agree of their forme, and choose their officers as they shall agree among themselves.

It is ordered, that all yᵉ Inhabitants in each Towne shall choose their Military Officers from among themselves on the first Tuesday after the 12ᵗʰ of March; and that eight severall times in the yeare, the Bands of each plantation or Towne, shall, openlie in the field be exercised and disciplined by their Commanders and Officers in the months of May, August, January and February excepted; and on the first Monday of yᵉ other months, all the Train Bands to make their personal appearances completely armed, to attend their colors, by 8 o'clock in the Morning, at the second beate of yᵉ Drum; and if any appear not they shall forfeit and pay five shillings into the hands of the Clark of yᵉ Band; and if any shall come defective in his Armes or furniture, he shall forfeit and pay yᵉ sum of twelve pence, after the Town Council have caused him to be supplied; and that all men who shall come and remaine yᵉ space of twenty days shall be liable to yᵉ injunction of this order; Provided, herdsmen, lightermen and such as be left of necessity at Farmes, shall pay two shillings and sixpence for every dayes absence. And that the two Chief officers in each Towne, to witt: one of the Commonweale, and the other of the Band upon the exhibition of the complaint by yᵉ Clark (which shall be within three dayes after the fault committed), shall judge and determine of yᵉ reasons of the excuses who upon the hearing thereof shall determine whether every such person shall pay five shillings, two shillings and six pence, or nothing; and according as they find any defective, shall give their warrants to yᵉ Clark to distrane their Goods if they shall refuse to pay what is ordered.

And if the Clarke shall neglect to gather up what is ordered, he shall forfeit and pay so much into the hands of the Captain, the next training day.

And that all the fines and forfeitures shall be employed to the use and service of the Band.

And the Towne Councils shall have power to cause those which are defective in armes to be supplied in an equal way according to estate and strength.

And if any of yᵉ Traine Band after his appearance shall refuse or neglect the command of his Captain, to be exercised and disciplined he shall forfeit as much as if he had not appeared.

And that the Town Council shall order the power of the Military Officers within the Towne, and in all cases of concerne yᵉ whole        the President and yᵉ foure assistants, and ye Captains of every Band shall be the Councill of Warr; that if any of the Officers of yᵉ Band be at any time left out they shall beare Armes again for yᵉ Constitution of our place will not beare the contrary; that every Inhabitant of the Island above sixteen or under sixty yeares of age shall always be provided of a Musket, one pound of powder, twenty bullets, and two fadom of Match, with sword, rest, bandaleers all completely furnished.

It is ordered, that in regard of yᵉ many incursions that we are subject vnto, and that an Alarum for yᵉ giving notice thereof is necessary when occassion is offered. It is agreed that this form be observed, Vidg't: Three Muskets distinctly discharged, and a Herauld appointed to go speedilie threw the Towne and crie Alarum! Alarum!; and the Drum beate incessantly upon which all to repair (upon forfeiture as the Town Councill shall order) unto the Town House ther to receive information of the Town Councill what is farther to be done.

It is ordered and agreed that if any person or persons shall sell, give, deliver or any otherwayes convey any powder, shott, lead, gunn, pistoll, sword, dagger, halberd or pike to the Indians that are or may prove offensive to this Colonie, or any member thereof, he or they, for the first offence shall forfeit yᵉ sum of five pounds; and for his second offence, offending in the same kind, and being lawfully convicted, shall forfeit ten pounds; half to the State, and half to him that will sew for it, and no wager of Law by any means to be allowed to the offender.

And it is further ordered, that if any person shall mend or repaire their Guns or he shall forfeit the same penaltie.

1650, May 23ᵈ.

It is ordered that Captaine Richard Morris, George Blisse, James Badcock, Peter Busserole, William Havens and Gabriel Hick, all excuses sett aparte shall mende and make all lockes, stockes and pieces that by order from the warden of each Towne shall be from any of the inhabitants thearof presented to them, for a just and suitable satisfaction in hand payed without delay vnder the penaltie of ten pounds, to be levied by distraint from the head officer to the use of the sayd Towne's milittia.

It is ordered that all men that have gunns and pieces to mend, and have need to have them mended for their present defence, shall forthwith accordihg to order carrie those pieces to mende upon paine of forferting ten ·shillings a piece, which shall be levied by distraint from the head officer of the Towne to the use of the sayed Towne's militia.

The Towne of Providence shall have in its magasine one barrell of good powder, five hundred pounds of leade, six pikes, and six muskets all in good case and fit for service.

The Towne of Portsmouth shall have in its magasine two barrells of good powder, one thousand weight of leade, twelve pikes and eighteen muskets, all in good case and fit for service.

The Towne of Newport shall have in its magasine three barrells of good powder, one thousand weight of leade, twelve pikes and twentie foure muskets all in good case and fit for service.

The Towne of Warwick shall have in its magasine one barrell of good powder, five hundred weight of leade, six pikes and six muskets all in good case and fitt for service; and all these magasines shall be thus compleately furnished by the last day of the month called August next ensuinge, under the penaltie of ten pounds sterling for each default therein, upon sufficient information of the default by virtue of a warrant from under thé President's hande, the Generall Sarjeant shall take it by distraint and forthwith returne it into the publicke Treasurie.

1665, May.

The Assembly taking into consideration the great defect in training, occasioned by the remissnes of some vnder the pretence of the burden of training soe often as eight dayes in the yeare, and other complaining of the great inequality in that the poorest being vnable to spare wherewith to maintaine armes and amunition, as powder, &c., yett are forced by law to beare armes as well as the most able; to redresse which grevances it is enacted and declared that the sixe dayes only in the yeare be ordered, and are hearby ordered for the military exercise in training, which shall be dilligently attended to in each respective towne upon penalty that each Captain or in his absence the Leftenant of each towne shall be fined in case he call not the listed souldiers together by warrant, to make choyce of Captain and other officers milletary, (at such time and in some sort as it is by a law made May 4ᵗʰ, 1664, it is provided) the summe of ten pound stearling to the Generall Treasury, to be by law recovered by the said Treasurer for the Collony; as alsoe fortye shillings for each defect in calling the said company together to traine on each of the training dayes hereafter appointed, or refusing then to exercise them in training; and the dayes prefired for the exercise of training are yearly to be the last Monday in May, the first Monday in September, the first Monday in November, the last Monday in March and the last Monday in Aprill. And for the incouradgement of the meaner sort, there shall be allowed yearly nine shillings in currant pay to ror each soldiare listed in the traine band, to be duely payed and discounted yearly by the Clarke or Treasurer of the traine band at the Captain's discretion for the repairing of armes, &c.; and the said nine shillings yearly to be payed and cleared by or before the last Monday in March, and delivered or ordered to such parents and masters as find armes and amunition (as they must doe) for their sones and sarvants that are listable, which are to be listed and to traine; as alsoe to such house holders or other men that find themselves armes and traine in their owne persones; which all men from sixteene years of age to sixtye yeares old are hearby required to doe both masters, parents, sones, sarvents, and others, excepting such as are in publicke office or are by former lawes exempted; and for every defecte in not duely attending the trainings, each one listed soe deficient, shall for every dayes defect pay three shillings fine, to be levied by distraint on the partyes goods, or on the goods of the master or mistress or parents of such sones or sarvents as are defective; and to the end the fines may be levied more certainly, the same course is to be taken to take the same as was ordered for the former fines in the said law made the 4ᵗʰ of May, 1664, and returned to the Clarke of the band for suply of drumes, collers and holbords, &c., at the discretion of the Captaine, Leftenant and Ensigne for the

20

company; and that care be taken to. gather all former fines; as alsoe the judging of
other defects in that sort to be left to the Counsell, &c., as by the said law of May 4th,
1664, is expressed, and for the raysing the aforesaid allowance of nine shillings a
yeare for each souldier that is or shall be listed, each towne shall in a towne meeting
yearly before the first Munday in November, choose a convenient number of men, and
authorize them to make a rate vpon each one ratable within the precinckes of the
towne with as much equality as may be according to each ones estate therein being;
and shall take care for the levying of the same by distraint in case of none paying,
that in time appointed by such as the majistrates in each towne shall be by warrant
authorized to gather the same with five shillings on the pound over and above for
distraining, to be for the vse of hee or they that distraine it, and the sum soe dis-
trained to be returned to the Clarke at or before the five and twentyeth day of
December, yearly; and the order for apprizing, redeeming and selling distringesses,
and returning the overpulse to the first owners formerly in vse to be observed by
such as distraine as alsoe offesetting with or for each persone the nine shillings before
allowed in case there be in the pertickelar rate soe much as and what either rate is
short is to be made vp and payed to each or for each person as abovesaid.

And as for choosing the Captaine and other military officers, every one that is
eighteene yeares old or more, and hath taken the oath or engagement of alegiance
shall vote if they please therein though not freemen, intending only the officers soe
chosen are only for the military exercise of training, there be power by the Charter
with the Generall Assembly, or in the intervalls of the Generall Assembly, then with
the Governor and Counsell, &c., in extreordinary cases to take care of and order the
militia as they find necessary for defence and safetye of the whole collony.

And the aforesaid order, however differing from former lawes or orders of this Collony consearning training or wherein it doth differ is to be observed and confirmed by
the authority of this Assembly, any law or clause in any former law to, the contrary
hearof notwithstanding; alwayes provided, that other rules in the former law of May
the 4th, &c., not contrary to this present law shall be observed.

1667.
Whereas the Generall Assembly, sitting in July last past, and taking into their
serious consideration the necessity of raysing a troope of horse in Rhode Island, did
then by the power of the Charter granted to this Collony by his sacred Majesty,
enact, order and betrust the Governor and Councill of the sayd Island to raise a troope
of horse; in pursuance of which authority and order the Governor and Councill meeting vpon the 24th of July last past, did conceive it to bee most requisitt to lay the
foundation in a voluntary way and therefore by the power committed to them did
nominate, choose and appoint Mr. Peleg Sanford, Captaine of the troope to be so
raysed, and Mr. John Almye, Lieftenant, who were to give notice for their assembling
and incorporating into such a body, and to make their appearance before the Governor and Councill, this present 10th of August, 1667.

Then appeared before the Govenor by and vnder (authoritie of) the Captain, Mr.
Peleg Sanford and Lt. Mr. John Almy, who were deputed and appointed the commanders of the troope of horse vpon the Island, and the commanders being chosen by the
Governor and Councill according to the Generall Assembly's act and the Charters
authority, wee the underwritten do subscribe as in obediente to the foresayd authority
and do approve of the choyce of our Captaine and Lieftenant to the full as witness
our hands.

Thcae following listed themselves:

The Governor, a horse, furniture and rider.

| | |
|---|---|
| Mr. Baulston, the like | James Barber, Jr., |
| Mr. Samuel Wilbur, the like | John Easton, Jr. |
| Mr. Wm. Reape, the like | William Smyton, |
| Henry Dyre, | Francis Brayton, |
| John Sanford. | Wm. Briggs, |
| Joseph Holdes, | David Leake, |
| Nath¹ Johnson. | Hugh Parsons, |
| Ralph Earle, Sr., | Thomas Briggs, |
| Joseph Wellington. | Samuell Albro, |

The commission granted to the Captaine and Lieftenant of the troope.

To Mr. Peleg Sanford; You being chosen Captaine of the troope of horse in this
Iland, called Rhode Island, in the Collony of Rhode Island and Providence Plantations,

by the Governor and Councill, according to the Charter and Generall Court order, and being accepted by the full approbation of the troop appearing before the Governor and Councill the 10ᵗʰ of August, 1667; These are therefore in his Majestys name Charles the 2ᵈ, King of England, Scotland, ffraunce and Ireland, with the dominions and territories thereto belonging, do require you and alsoe-impower you to mannage and discipline the sayd troope according to your best skill and understanding; at and vpon such dayes and times as you shall think fitt or find expedient not exceedinge six times in the yeare, except extraordinary occasion shall present, and then by order from the Governor or Governor and Councill, you and your troope to be in readiness also if invasion or endanger of surprize by his Majestyes enemyes, bee or likely to bee, you are forthwith to mount your troope, and give your vtmost abilitie and strength to defend, make resistance and oppose; and alwayes and at all times, especially in time of danger, to be attent and observante of such orders, directions and instructions, as you shall receive from the Governor or Governor and Councill; and in so doing this shall be your sufficient warrant and discharge as to all and singular the premises, Given vnder our hands, with seale of the Councill, this 10ᵗʰ of August, 1667.

WILLIAM BRENTON, Govenor.
WILLIAM BAULSTON, Assistant.
WILLIAM REAPE, Assistant.
SAMUEL WILLBURE, Assistant.

The like commission was by the Governor and Councill vnder the hands and seale of the Councill, to Mr. John Almye, as Lieftenant to Captaine Peleg Sanford, of the troope, thus and as aforesaid rayzed joyntly by the Iland called Rhode Island.

ARTHUR FENNER, Assistant,
JOHN GREENE, Assistant.

1669, August 26ᵗʰ.

The Councill takeing into consideration an information formerly given vnto them by Mr. William Baulston, Generall Assistant, that there are noe military officers chosen for the towne of Portsmouth, by reason of the decease of the late Captaine; and alsoe foreseeing of what consequence it is, that prouision bee forthwith made in that behalfe, especially considering the present fears of the country; doe therefore order and ordaine that the said Mr. William Baulston, Assistant, bee heerby required and authorized to issue out warrants vnder his hand, directed to such person or persons as hee shall thinke fitt to warne all persons of the towne of Portsmouth that are capable to vote in the election of military officers to appeare at the vsual place in the said towne on the first Munday in September next, at nine of the clock in the morning, then and there to make choice of their said officers accordingly; and Mr. Baulston is alsoe desired to signifie vnto the said towne that the Councill doe hope and expect that they will proceed to the said choice, or otherwayes they will force the Councill to impose officers vpon them which they earnestly desire they may not bee constrained to doe; and a copy of this order vnder the seale of the Councill shall bee Mr. Baulston's warrant in this behalfe.

# PROFESSIONAL LISTS.
## 1636—1700.

## CLERGYMEN.

| Name of Town. | Name of Clergyman. | When Settled. | When Dismissed. | Cause of Dismissal, or Place of Removal. |
|---|---|---|---|---|
| Newport— | Robert Lenthal<br>John Clarke<br>...... Lockyer | ...... 1640<br><br>about 1698 | | |
| New Shoreham— | Samuel Niles | March, 1700 | | Braintree. |
| Providence— | Roger Williams<br>Wm. Blackstone | ...... 1636 | ...... 1683<br>May 26, 1675 | Death.<br>Death. |

Note.—Lenthal and Lockyer were Episcopal Clergymen, and Clarke a Baptist. A Quaker meeting was established at Newport in or before 1676, and that form of worship had existed there from about 1643. A second Baptist church was organized in 1656. William Blackstone resided within the limits of Plymouth Colony, but the proof is reasonably conclusive that for a time he preached in Providence, R. I.

## PHYSICIANS.

| Where Located. | Name. | Term of Practice. |
|---|---|---|
| Newport— | John Clarke<br>John Cranston | From 16.., to Death, April 20, 1676.<br>March, 1664, to Death, March 12, 1680. |
| New Shoreham— | Sarah Sands | |

March, 1664.

Wheras the Court have taken notice of the great blessing of God on the good endevers of Captayne John Cranston of Newport, both in phissicke and chirgery, to the great comfort of such as have had occasion to prove his skill and practice, &c. The Court doe therfore vnanimously enacte and declare that the said Captayne John Cranston is lycenced and commistioned to administer phissicke and practice chirurgery throughout this whole Collony, and is by this Court styled and recorded Doctor of phissicke and chirurgery, by the authority of this Collony.—*Rhode Island Colonial Records.* Vol. iii. p. 33.

## CORRECTIONS.

Page 11.　Daniel *Cole*, instead of Daniel "Doane" was Town Clerk of Eastham 1676 to 1703.
Page 94.　In 2d line under the cut, for "July" read *August* 8.
Page 119.　Cranston's term of service as Governor ended *March* 12, 1680, instead of "May 5."
Page 141.　Cranston's term of service as Major began April 11, 1676, instead of "1679."

# INDEX.

# 156 INDEX.

www.ingramcontent.com/pod-product-compliance
Lightning Source LLC
Chambersburg PA
CBHW061743270326
41928CB00011B/2356